W9-AOZ-036

EMERGENT LEARNING FOR WISDOM

EMERGENT LEARNING FOR WISDOM

Marilyn M. Taylor

palgrave
macmillan

EMERGENT LEARNING FOR WISDOM
Copyright © Marilyn M. Taylor, 2011.

First published in 2011
by PALGRAVE MACMILLAN®
in the United States – a division of St. Martin's Press LLC,
175 Fifth Avenue, New York, NY 10010.

Where this book is distributed in the UK, Europe and the rest of
the world, this is by Palgrave Macmillan, a division of Macmillan
Publishers Limited, registered in England, company number 785998,
of Houndmills, Basingstoke, Hampshire RG21 6XS.

Palgrave Macmillan is the global academic imprint of the above companies
and has companies and representatives throughout the world.

Palgrave® and Macmillan® are registered trademarks in the United
States, the United Kingdom, Europe and other countries.

ISBN: 978–0–230–60367–7

Library of Congress Cataloging-in-Publication Data

Taylor, Marilyn M.
  Emergent learning for wisdom / Marilyn M. Taylor.
      p. cm.
   Includes bibliographical references.
   ISBN 978–0–230–60367–7
   1. Transformative learning.   2. Experiential learning.   3. Learning,
Psychology of.   I. Title.
   LC1100.T39 2011
   370.15'23—dc22   2010039070

A catalogue record of the book is available from the British Library.

Design by MPS Limited, A Macmillan Company

First edition: April 2011

10 9 8 7 6 5 4 3 2 1

Printed in the United States of America.

For my brother Norman and all those who leave the world better than they found it, whatever the challenges.

Contents

List of Figures and Tables

Figures

Table

ACKNOWLEDGMENTS

This book has been in progress for many years and has been generously supported by many people. I am fortunate to have worked and studied in imaginative university organizations that have inspired innovation in learning and leadership. I am grateful for mentoring in social science that makes a difference from people like Richard McDonald, Hedley Dimock, Roby Kidd, Matt Miles, Diana Ironside, Virginia Griffin, Edmund O'Sullivan, David Hunt, Edith Whitfield Seashore, Charles Seashore, and Bill Bergquist. Over the years, I have enjoyed learning with colleagues who have enriched my practice and my thinking, among them, Gord Hodge, dian marino, Don de Guerre, Margaret Douek, Marilyn Laiken, Raye Kass, Jim Gavin, David Kelleher, Bev Patwell, and a number of those named below. Most recently, I have been sustained by the continuous encouragement and tangible contributions from my family, especially Mary (Louie)Walton-Ball and Isabelle and Donald Popple, as well as friends and colleagues Jan Jeffers, Heather Maclean, Susan Joiner, Deborah Sheppard, Richard Barrett, Marge Denis, Mary Stacey, Dorothy MacKeracher, Maggi Feehan, Karen Engle, Marilyn Hamilton, Cathy Fulton, Mark Fulton, Mal Jeffers, and Gabrielle Lacelle. I am especially appreciative of the support of the Royal Roads University, particularly the Office of Research, the Todd Thomas Institute for Values-Based Leadership, Library Services, and in particular, Mary Bernard, Bev Hall, Isabel Cordua-Von Specht, Pedro Márquez, Diane Carpenter, and Carolin Rekar-Munro. A special note of gratitude is extended to Dawn Martin for her careful and comprehensive work as my own editor for this volume.

INTRODUCTION

What was scattered gathers.
What was gathered blows apart.

Heraclitus, in Haxton (2001, p. 27)

Heraclitus, you're okay!

dian marino[1]

We find ourselves poised at the outer edge of the modern age, glimpsing its limits and sensing the unknown beyond it. Life in our times is often puzzling, sometimes astonishing, and frequently overwhelming. We experience a dizzying pace daily. What we do to save time seems, paradoxically, to create even more accelerating demands on us. Electronic communication enables us to get our messages to others instantly, but it also rapidly loads our "inboxes" with demands for our attention. Communication technologies combine with rapid global transit to expose us to diverging worldviews of people around the globe—whether we leave home or not. The same sciences that have amplified our ability to describe and measure the vast expanses of space and the infinitesimal elements of the material world have vanquished our expectations of predictability. Control eludes us like never before. The more social and medical knowledge we generate, the more poverty and illness abound.[2] Not only are our ways of doing things coming up short, but the rate at which we face paradoxes and conundrums suggests that our current perspective is inadequate to describe our world. Nearly 15 years ago, Imparato and Harari (1994) observed that we are in "a moment of epochal transformation," like the Enlightenment and the fall of the Roman Empire, in which change "goes to the core of what our lives and institutions are about" requiring us "to rethink . . . core assumptions" (p. 4). More than a decade later, Thomas Homer-Dixon (2006) provided a compelling comparison between the end of Rome and signs of the end of our current era.

The purpose of this book is to illuminate the experience of emergent learning and its practical significance in our current environment of exponential change. Emergent learning is a process through which we create a shift of mind, a fundamentally new perspective and approach to acting in the world; it begins when we are confronted with something that we did not know we did not know. This experience is increasingly common as spiralling sociocultural, political, economic, and environmental change impacts on our daily experience with the unexpected. Much of what we consider commonplace today—how we travel, communicate, live, and work—was unimaginable several decades ago. We have both rapidly expanding opportunities and enormous challenges, some of which threaten life on this planet as we now know it. The critical challenge of our times is to become experts at fostering emergent learning in ourselves and others. Without it we will not develop the resilience and wisdom needed to lead ourselves through these perilous times to a sustainable future.

My work on emergent learning began just over 30 years ago. Momentous worldwide change in the interim has repositioned emergent learning from an interesting concept to a vital project. One of the most frequent quotes heard in the past few decades has been that of Albert Einstein's—"No problem can be solved from the same level of consciousness that created it." There is growing recognition that a shift of mind is essential for our survival in a twenty-first-century world.

Robert Kegan and Lisa Lahey (2009) offered three orders of "mental complexity" in response to what Kegan (1994) earlier called the "hidden curriculum" of culture and its mental demands. "When we are experiencing the world as 'too complex' we are not just experiencing the complexity of the world. We are experiencing a mismatch between the world's complexity *and our own at this moment*" (Kegan and Lahey, 2009, p. 12). They observed three distinctive "plateaus in adult mental complexity." "The socialized mind" (p. 17) is about being "shaped by the definitions and expectations of our personal environment," and our sense of self comes from "alignment with, and loyalty to" (p. 17) external points of identification. We work on the agenda of others. We might expect that if we remain at this plateau, our rapidly changing world will be increasingly overwhelming and frightening. "The self-authoring mind" is evident by being able "to step back enough from the social environment to generate an internal 'seat of judgment' or personal authority that evaluates and makes decisions about external expectations" (p. 17). We recognize that competing positions, and the extraordinary amount of energy that is consumed in maintaining them, have little practical benefit. "The self-transforming mind" is evident in being able to "step back from and reflect on the limits of our own ideology or personal authority," being able to notice that we are "incomplete," in being comfortable with "contraction and opposites," and in being capable of "hold[ing] on to multiple systems" (p. 17).

The central theme of this book is that the critical challenges we are experiencing in this millennium require self-transforming minds. We have to be able to let go of "theories" that are not bringing the results that we are seeking. We have to acknowledge that we are "works in progress." We have to be able to transcend opposites and differences rather than collapse or ignore them. Since Kegan and Lahey observe that less that 8 percent of the American population is close to this level of mental complexity, this sounds like a very tall order. I suggest that this is a difficult challenge, but that it is not exotic—something that requires specialists and consultants, accessible only to a few. The opportunities for learning our way to a new plateau of mental complexity are within our daily experience. This book is an invitation to use experiences of disruption and distress in a positive way to learn our way through to a demanding future. It makes the following audacious propositions: it is precisely our experiences that begin in profound confusion that enable us to transcend our limits of understanding; it is experiences that begin in loss that bring us previously unseen advantages; it is experiences that begin in fear that yield a new confidence; and it is experiences that begin with a sense that our world is crumbling that generate new possibilities.

Emergent learning arises from our direct experience of the practical world; it is triggered by an unpredicted event. The process that follows has the possibility to create not only knowledge but also the *wisdom* we need to engage productively and effectively in a world of uncertainty. Learning that leads to wisdom involves the whole person and new dimensions that have been banished from public life in the modern era. It requires attention to our right-brain processes—sensing, feeling, imagination, metaphor, and context—as well as left-brain processes—analysis, logic, strategy, and application. Gisela Labouvie-Vief (1990) noted: "One mode provides experiential richness and fluidity, the other logical cohesion and stability" and "smooth and relatively balanced dialogue between the two modes . . . I define as wisdom" (p. 53). The process also requires us to attend to unconscious and preconscious processes, as well as conscious processes. Finally, *the pattern that can serve as a map through unpredictability is only fully evident from "the inside-out,"* a vantage point not often taken in traditional social science. "We are only beginning to realize the adaptive significance and heuristic importance of . . . the inward turn" (Labouvie-Vief, 1990, p. 72).

Order is inherent in our own experience. It can serve as a map with which to navigate unpredictability, exercising influence without needing or expecting to control. It means a shift in value priorities from product to process, from knowledge and performance to learning, from theoretical to practical.

THE PLAN OF THE BOOK

The significance of emergent learning derives from our context. We begin in Chapter 1 by examining briefly the current context highlighting its critical challenges. We conclude the chapter considering the kind of learning implied by those challenges that would enable us to engage the challenges constructively.

In Chapter 2, we consider how the meaning of "learning" has evolved over the past four decades. The refined thinking of some scholars and scholar-practitioners beginning with Gregory Bateson (1972) and William Torbert (1972), followed by Chris Argyris and Donald Schön (1974), Paulo Freire (1973), and Robert Kegan (1994), has provided critical conceptual "tools" to distinguish orders of learning and to illuminate shifts of mind or consciousness. We then look closely at consciousness as value-perspectives through which we become aware, choose, and act. Finally, we look briefly at the direction of changing orders of mind or consciousness (Wilber, 2000a) and locate the emergent learning process described in this book in the developmental schemata of Robert Kegan (1982), Jane Loevinger (Loevinger and Blasi, 1976), Beck and Cowan (1996), William Torbert (2004), Abraham Maslow (1943), and Richard Barrett (1998).

The emergent learning process pattern offered in Chapter 3 is a detailed description developed through careful documentation of learners' experiences over the duration of a graduate course (Taylor, 1979). The setting turned out to be a laboratory setting that replicated our current wider cultural experience of being in the face of uncertainty. The common emergent learning process pattern is constructed from a comparative inductive study of "inside-out" commentaries gathered at frequent and regular intervals.

Chapter 4 is a celebration of all the work done over the past four decades to illuminate emergent learning processes in a wide variety of settings, accomplished by Kurt Lewin and Edgar Schein (1995a), Charles Hampden-Turner (1971), David Kolb (1984), Jack Mezirow and his colleagues (1978), William Bridges (2004), Donald Beck and Chris Cowan (1996), and Otto Scharmer (2007). This work exists as a rich resource for us to use in our own map-making. It also provides an opportunity to look for common patterns across settings. While the emergent learning process pattern has been recognized widely by men and women as reflective of their experience in a variety of life settings, juxtaposing the sequence in Chapter 3 with other process formulations highlights an underlying common structure. We conclude the chapter with a similar change process model observed in the natural world—Lance Gunderson and C. S. Holling's (2002) Panarchy Model—that suggests that understanding and relating to our own process of emergent learning may enable us to identify and learn from the equivalent patterns in our environment.

Chapter 5 is an invitation and a resource to "lead ourselves" by developing composite strengths in emergent learning. We briefly explore 12 practices that enable us to enhance our abilities as emergent learners, including mindfulness, complementarity, self-esteem and self-compassion, emotional intelligence, social choreography, right-brain thinking, collaborative inquiry, reflection, presence, vision and flow, wisdom, and values fluency. Each practice is introduced, offering a brief description and pointing to resources for further exploration.

The final chapter highlights the relevance of emergent learning to specific items on our twenty-first-century learning agenda set out in Chapter 1, and a consideration of the relationship between emergent learning and the new leadership that is being identified with our postindustrial era.

A Word about Words: Learning, Change, Emergent, Transformation, Transition, Development

As in any recent domain of discourse, words are used differently, sometimes interchangeably, by different writers and practitioners. One of the key words in this book is "learning," a word for which there are several cognate terms—change, transformation, and transition. "Change" is used as "individual change" (e.g., Mahoney, 1991), "organizational change" (e.g., Burke, 2008), or "social change" (e.g., Rosenberg, 2005) to mean growth, evolution, maturation, and development. However, it is in the broadest of terms defined as "substitution of one thing for another; succession of one thing in place of another" (*Oxford English Dictionary*), without necessarily being a change for the better. Similarly, "transformation," defined as "the action of changing in form, shape, or appearance; metamorphosis" (*Oxford English Dictionary*), does not necessarily mean improvement. "Transition," defined as "a passing or passage from one condition, action, or (rarely) place, to another; change" (*Oxford English Dictionary*), is another term often used to describe the human experience we are examining. However, "transition" is understood by some to be a contrast to "transformation" (de Guerre, 2001); transition is the pursuit of a *known* desired state, while transformation is a process through which the end state emerges. Finally, "development" has wide currency as a term applied to individuals, groups, organizations, communities, and regions to signify positive change. While helpful, this term does focus our attention exclusively on the growth side of the process. On a wider social scale, development is also a controversial term, often associated with the predominance of one group over another and exploitation of resources by powerful interests (e.g., Krueger and Gibbs, 2007).

The choice here is to use the term "learning." There is the risk that some of us may interpret this narrowly as synonymous with "teaching" and "school," but it is part of the whole term, "emergent learning," and the distinction will, hopefully, be obvious. There are several compelling reasons for selecting "learning" as the primary term. First, while a restrictive term in the traditional sense, there has been a 40-year history of enhancing its relevance and meaning, starting with Gregory Bateson (see Chapter 2). Second, it is a term that implies responsible agency in a change process in which we exercise choice. Third, "learning" is a term that, in the past several decades, has been applied to human systems—teams and organizations—in a systems perspective (e.g., Senge, 2006), linking individual learning to effective adaptation on a larger scale. The "reach" of learning has been expanded in this discourse. Fourth, learning is a concept associated with enabling us to accomplish more in the future than we can now; this positive association is critical. Fifth, as it is redefined to include second- and third-order learning, it can be reframed to include *all* phases and features of emergent learning including, paradoxically, the accomplishment of "unknowing" that we need in order to transcend a more limited way of interpreting the world.

Finally, I propose that we call the process "emergent learning." Many (e.g., Mezirow, 2000; O'Sullivan, 1999) have called it "transformation" or "transformative learning," which it is certainly in its outcome. But if we focus on the *process*, it is more than that. I suggest that "transformation" is the third and final phase in which we understand our world from a new perspective that Mezirow called "perspective transformation." It is the moment in which we consciously realize the "big picture" that redefines our world and our place in it. It is understandable that our attention is drawn to that moment, both because it is dramatic and also because in this culture we give most importance to *conscious* aspects of learning and the world of defining ideas. In practical terms, however, we first engage a new perspective *as an experience* and give it significance long before we conceptualize it. In our twenty-first-century context, unless we can step out of our cultural "comfort zone" and recognize what *emerges* as learning, beginning with the surprising experience of *not knowing* out of which knowing emerges, we will be unable to use our talents to their best effect in meeting the challenges of the current era.

I have used the first person plural, "we," to emphasize a sense of collective responsibility in which I include myself. I do not presume all of the statements here apply necessarily in the same way to everyone, but I invite us all to think of ourselves on similar journeys.

CHAPTER 1

---◆---

A TWENTY-FIRST-CENTURY LEARNING AGENDA: CHALLENGES AND POSSIBILITIES

One of humanity's constant nightmares has been that technological growth . . . has always run ahead of . . . growth of wisdom, care and compassionate use of that technology.

Ken Wilber (2000b, p. 103)

We need the sagacity, as well as immense energy, to find our way into a new cultural synthesis of planetary proportions. People say we cannot do it, and the answer is that we must do it.

Edmund O'Sullivan (1999, p. 39)

OUR GLOBAL CONTEXT OF EXPONENTIAL CHANGE

We now recognize not only that we are in an age of continuous change, but also that change, itself, is continually accelerating. Fred Emery and Eric Trist (1965) were among the first to recognize this as the defining quality of a fundamentally new age. They observed more than 40 years ago that we were moving out of an age in which, as organizational and community leaders, we could predict successful results from wise strategies and the power to compete effectively, and we were entering an age that is inherently unpredictable. Emery and Trist called this a "turbulent field" created by a growing multiplicity of competitors for resources, buyers, and the like; their simultaneous and intensifying interactions were generating a qualitatively different environment. Few would have regarded these observations as critical then, but most of us now would recognize this theme as a defining feature of nearly every aspect of our human experience today. In fact, many of us would recognize features of what Emery and Trist speculated as a subsequent type of environment, a vortical environment, which would rise in the absence of effective adaptations to turbulence. Without a thoughtfully formulated desirable direction for change, guided by explicit values and engaging those who have a stake in the outcome, turbulent environments turn to a vortical pattern that draws more into it as it accelerates.

Forty years later, Thomas Friedman (2005) published his encyclopedic examination of how the Emery and Trist commentary has become manifest in our twenty-first-century world. Like Emery and Trist, he highlighted the impact of technological innovation not only on how we do things but also on its implications for how we organize ourselves to do things—transformations of the social, organizational, and cultural order. Friedman spoke of a "flattening process" globally—the creation of a more level playing field. "Because it is a flattening and shrinking of the world, [the new] globalization . . . is going to be more and more driven not only by individuals but also by a much more diverse—non-Western, nonwhite—group of individuals. Individuals from every corner of the flat world are being empowered" (p. 11). At home, we are experiencing a flattening of our own social and organizational structures, and the diminishing effectiveness of centralized authority keeping pace with new opportunities and challenges. These reconfigurations of global and local social realities confront each one of us, as participants in the twenty-first century, and require us to reframe our perspectives, assumptions, and expectations about our world, our nation, our organizations and communities, our knowledge and learning, leadership and authority, and ourselves.

GLOBAL CONNECTIVITY

A series of electronic innovations have transformed our workplaces and, more generally, our world, by enabling us to communicate and, indeed, collaborate with almost anyone in the world. We are now living in the "global village" that Marshall McLuhan (1962) named nearly 50 years ago.

My initial work on emergent learning was written on a typewriter at a time when the most rapid transfer of written work across distance was by courier. IBM's original personal computer was released by 1981. At that time, Bill Gates of Microsoft believed that his

64-kilobyte floppy disks provided more memory than anyone would need (Harris, 1998). I am currently writing on a computer with 400 gigabytes of memory, over 6 million times that of the floppy disk, and I back it up on a terabyte external hard disk. In 1981, the first public access Internet system became available. While email predates the Internet, its use as the primary medium for correspondence has become a reality through this electronic network of networks. By 2008 there were 1.3 billion email users (Royal Pingdom, 2010). The World Wide Web, the system of electronic documents and related search engines, emerged in the early 1990s, less than 20 years ago. There are now over 1.8 billion Internet users worldwide, with the highest proportion by region being North America (76.2 percent), Oceania/Australia (60.8 percent), and Europe (53 percent). The highest rates of growth in 2000–2009 were in the Middle East, Africa, and Latin America/Caribbean (Internet World Stats, 2009). Amplifying the connectivity of the Internet, satellite-based telephone communication makes it possible for us to be in daily, virtually instantaneous, contact with people around the world at minimal cost. Satellite-enabled wireless technology means that we can speak to anyone virtually anywhere from nearly anywhere. Use of mobile telephones worldwide increased over eightfold from 2000 to 2009 as reported by the International Telecommunications Union.[1]

Satellite communication technology permits the instantaneous transmission of images from any part of the world to any other. The turn of the millennium was viewed in real time as one global event—a "first" in history—through the televising of culturally distinct celebrations in each country as the first day of the twenty-first century dawned around the Earth. Images of natural disasters, wars, terrorist attacks, rescues, and airplane crashes can be witnessed in our homes within minutes of their occurrence. World championships are watched live by each country's cheering fans from virtual bleachers around the world.

From the "platform" of space, too, within the past 40 years, we have had our first images of our planet as a whole, which some have suggested compels us to see ourselves differently. American space tourist Anousheh Ansari commented: "The sheer beauty of it just brought tears to my eyes. . . . If people can see Earth from up here, see it without those borders, see it without any differences in race or religion, they would have a completely different perspective. Because when you see it from that angle, you cannot think of your home or your country. All you can see is one Earth" (Keim, 2007).

The virtual workplace, too, has arrived. This book was written primarily in Victoria, British Columbia, but it was also written in

Toronto, Vancouver, Calgary, and Stockholm. I was unable to lift all the components of my first-generation IBM computer together at one time; I now work on a laptop that goes everywhere with me and can store this book and its related literature on a memory stick that is not much larger than my little finger. I not only accessed vast databases of articles through my library at Royal Roads University, but also delved into "the ebrary," electronic books at my fingertips available to me from anywhere that I access the Internet. This book was submitted as a manuscript to my publisher, Palgrave Macmillan in New York, a global academic publisher that is part of the Macmillan Group, which is connected throughout Europe, North America, Australia, the Far East, Japan, the Middle East, India, Africa, and the Caribbean. The approved manuscript was sent to Bangalore in India, where it was packaged. Then again from New York, the book was distributed through a worldwide network of book sellers and academic conferences. This is one small example of what Friedman (2005) called the "web-enabled platform."

> This platform enables individuals, groups, companies, and universities anywhere in the world to collaborate—for the purposes of innovation, production, education, research, entertainment, and, alas, war-making—like no creative platform ever before. This platform now operates without regard to geography, distance, time, and, in the near future, even language. Going forward this platform is going to be at the center of everything. (p. 205)

With the remarkable advantages of digital and electronic communication have come unexpected demands and challenges. Thirty years ago, communication by mail, even courier, meant that I could forget about the subject of the correspondence for at least another week and turn my attention to other things. Today, I can send an email to the other side of the world and can receive a response within a few minutes. It is not uncommon for people to spend hours just managing email—responding and filing—let alone managing the rapidly accumulating tasks generated by them. Email, text messaging, and other forms of instant communication seem to be compelling and seductive to the extent that they are seizing our attention and taking over our agendas.

Kevin Kelly (2008), founding editor of *Wired Magazine*, observed:

> Everything that we have—satellite images of the earth, your family tree, all patents, anything to do with anyone's phone number, anything

for sale, government forms, weather everywhere, all your friends, real time stock quotes, newspapers, sports scores, real estate prices, library books, street maps, all movies, all regulations . . . has happened in 5000 days. . . . It does about 100 billion clicks per day. It contains about 55 trillion links between all the web pages in the world. There is about a billion PC chips. It does 2 million emails and 8 terabytes of traffic in a second. . . . It uses 5% of the world's electricity to keep it going. . . . The order of magnitude of this machine is very equivalent to the size and scale of the human brain.

Kelly pointed out that the Web works in an associative manner similar to our brain, but the difference is that our brain will not double in capacity every two years, as will the Web. He expects that in 30 years the Web will have outgrown the capacity of the whole human race put together. He predicted that by about 2012 we will see Web 3.0, the Semantic Web, which will link data, ideas with "a much finer resolution." "We're going to live inside the Web because everything will be connected to it."

Poscente (2008) observed, "With the boom in technology enabling us to achieve speed in almost every imaginable way, speed is no longer a luxury—it's an expectation. And the more we get, the more we want. Email, PDAs, self-checkout, downloadable music, real-time news, ATMs, digital cameras: technology has driven speed into every aspect of our daily lives" (p. 13). Paradoxically, while technology can amplify options, it can also impact employees and the workplace in unintended negative ways. An expert on stress in the workplace, Marc Chenais, suggested, "increasing reliance on technology is one of the biggest causes of work-related depression" (Hollinger, 2008). While some have observed that, on one hand, electronic communication in the workplace can diminish employees' sense of autonomy, others have noted that curiosity-based, rather than task-related, use of the Internet is compromising productivity. "A kind of communications anarchy is breaking out in offices all over the world and managers are feeling powerless to intervene" (Donkin, 2008). One great danger is that individuals and organizations lose focus and their purpose, simply reacting and running to catch up with the pace of change.

The access to instantaneous information also affects our lives in communities. On one hand, citizens have been enormously empowered through immediate access to public policy and governance decisions, research and public records, best practices, and documentation of social issues around the world. We are able to access health and medical knowledge when concerned about our physical well-being, product information and sources when interested in purchasing goods and services, and detailed information about recreational opportunities around the world when making decisions about our leisure pursuits. On the other hand, the same connectivity has amplified the dissemination of child pornography, the perpetration of scams, breaches of privacy, and facilitation of serious, often deadly, threats to safety and security. Child pornography has been prevalent on the Internet; distributors were early adopters of Internet benefits. Recently, Wortley and Smallbone (2006) noted, "At any one time there are estimated to be more than one million pornographic images of children on the Internet, with 200 new images posted daily" (p. 12). Finally, in December 2010, the WikiLeaks Web site posed the most dramatic and far-reaching instance of what many consider to be misuse of the Internet by exposing 250,000 diplomatic cables to leading newspapers. As authorities moved against the Web site's founder, Julian Assange, his supporters targeted other Web sites seen to be opposed to him; they managed to render some inaccessible and others less operable. The WikiLeaks events highlight new ways in which the Internet can be used aggressively; they raise spiraling concern about cyber security and control.

Thomas Homer-Dixon (2006) sees global connectivity as a "multiplier," a kind of accelerant for what he calls "tectonic stresses" facing us in the twenty-first century, some of which are explored in the following pages.

Global connectivity has triggered change in every imaginable corner of our world, and our lives and these effects are expected to accelerate. However, our greatest learning challenges are not technological in nature. Rather, they are the radical shifts in reinventing how we relate to each other in organizations and communities locally and globally, and how we relate to our environment, the natural world. Implicit in the reconfiguration of these fundamental relationships is learning our way into a new understanding of ourselves. We turn to these now.

EXPONENTIAL ECONOMIC UNCERTAINTY

No evidence of international interdependence and unpredictable turbulence has been more palpable and dramatic than the global economic collapse of 2008. Relaxed credit conditions and low interest rates introduced by the U.S. Federal Reserve after the stock market crises of the "dot-com" bubble and the 9/11 terrorist attacks enabled American consumers to extend their borrowing power beyond their means in normal credit conditions. In addition to accelerated home purchases, billions of dollars were withdrawn from home equity through refinancing. The American economy became driven by, and dependent on, the U.S. consumer. When subprime mortgages came to term, more than a million U.S. homes were in foreclosure in June 2008 (CNNMoney.com),[2] and by September of that year, huge financial institutions were being taken over (Fannie Mae and Freddie Mac with $5 trillion debt) (*New York Times*),[3] or receiving government bailouts (AIG for $85 billion) (*Wall Street Journal*),[4] or going bankrupt (Lehman Brothers, one of the largest bankruptcies in American history) (*New York Times*).[5] September 29, 2008, saw the largest single-day drop on the DOW in its history (778 points), wiping out $1.2 trillion of market value at the thought that massive government bailouts would not be forthcoming (CNNMoney.com);[6] the DOW continued to fluctuate and ultimately decline to its lowest level—6469.95—on March 6, 2009 (CNNMoney.com).[7] Millions of Americans suddenly lost their homes and many more lost their jobs. In spite of the largest government bailouts in U.S. history, from the start of the recession in December 2007 to June 2009, the unemployment rate more than doubled (7.2 million to 14.7 million—4.6 to 9.5 percent) with large declines in manufacturing, professional and business services, and construction (U.S. Bureau of Labor Statistics, 2009).

The collapse of the U.S. housing bubble was predicted by many, but its far-reaching effect around the world was expected by few. The extent to which the world economy is hinged on the U.S. economy and, indeed, the American consumer, was revealed through the 2008–2009 global market collapse, seen as the worst since the Great Depression. The effects from the burst of the subprime mortgage bubble in the United States rippled around the world, exploding similarly vulnerable banking practices especially and generally devastating world markets with sharply dropping stock market indices. By October, Iceland was on the verge of bankruptcy. Bankruptcy was prevented only by a $10 billion bailout from the International Monetary Fund. By the end of 2008 and closing in their worst years ever, Japan's Nikkei lost 42 percent of its value; Chinese stock exchanges dropped 20 trillion yuan or US$3 trillion; and the UK's FTSE 100 declined 31 percent, wiping out £500 billion. The Canadian TSX dropped from a high of 14,714.73 in April 2008 to a low of 7591.47 by March 2009, a decline of 51.6 percent of its value, and along with it a significant proportion of my retirement investments. I, along with millions of individuals and their families, was surprised by the extent of this downturn and its devastating results in lost homes, jobs, and retirement savings. Over time, economists, financial analysts, and business leaders confessed that this global event was new territory for them also. American mortgage debt had been distributed through financial institutions around the world, and as a result, the United States had a disproportional influence on the international banking system that had been propping up the U.S. banking system (Soros, 2008).

While the economic collapse well beyond a relatively predictable expected market correction came as a surprise to most of us, Soros (2008) dates the pervasive "dot-com" downturn in 2000—the advent of hedge funds, and the radical reduction in interest rates to soften the effects of the 9/11 terrorist attack. He describes this collapse as a "super-bubble," which he says "marks the end of an era of credit expansion based on the dollar as the international reserve currency" (p. vii). The 2008 economic collapse has been followed by a rather rapid recovery of stock markets, but a high level of uncertainty continues as the other aspects of national economies, such as the resulting rates of unemployment and of national debt, remain perilously high. In late 2009, debt levels and fragile economies in Greece, Portugal, and Ireland along with mega-bankruptcies in Dubai, precipitated debt restructuring and bailouts—all with consequences in a highly interdependent and increasingly unpredictable global economy.

RECONFIGURING SOCIAL RELATIONS

Redefining Leadership, Authority, and Organization

In the current context of an astonishing rate of change, an explosion of knowledge in every sector and an increasingly informed global citizenry, the intelligence to effectively decide and provide direction in organizational life can no longer originate with only the few "at the top." Friedman (2005) sees organizations and institutions having to flatten along with the twenty-first-century world:

> As the world starts to move from a primarily vertical—command and control—value creation model, and as we blow away more walls, ceilings, and floors at the same time, societies are going to find themselves facing a lot of very profound changes all at once. But these changes won't just affect how business gets done. They will affect how individuals, communities, and companies organize themselves, where companies and communities stop and start, how individuals balance their different identities as consumers, employees, shareholders, and citizens, tell people to find themselves politically, and what the role of government plays in managing all of this flux. This won't happen overnight, but over time many roles, habits, political identities, and

management practices that we had grown used to in the world are going to have to be profoundly adjusted for the age of flatness. To put it simply, following a great triple convergence that started right around the year 2000, we're going to experience what I would call "the great sorting out." (p. 234)

In the workplace, the attention to developing relevant adaptations to twenty-first-century realities has been largely on redesigning organizations and on creating work teams to respond effectively to the rapidly and continuously changing demands for services and products. Nearly 20 years ago, Beckhard and Pritchard (1992) noted: "This 'white water' turbulence is forcing most leaders to examine the very essence of their organizations—their basic purposes, their identities, and their relationships with customers, competitors, and suppliers" (p. 1).

Simple rearrangements according to traditional organizational principles have frequently proven ineffectual, as evidenced by recurrent, unsatisfactory restructuring. We have reached the limits of our traditional bureaucracy generated by a nineteenth-century imagination—silos with vertical top-to-bottom, one-way communication. Simply downsizing current organizational structures or shifting traditional responsibilities around has resulted in unrealistic expectations of fewer people producing more and doing so more quickly. Recent National Values Assessments[8] highlight bureaucracy and long hours as the most common issues in workplaces in the United States, UK, Canada, Sweden, Denmark, and Iceland. Employees become overwhelmed, feeling hopeless and cynical about the recurrent change efforts that are seen as minimally successful, at best.

It is not clear what new forms of organization will prevail and endure, but there are some definite trends. Organizations that thrive in the future are likely to reflect

1. significant decentralization of responsibility and decision-making in order to be flexible and responsive to changing demands;
2. workplace engagement of employees in the creation and intelligent use of knowledge in planning and decision-making; and
3. continuous adaptation and reshaping of themselves as their challenges emerge and change.

A critical challenge is to manage organizational change so as to unleash confidence, enthusiasm, and satisfaction of employees in the process of effectively engaging with the new opportunities. Movement to distributed leadership and decision-making requires organizational change processes that model that new configuration; in that vein, there have been fundamental changes to organizational change, itself. Peggy Holman and Tom Devane (1999) have drawn together four methods for planning, four for organizational restructuring, and ten adaptable to a range of organizational change objectives, all of which enact two radically different sets of assumptions, beliefs, and values. The first is "*intelligently involving* people in changing their workplaces and communities" and the second is "a *systemic* approach to change" (p. 6). These new approaches imply shifts in a worldview that are radical in nature, that is, change at the root of our culture.

Intriguingly, social values seem to be shifting in most of the more developed world in synch with demands for organizational "flattening." Adams (2007b) reported significant social values shifts among Canadians from "deference to authority" to "autonomy," from "patriarchy" to "equality," from "hierarchy" to "heterarchy," from "rigidity" to "flexibility," and from "follow the rules" to "think for yourself." He described a strong shift away from patriarchal values in Canada and many other Western nations (including France, Italy, Britain, Spain, Germany, and Sweden), the exception being in the United States, where support for patriarchal authority has been increasing (Adams, 2003, 2006).[9] However, House and his colleagues (2004) found that the practice of distributed leadership is more often valued than actually practiced. In their prodigious global study of culture and leadership, based on interviews with 17,300 managers in 951 organizations in 62 countries around the world, they found that with respect to power distance, "the degree to which members of an organization or society expect that power should be distributed equally" (p. 30), the value was the most discrepant from the perceived practice compared to the other eight value clusters. "The GLOBE sample of societies shows that Power Distance is the most strongly practiced, yet the most strongly despised dimension of societal cultures" (p. 559). This contradiction represents one of the most critical ongoing struggles in organizational life.

So whether driven by global flux or by social values trends or by both, there is pressure to reimagine leadership and, in particular, to redistribute authority, responsibility, and accountability. For those holding positions of authority, perhaps even more than for their employees, this is an enormously difficult change—perhaps because it begins with themselves.

In order to make change happen, executives have to break a longstanding behavior pattern of their own: providing leadership in the form of solutions. This tendency is quite natural because many executives reach their positions of authority by virtue of their competence in taking responsibility and solving problems. But the locus of responsibility for problem solving when a company faces adaptive challenge must shift to its people. Solutions to adaptive challenges reside not in the executive suite but in the collective intelligence of employees at all levels, who need to use one another as resources, often across boundaries, and learn their way to those solutions" (Heifetz and Laurie, 2001, p. 132)

Rooke and Torbert (2005) suggest that only 5 percent of leaders currently operate as dynamic change leaders, transformational leaders at the organizational level and beyond. George and McLean (2007) found that the shift of mind they identified as "'I' to 'we,'" leaving the heroic, egocentric orientation to leadership behind and moving to a focus on engendering leadership in others, is not easily accomplished but is the outcome of a very demanding journey with painful moments and many ups and downs.

The Intersection/Clash of Cultures

The virtual workplace is made possible through global connectivity. Combined with increasing ease of travel and increases in migration around the world, it has amplified our contact with cultural differences and ways of life.

International travel across all continents is skyrocketing, most of it over and above business-related travel, reflecting growing international interest and intercultural contact. The World Tourism Organization (UNWTO) reports that, when considering all countries, international tourist arrivals nearly doubled between 1990 and 2006, and it projects that the rate will almost double again between 2006 and 2020. The greatest annual increases in 2006 were to Africa, Asia, and the Pacific. In 2006, 51 percent of the 846 million arrivals were identified as leisure, recreation, and holidays, and a further 27 percent related to visiting friends and family; business travel accounted for 16 percent.

According to the Global Commission on International Migration (GCIM), migration doubled from 99.3 million to 190.6 million in the period between 1980 and 2005, though accounting still for only 3 percent (1 in 35) of the world's population (GCIM, 2005).[10] The Commission noted that migration has been facilitated by more developed global communication, increasing ease of global transportation, and growing social networks worldwide. The government of Switzerland's Federal Office of Migration reported that the current unprecedented levels of migration are driven largely by economic necessity. "The growing gap between rich and poor is the most significant driving force for global migration. In 1960, the income of the richest fifth of the world's population was, on average, 30 times higher than the poorest fifth. By the year 1990, it was already 60 times higher" (Schweizerische Eidgenossenschaft, n.d.). Significantly decreased birth rates in more developed countries have led to immigration policies in these regions, which are intended to attract foreign-born workers to compensate for their drop in population. So it is not surprising that the GCIM (2005) reports that 60 percent of immigration is in the developed world, with a 20-year trend indicating that there is increasing flow (2.3 percent increase) toward the more developed regions of the world, compared to migration toward the developing world (1.2 percent increase).[11] In launching the Organization of Economic Cooperation and Development's (OECD) 2008 *International Migration Outlook,* Secretary-General Angel Gurría confirmed this trend continuing with a 5 percent increase in immigration to OECD countries over the previous year, only to be interrupted the next year due to the economic crisis (OECD, 2009).

While human migration strengthens our societies and economies, it also amplifies confrontation with the unfamiliar, in this case, cultural values, beliefs, and practices. The GCIM (2005) developed a series of "principles for action to maximize the benefits of and minimize the negative consequences of migration; these included the need for a mutual process of adaptation and integration that accommodates cultural diversity and fosters social cohesion" (p. 4). Both immigrants and the host country's citizens are faced with a complex process of engaging with the culturally unfamiliar. As an example, in my country, the 5.4 percent population increase between 2001 and 2006 was due in large measure (69.3 percent) to immigration (Statistics Canada, 2007a). Further, these new neighbors most likely came from Asia (58.3 percent), while in 1971 they were more likely to come from Europe (61.6 percent) (Statistics Canada, 2007b). An overwhelming majority of Canadians (79 percent) feel that "cultural diversity gives Canada a distinct advantage, especially with respect to innovation" and "flexibility and adaptability to a changing marketplace." Specific advantages were seen to "encourage a more balanced view of problems . . . strengthen the overall corporate culture, enhance corporate reputations, enhance service levels, reduce turnover, lower absenteeism rates and improve a company's global management capacity" (Bowes, 2007/2008, p. 14, 15). Sixteen years ago, Matt Barrett (1994), then president of Bank of Montreal (BMO), placed Canada's diversity as an asset in the global economy; it meant BMO employees could represent the bank in almost every country in the world in their own mother tongue.

Michael Adams (2007a) of Environics Research and Communications observed that attitudes toward immigration vary among host countries. Quoting an IPSOS MORI study in 2006[12] in which the question "Overall, would you say immigrants are having a good or bad influence on the way things are going in [country]" was posed to 1000 respondents in eight more developed countries, he noted that 75 percent of Canadians say their contributions are positive compared with 54 percent of Australians, 52 percent of Americans, 47 percent of Germans, 45 percent of Spaniards, 45 percent of French, 44 percent of Italians, and 43 percent of Britons. Perhaps more significantly, 40 percent or more of the respondents from the United States, Britain, and countries in Europe viewed immigrants' influence as negative. Countries with under 40 percent of respondents viewing immigrants' contributions as negative were Australia at 39 percent and Canada at 20 percent. Nevertheless, even in a considerably immigrant friendly country like Canada, a mutual adaptation process demands intercultural understanding and accommodations. Adams cites specific examples of Canadian experiences—how to fit a turban into a military or a police uniform, how to enable girls to play soccer safely while wearing a hijab, and how to enable women to vote with their faces concealed by a niqab. These are examples of daily differences that confront us, and demand that we find common ground. These new conditions of life in workplaces and communities demand collaboration and dialogue among people who see and approach things differently and the negotiation of changes in taken-for-granted social and organizational practices.

The more subtle and profound demand on us is to fully embrace multiple cultural perspectives and life in pluralistic nations. Those of us who have lived and worked in culturally homogeneous communities and organizations are like the fish that does not know what water is; we are typically unaware of our perspective, assumptions, and values that give meaning to our way of life, until we encounter different people with very different viewpoints, values, and expectations. It becomes clear that there are many interpretations and ways of doing things. We are provoked to examine *why* we see things the way we do. Ultimately, we have to recognize that the infusion of different cultural perspectives will change our organizations and communities and also that mutual adaptation means change, for both those who are immigrants and those who are current citizens.

Human Rights and Equality within and across Nations of the World

In the context of the United Nations' Universal Declaration of Human Rights in 1948, in the past 50 years a series of international conventions have defined a human rights agenda worldwide. They include the International Convention on the Elimination of All Forms of Racial Discrimination (ICERD) (adopted in 1965 and enforced in 1969), Convention on the Elimination of All Forms of Discrimination against Women (CEDAW) (adopted in 1979 and enforced in 1981), and the Declaration on the Rights of Indigenous Peoples (adopted by the UN in 2007). The past 30 years have been characterized by a continuing struggle to establish human rights and equality among people everywhere in nations around the world. Attention to human rights in recent decades is reflected throughout the Western world in new and updated legislation and enforcement infrastructure with respect to fair employment practices, antidiscrimination, and harassment prevention across sectors, jurisdictions, and institutions.

Taking employment equity as an example, the International Labour Organization (ILO) reported that the percentage of women participating in the labor force continues to climb in all regions of the world, and their percentage of total employees increased slightly between 1995 and 2004 in every region of the world except in sub-Saharan Africa and in the non-EU states and Central Asia. Women's participation in high-status positions (legislative, senior official, and managerial jobs) has increased in all regions of the world, but still remains at 28 percent, with the greatest increases being in South Asia and East Asia/Pacific regions (ILO, 2007). Overall, gender pay inequity is a most intractable challenge. "Even though the gender pay gap narrowed in some places and stagnated in others, women continue to work, on average, for lower earnings than men. This trend continues despite striking advances of women in educational attainments relative to men" (ILO, 2007, p. 20). Racial and ethnic discrimination also continues to persist in the workplace worldwide. Highlighting the cases of people of African descent, ethnic minorities, and indigenous peoples, the ILO report (2007) noted, "Centuries of unequal treatment in all spheres of life, combined with persistent and deep ethnic socio-economic inequalities, explain their low educational and occupational attainments" (p. 24). The report pointed out that ethnic and racial discrimination are closely linked to poverty and chronic poverty in particular. Progress on the United Nations

Millennium Development Goals established in 2000 to be achieved in 2015 has been mixed, according to the Secretary-General's 2010 report to the General Assembly (United Nations, 2010). While poverty is decreasing by some measures, the improvements are unevenly distributed worldwide—mostly in China. Gradually, the number of hungry people had been increasing in the period between 1990–1992 and 2004–2006 (3.7 percent) but sharply in the three years ending in 2009 (16.8 percent) due to rising food prices and the global economic crisis.

Commentaries on the enormously beneficial possibilities of globalization are accompanied with concerns about its dangers to the well-being of populations and the environment (Homer-Dixon, 2006). It is too soon to know which will outweigh the other, but it is vital to track its effects. There are those who are optimistic that globalization will foster the advancement of democracy and human rights worldwide through innovation and open trade (e.g., Cuervo-Cazurra and Dau, 2009; d'Aquino, 1996), though concerns are simultaneously expressed about social disruptions, the potential for exploitation, and impacts on the environment. While global connectivity has created access to information and tools for collaboration for hugely expanded circles of people, the conditions for empowerment and enhancing life are complex combinations of government, culture, education, and capital (Friedman, 2005). Arjun Appadurai (2006) has articulated a deeper analysis of the challenges of the global era as he searches for an understanding of cultural violence on a large-scale manifest in the 1990s.

> Where the lines between us and them may have always, in human history, been blurred at the boundaries and unclear across large spaces and big numbers, globalization exacerbates these uncertainties and produces new incentives for cultural purification as more nations lose the illusion of national economic sovereignty or well being. This observation also reminds us that large-scale violence is not simply the product of antagonistic identities but that violence itself is one of the ways in which the illusion of fixed and charged identities is produced, partly to allay the uncertainties about identity that global flows invariably produce. (p. 7)

Appadurai's observations go to the heart of human response to change, which, as an individual expression, is the theme of this book. However, his is a consideration of its destructive potential on a grand scale. While pursuing the benefits of globalization and global connectivity, it is clearly urgent that we accelerate our understanding and capacity to wisely engage this world of change and its uncertainties.

FAILURE TO REDEFINE OUR RELATIONSHIP TO NATURE

Perhaps the most demanding and far-reaching changes required, and the far too gradual recognition of the need for them, are those that relate to our planet being endangered by our own way of life. While environmentalism is almost as old as industrialism, the environmental movement over the past 30 to 40 years has become a growing feature of our public attention, as the magnitude of the current environmental crisis becomes more apparent to more and more people. The movement has evolved to generate political parties, environmental policies and legislation, interdisciplinary domains of education and research, and an advocacy agenda that is front and center in our media.

The past 30 years have been punctuated by marker events that have characterized this period as one of mounting environmental threat. They include the Three Mile Island's near meltdown (1979); the Chernobyl nuclear plant disaster (1986); a continuing series of oil spills such as that of the Exxon Valdez (1989)—all of which are dwarfed by the largest oil spill in U.S. history, with an estimated 60,000 barrels pouring into the Gulf of Mexico from a BP deep water oil well that exploded on April 19, 2010; the effects of climate change, including observable reductions in the north and south polar ice caps that threaten highly populated land masses with rising ocean levels; regular smog alerts in our cities, due to increasing levels of air pollution; and increasing frequency of destructive changes in global weather patterns. For the first time in human history, we are confronted with the news that our expectation that our natural world will always be there for us is an assumption not supported by the evidence. The air we breathe; the food we eat; the water we drink; the forests, lakes, and streams we enjoy; and the wildlife we marvel at are all compromised by our industrial and postindustrial production and transportation activity.

Yet, to date, our individual daily lives have been changed only in very small ways as the scale of environmental damage unfolds. We are more likely to recycle to reduce the accumulating waste we generate. We may use energy-conserving products such as light bulbs and better home insulation, and look for other ways to reduce our consumption of energy. These initiatives, while helpful, fall short of addressing, and even perhaps mask, the enormity of the challenge.

Recognizing that a global problem requires a global response, we look to international organizations and national governments whose mandates are to act on behalf of the well-being of their citizens and communities. Here we find the collective response through legislative change typically paralyzed in a maze of competing economic and political interests.

Taking climate change as one of the most critical cases in point, the United Nations Earth Summit held in Rio de Janeiro in 1992 generated the United Nations Framework Convention on Climate Change (UNFCCC) (United Nations, 1992), the name of both a treaty and a UN secretariat, intended to "achieve . . . stabilization of greenhouse gas concentrations in the atmosphere at a level that would prevent dangerous anthropogenic interference in the climate system" (United Nations, 1992, p. 4). Signatories agreed, among other things, to provide national data for periodic updates in greenhouse gas emissions, to promote and provide updates on preventive measures to reduce emissions, and to promote education and public awareness. The UNFCCC, though a legally nonbinding treaty, did generate a greenhouse gas inventory and the Kyoto Protocol that did set mandatory greenhouse gas emission levels (agreed in 1997 to come into effect in 2005). By 2007, several signatory nations had not ratified the agreement, one of them being the United States. It took until 2007 to even get unanimous agreement of member nations of the Intergovernmental Panel on Climate Change (IPCC) that stated: "Warming of the climate system is unequivocal, as it is now evident from observations of increases in global average air and ocean temperatures, widespread melting snow and ice and rising global sea level" (IPCC, 2007, p. 2). And the IPCC further agrees that ". . . many natural systems are being affected by regional climate changes, particularly temperature increases" (p. 2). The urgency of dealing with the climate change problem is, perhaps, symbolized in the awarding of the Nobel Peace Prize to Al Gore, author of *An Inconvenient Truth* (2006), for his research and global initiative to educate people about the dangers of global warming. Yet the Copenhagen Conference on Climate Change in 2009, while it drew unprecedented participation, including visits by 115 heads of state, and raised for the first time some of the most difficult issues, failed to establish the kind of binding agreements that would launch a turnaround in global warming. A subsequent conference of

190 nations in Cancun in December, 2010, achieved modest gains in the form of all, for the first time ever, agreeing to reduce pollution as well as working out ways to create a $100 billion fund that will enable poorer nations to comply. However, as Rob Edwards, environmental editor of the *Herald-Scotland* noted, "The world, in other words, may not be dying, but it is still on life support" (*The Herald,* 2010).

DIMINISHING CAPACITY FOR RESILIENCE

We have been reviewing the trends of challenge—the "what"—that we faced in the first decades of the twenty-first century. There is also a second "layer" of threat that cuts across the foregoing domains of challenge.

Comparing the current state of Western civilization to the last days of Rome, Thomas Homer-Dixon (2006) argued that we lack the flexibility it takes to successfully address the "stresses" we are facing. We lack resilience, or the capacity to rebound or spring back (*Oxford English Dictionary*) from events that challenge us. Resilience is a central theme of this book, both as a quality, and in and of itself, and as an outcome of individual emergent learning.

Homer-Dixon drew our attention to the question of resilience of the economic, social, and political dimensions of our civilization. He examined the energy that it takes to run current "developed" and "developing" societies—their "thermodynamics"—and "the link between energy and complexity" (p. 37). Living systems create order and complexity within them to accomplish efficiencies: "Cities build elaborate transportation, water, and energy infrastructures; ecosystems become more biologically diverse as new species evolve; and human embryos develop into people with all their complex organs and structures" (p. 41). These complex systems "must have a constant input of high-quality[13] energy to maintain their complexity and order . . . in the face of nature's relentless tendency toward degradation and disorder" (p. 41). Homer-Dixon cited energy "experts" term "energy return on investment (EROI)" (p. 51) as a critical measure for societies; anything less than a one-to-one ratio of energy created to energy consumed means that a society is unsustainable over time. He and his researchers painstakingly conducted a study to estimate the amount of energy that the Romans required in the late phase of their civilization; they concluded, "the Roman Empire was eventually unable to generate enough high-quality energy to support its technical and social complexity. This shortfall . . . was the fundamental cause of Rome's fall" (p. 42). He offered two lessons from the fall of the Roman Empire.

> Without constant inputs of high-quality energy, complex societies aren't resilient to external shock. In fact, they almost certainly can't endure. These ever present dangers . . . drive societies to relentlessly search for energy sources with the highest possible return on investment (EROI). They also drive societies to aggressively control and organize the territories that supply energy and to extend their interests, engagements, and often their political economic domination far beyond their current borders . . . The second lesson is [that] . . . without dramatic new technologies for finding and using energy, a society's return on investment to produce energy . . . starts to decline. . . . [Currently, like Rome] . . . we're finding that we are steadily spending increasing amounts of energy to get energy. (pp. 54–55)

Homer-Dixon's analysis focused on the enormity of our challenge and risks by elaborating the energy issue to the structure of our economic system and central tenets of our worldview. The lack of resilience in the economic system becomes matched by our lack of culture resilience through increasingly strenuous denial of the signs of decline and vulnerability. One of a series of origins of denial he noted is our tendency "to ignore things that scare us or that threaten assumptions that give our lives meaning and security" (p. 214).

The development of expertise in emergent learning is significant at this point in our history precisely because it generates individual resilience that impacts social processes of adaptation. Homer-Dixon refers to C. S. Holling's work on environmental and institutional adaptation processes, which we examine in Chapter 4, as analogous to individual emergent learning.

A LEARNING AGENDA FOR THE TWENTY-FIRST CENTURY

While the challenges of our age, as illustrated so far, imply a "growth agenda" for us, the pivotal, and perhaps the defining, challenge of our new millennium seems to be for us to accept constant change and uncertainty, to engage constructively with the unfamiliar, and to adapt and learn in a continuously emergent context. Appadurai (2006) has reminded us of the alternative, namely, spiraling fear of uncertainty, which generates desperate attempts to control and eliminate the unfamiliar. The stakes are high. An inability to meet this fundamental challenge as persons, as organizations, and as nations will bring further social, environmental, and economic deterioration in the forms of weakening cultures and social infrastructures, small- and large-scale violence, loss of critical gifts of the biosphere, and the shrinking possibilities for prosperity that can be sustained over time. Some of the interrelated themes in our twenty-first-century learning agenda include:

- *The capacity to surmount fear to engage change and challenges with confidence, while in the midst of uncertainty and ambiguity*
  We have to make friends with change, since it will be a constant feature of our experience; it will be our way of life. We will need to become comfortable with not knowing and accept that we will often not even know what we do not know.

- *Values-based leadership with "global intelligence"*[14]
  Sustainability on the planet will require the influence of those who are guided by values that endure in a time of flux and that serve the interests of the whole; twenty-first-century leadership will need to transcend self-interest, self-doubt, and immediate narrowly focused concerns to serve the common good.

- *Widely practiced informed and responsible participation in communities and organizations*
  Active engagement based on a sense of personal agency, creative thinking informed by diverse perspectives, and commitment accomplished through participation in decision-making are needed throughout organizations and communities in a rapidly changing and challenging environment.

- *Respect for cultural, gender, and generational difference and equitable world citizenship with differences appreciated as a potential source of innovation*
  The courage to engage differences across cultures, welcome generational perspectives, and integrate feminine and masculine strengths is required for building a constructive global future.

- *The natural world cared for and recognized as our home*
  The serious environmental challenges demand a fundamental repositioning of ourselves *within the natural world* from our illusory stance as external observers and benign beneficiaries of its riches.

The foregoing themes are about adapting to the social and cultural consequences of accelerating technological change, a shrinking global context, and our capacity to impact the natural environment. To survive and thrive in this fundamentally different world, we have to reframe our expectations and perspectives and, indeed, understand ourselves differently. Perhaps Albert Einstein (n.d.) captured the task when he said:

> A human being is part of a whole called by us "Universe," a part limited in space and time. He experiences himself, his thoughts and feelings, as something separate from the rest—a kind of optical delusion of his consciousness. This delusion is a kind of prison to us, restricting us to our personal desires and to affection for a few persons nearest to us. Our task must be to free ourselves from the prison by widening our circle of compassion to embrace all living creatures and the whole of nature in its beauty. We shall require a substantially new manner of thinking if mankind is to survive.

The remainder of this book is an exploration of the kind of learning that is likely to assist in addressing these enormous twenty-first-century challenges and to lead to the kind of perspective and practices that appear essential in meeting them.

CHAPTER 2

LEARNING IN THE TWENTY-FIRST CENTURY: EMBEDDED, EMERGENT, AND EMBODIED

Real learning gets to the heart of what it is to be human. Through learning we re-create ourselves. Through learning we become able to do something we never were able to do. Through learning we re-perceive our world and our relationship to it. Through learning we extend our capacity to create, to be part of the generative process of life.

Peter Senge (2006, pp. 13, 14)

"Learning" has gained significance over the past four decades and it is all about living in a world of swirling novelty and surprise. Our unpredictable global environment is forcing us to reposition learning to the center of daily life—to shift the balance from being knowledge focused to being learning focused. The world demands *thoughtful action* globally and locally, based on current knowledge of ever-changing conditions. Shifting gears to generate knowledge with a radically decreased "time to use" requirement means reconceiving learning itself from something we do once and for all at one time in our lives to something that is continuous. The phrase "lifelong learning" may have appeared first in the lexicon of adult educator Eduard Lindeman (1926) in the 1920s, but in the past 30 years it has become a part of our everyday discourse.

Emergent learning means more than acquiring knowledge over a lifetime; it means that we *create* new knowledge continuously as we encounter new conditions and challenges. This implies two other qualities of the new learning. Learning emerges in relation to a specific context; it arises from a particular setting. So what we come to know is *embedded*, and its meaning and value are linked to a particular time and place. In their groundbreaking book published over 40 years ago, Peter Berger and Thomas Luckmann (1966) proposed that our reality is a social construction and, therefore, contextually contingent—"specific agglomerations of 'reality' and 'knowledge' pertain to specific contexts" (p. 3). One of the painful tasks we face in a global village is to let go of the belief that reality is "a given" and knowledge of it is immutable. We have begun this journey, but we are still often surprised when we find that what we take for granted as true may well not be true for others. Yet this fundamental recognition is critical to peaceful and mutually respectful coexistence on the planet. Finally, symbolized by physicist Werner Heisenberg's (Lindley, 2007) groundbreaking discovery that, at a subatomic level, we cannot observe matter without changing what we are observing, we have come to realize that we shape reality by our very presence. We are *embodied* as an integral part of what we seek to understand.

This chapter begins with a consideration of the predominant twentieth-century Industrial Age perspective on learning and an overview of the new perspectives generated over the past 40 years that are relevant to the twenty-first-century learning agenda set out in Chapter 1.

THE NEW MEANING OF "LEARNING"

Learning in the Modern Industrial Imagination

Most us who have been adults in the Western world for a few decades are likely to associate the word "learning" with "school," "college," "university," and, possibly, workplace-related training. Learning in this sense is about ideas and information that are transferred by teachers to students, or trainers to participants. What was learned is what is taught. We had become so immersed in the "schooling" interpretation of "learning" that a little over 30 years ago, Allen Tough (1971) astonished even many adult educators by highlighting the independent learning projects that adults undertook without teachers and outside of formal educational settings.

Traditional assumptions about knowledge and skill learning as commodities that can be passed on from one person to another are reflected in our language—"I'm going to take science or communications." The assumption here is that knowledge comes from outside ourselves. Knowledge is also likely to be identified primarily as the written or spoken word stored in books and memories and made available in libraries and classrooms. It is something organized as subject matters within distinct disciplines. Knowledge or skill sets are packages that are selected for transfer as part of a curriculum—as teachers, we "cover a topic."

In this perspective, our focus has been primarily on the "what," a commodity that was learned. We test to see how much knowledge has been *acquired* from that which the instructor has *covered*. Learning, to be real, has to be reliably measureable. Paulo Freire (2000) called this the "banking" notion of education.

Exemplifying the tradition of thought that shaped twentieth-century education, Ernest Hilgard, who, in 1975, published the fourth edition of his classic work *Theories of Learning,* presented "modern learning theories" (p. 13) as deriving from either the empiricist or the rationalist schools of thought—variations of either behavioral or information processing or both. His definition ruled out developmental learning.

> Learning refers to the change in a subject's behaviour to a given situation brought about by repeated experiences in that situation, provided that the behaviour change cannot be explained on the basis of native response tendencies, maturation, or temporary states of the subject (e.g., fatigue, drugs, etc.). (p. 17)

More complex and engaging theories of learning were mentioned in this classic text, but were presented as being only peripherally relevant. Pioneering Swiss psychologist Jean Piaget's (1951) developmental theory and Gestalt theory were mentioned only for their significance for assessing the capacity for mental functions, such as memory and recall. Philosopher John Dewey's (1967) discovery learning was also mentioned but was seen as having limited value since "one of the roles of education is the *transmission* of culture" [italics added] and was "inefficient if it had to carry the burden" of the curriculum (p. 345). Freud's (Brill, 1995) psychodynamic perspective was regarded as a less central concern because "the problems he worked on were not those with which learning theorists have been chiefly concerned" (p. 347). Hilgard's text is illustrative of the marginalization of holistic and practice-based approaches in conventional education; they did not fit. Schools, colleges, and universities are seen as preparation for later use in the world; theory and knowledge are accumulated in one setting for application to practice in another (Raelin, 2007). While postsecondary education, especially professional education, incorporates field practice and projects, as well as internships, they are often added at the end of the programs, with the integration of theory and practice left to the student.

In this perspective, common unspoken assumptions about learning and knowledge include:

a. what is to be learned is "outside" us;
b. knowledge is best generated in controlled settings independent of practice;
c. it has to be codified before it can be disseminated;
d. knowledge and skill are discrete entities that can be transferred from one person to another;
e. learning occurs through sensory observation and/or assimilation of information;
f. learning is largely headwork;
g. subject matter can be transferred in the same way to all learners in all settings;
h. knowledge and skill are "added to the learner from outside" without changing anything else about the learner; and
i. institutional authorities are those that are best qualified to determine what should be learned.

At the heart of every civilization is a set of assumptions about how we know and learn; we have an implicit theory of knowledge. Assumptions about learning and knowledge are consistent with the cultural assumptions about what is real. Our cultural assumptions become apparent to us when they become problematic. The epochal change we have been experiencing in our civilization for the past 30 to 40 years is of such enormous proportions that we are being challenged to radically revise how we see the world and our place in it; we are gradually realizing that our traditional cultural assumptions *have* become problematic. The predominant twentieth-century perspective on learning in Western society is a cultural expression of the Enlightenment that began over 300 years ago and that generated the Industrial Age, the modern era. All were rooted in what many have identified as a mechanistic metaphor (Pepper, 1961; Wheatley, 1999), which suggests that, in order to understand something, it is possible and necessary to reduce it to its component parts. In that perspective, knowledge is generated through detached, disinterested observation, and controlled experimentation according to the canons of scientific method (positivism); results are codified and disseminated. Underpinning these practices is the metaphysical assumption that reality is a configuration of primarily solid objects, stable states, and their discrete movements, which can be measured. A second assumption is the mind-body dualism that leads to the view that the knower and her thoughts are separate from the observed objects—the known. And, finally, there is the presumed preference that thoughts scientifically formulated into theories exist independently of the concrete world of particulars; they take on "a life of their own." Indeed, the whole Enlightenment enterprise has been dedicated to transcending the confusion of the practical world with disciplinary orthodoxies that establish intellectual order.

Twentieth-Century Roots of the Epochal Shift

Our enormously accelerated and globally connected world has shattered any dreams we might have had of imposing order through our minds. It provokes us to turn most of our Enlightenment/Industrial Age assumptions upside down and to pursue the practical and educational significance of new perspectives that have begun to emerge in the twentieth century about our world and our place in it, and its implications for how we learn and know.

In his lucid examination of the evolution of Western thought, Richard Tarnas (1991) locates the beginnings of a shift out of the modern synthesis, primarily in the first half of the twentieth century, with the emergence of diverse intellectual streams—the pragmatism of Pierce and Dewey, the existentialism of Sartre and Camus, Marxism, the psychoanalytic thought of Freud and Jung, and the "new sciences" of Einstein, Bohr, and Heisenberg, to name a few. He summarizes the key convergent themes in what has now become known as the postmodern era. Contrary to a focus on stable forms, the search for the truth through rational empiricism, the preeminence of codified (written or spoken) knowledge, and the expectation of clarity and enduring conclusions, Tarnas stated:

> There is an appreciation for the plasticity in constant change of reality and knowledge, stress on the priority of concrete experience over fixed abstract principles, and a conviction that no single *a priori* thought system should govern belief or investigation. It is recognized that human knowledge is subjectively determined by a multitude of factors; and that objective essences, or things-in-themselves, are neither accessible nor plausible; and that the value of all truths and assumptions must be continually subjected to direct testing. The critical search for truth is constrained to be tolerant of ambiguity and pluralism, and its outcome will necessarily be knowledge that is relative and fallible rather than absolute and certain. Hence the quest for knowledge must be endlessly self-revising. (p. 395)

Discounting the neutral, detached researcher or learner, Tarnas wrote:

> One cannot regard reality as a removed spectator against a fixed object; rather, one is always and necessarily engaged in reality, thereby at once transforming it while being transformed oneself. Although intransigent or provoking in many respects, reality must in some sense be hewed out of by means of the human mind and will, which themselves are already enmeshed in that which they seek to understand and effect. The human subject is an embodied agent, acting and judging in a context that can never be wholly objectified, with its orientations and motivations that can never be fully grasped or controlled. The knowing subject is never disengaged from the body or from the world, which form the background and condition of every cognitive act. (p. 396)

Ironically, it was from the scientific world, seen at one time to epitomize positivism, from physicists like David Bohm (1996) that the groundbreaking corollary about knowledge and inquiry emerged:

> Relativity and quantum theory agree, in that they both imply the need to look on the world as an undivided whole, in which all parts of the universe, including the observer and his instruments, merge and unite in one totality. In this totality, the atomistic form of insight is a simplification and an abstraction, valid only in some limited context. (Bohm, 1996, p. 11)

Joseph Raelin (2000), whose work is contributing to the intellectual foundation that restores the inherent connection between theory and practice, has described some of the features of professional education practice that support seamless theory-practice integration.

> The classroom will no longer need to be the sanctuary for learning. Indeed, the workplace can be viewed as the prime location for learning. . . . In the new learning . . . teachers are just as likely to be mentors, group project leaders, learning team facilitators, and designers of learning experiences. With the new learning comes the realization that learning involves active engagement in the action at hand. (2000, p. 14)

Continuous Flow as Root Metaphor for New Age

We have been working out the implications of this perspective shift in every domain of human endeavor through the last half of the twentieth century and into the first decade of this one. Pepper

(1961), whose first edition of *World Hypotheses: A Study in Evidence* appeared in 1942, offers a thorough discussion of root metaphors, "a traditional analogical method of generating world theories" in which one "desiring to understand the world looks about for a clue to its comprehension." Pepper's "historic event" seems most descriptive of the new age into which we are moving. This analogy is distinct from the notion of an event in past history. Rather, as he explains:

> The real historic event, the event in its actuality, is when it is going on *now*, the dynamic dramatic active event. We may call it an "act," if we like, and if we take care of our use of the term. But it is not an act conceived as alone or cut off that we mean; it is an act in and with its setting, an act in its context. (p. 232)

Pepper identifies this root metaphor with the foundational perspective of "contextualism" that pulls us powerfully into the dynamic, continuously changing present, the world of concrete particulars, a focus on relationships among particulars yielding the distinctive character of the whole. Contextualism implies a "horizontal cosmology" with "no top or bottom" with significance defined by purpose. In this understanding of ourselves and our world, we are *embedded* in a context as fully *embodied* learners; as such, change and learning *emerge* out of that experience of the present.

A related metaphor with properties also relevant to our times was elaborated from the work of biologist Stuart Kauffman (1991) and educator William Bergquist (1993) in illuminating the contrasts among premodern, modern, and postmodern organizations. These authors from very different disciplines explored states of water as a means to understand and represent the complexities of this new age. Kauffman, building on the earlier work of computer scientist Christopher Langton, was concerned about the simultaneous states of order and disorder and how they may be related. He compared highly ordered or solid states to the frozen state of water and the disorder as its gaseous state, and observed that, usually but not always, water as a fluid is an intermediary state between the two others. Bergquist highlights the fluid form of water as an analogous physical form that might inform how we can think about organization and learning in a new age:

> The third state (most interesting) is one of transition between order and chaos, which Kauffman identifies with the liquid state of water (though he notes that true liquids are not transitory in nature but are instead a distinct form of matter). . . . We must look not only at

ordered networks (the so-called solid state) and at chaotic networks (the so-called gaseous state) but also at liquid networks that hover on the brink of chaos if we are to understand and influence our unique postmodern institutions. The third state holds particularly great potential when we examine and seek to understand confusing and often illusive organizational phenomena such as mission, leadership, and communication. Turbulent rivers, avalanches, shifting weather patterns and other conditions that move between order and chaos to the liquid state and liquid systems contain chaotic elements as well as elements of stability. . . . The liquid state is characterized by edges and shifting boundaries. The liquid, edgy state is filled with the potential for learning. (p. 9)

The quality of *continuous flow* is common to both water and the historic event, the story, both unfolding as we go. The historic event clearly implies our full engagement in the shaping of the future, and water, as Bergquist observes, points to our "edgy state" on the boundary between order and chaos, "filled with the potential for learning." The rest of this chapter highlights some of the key contributions emerging in the last half of the past century that point us to an understanding of "learning" that potentially better prepares us for our twenty-first-century challenges.

PERSPECTIVES ON "LEARNING" FOR AN AGE OF COMPLEXITY

Bateson's Ecology of Mind

Gregory Bateson, in *Steps to an Ecology of the Mind* (1972), was one of the first to pose a radical reframing of learning and the learner relevant to our dynamic times. He introduced the notion of different *levels* of learning based on his studies of mind in wide-ranging phenomena, such as laboratory experiments, cultures, and illnesses (such as alcoholism and schizophrenia). He was an anthropologist and a communications theorist whose breakthrough thinking became influential with people from an equally wide range of disciplines and domains of practice who were trying to make sense of increasingly frequent encounters with a more profound experience of learning than traditional schooling theories could have explained.

Bateson introduced the concept of "system" to the discussion of learning and defined learning as a *process*. It is in attending to qualitative differences in learning *processes* that we are able to distinguish significantly different levels of learning. It was, perhaps, because we had been focused primarily on content (the "what") of learning—subject matters—that we did not have a conceptual perspective on learning that could have revealed differences in orders of learning and their relationship to one another. Bateson saw shifts in levels of learning as *emerging* from "contraries" that arise in the previous level of learning. As such, learning is not controlled or predictable but arises from a problematic circumstance that we encounter. The second key element of Bateson's perspective was that of "context" for learning. He linked learning to systems thinking, coining the term "an ecology of mind"; our learning is co-constituted in our relationship with an environment. Learning is *embedded*; it *emerges* through relationship within a context.

Bateson highlighted the difference between learning and performance, a distinction later amplified by writers like Robert Fritz (1991). If we are able to reliably repeat behavior in the same context, we are not learning, we are performing. Bateson called activity in which error is unlikely "zero learning." In conversing with a person with whom I have worked successfully for years in the same organization fostering effective teamwork, we are unlikely to mistake each other's messages. Without changing the conversational theme, the speaker, the language, and/or the workplace context, we are not learning anything new from each other.

The first order of learning, "Learning I" for Bateson, is a "class of phenomena that are *changes* in zero learning" (p. 287). Examples of Learning I include rote learning and forms of conditioning, such as becoming habituated to something new or learning not to respond to an event one has come to know is of no consequence. The emphasis here is on being able to assume an unchanging context. He introduced us to the notion of a "context marker" (e.g., sirens announcing danger, social etiquette), which enables the learner to identify similarity of context. Bateson directed our attention to successive layers of context (the context of the context), which generate different levels of learning. Continuing with our example, "Learning I" would be exemplified by us having the same conversation about teamwork in the same workplace sector, with the same colleague who shares the same cultural and professional experience but, this time, as Anglophones, we and our colleague are both trying to conduct the conversation in Spanish. This requires us to memorize clearly defined Spanish language conventions and vocabulary in order to translate correctly the same topic into Spanish. We have identified something we do not know and have set out to learn it. The learning challenge is clear.

"Learning II" that Bateson called "deutero-learning" (second order) is about learning to learn. While "Learning I" is "change in specificity of response," "Learning II" is "change in the process of "Learning I" (p. 293), which is required by a change in the context. Here, the context becomes ambiguous and cannot be assumed, so becomes, itself, a focus for learning. If, instead of a known colleague, our Spanish conversation is taking place with a person from Mexico, for example, the communication challenge shifts from simply Spanish syntax and vocabulary to one that requires us to learn different cultural meanings of language about work and collaboration. The context for our Spanish-speaking colleague, which now becomes ours to engage in, is the Mexican culture from which our colleague interprets her experience. We come to realize that we cannot assume that teamwork would be acceptable in the same way under the same circumstances as in our familiar workplace; we now have to learn a different context and how to introduce teamwork, and adjust our expectations about how teams will function. It may be that learning about cultural differences in the application of teamwork in the workplaces opens out for us a wider engagement with Mexican culture as a whole. Let us assume that we become associated with an international agency that is interested in promoting a teamwork approach in workplaces around the world. We are invited to bring our expertise to a similar task in Zimbabwe. Here again, we have to learn how to foster teamwork in another new culture and we have to learn that culture. What is different this time is, while we do not know the culture, we have *learned what it is to learn a new culture* and to deal with these kinds of contextual ambiguities and unknowns.

Bateson saw "Learning III," what we are calling third-order learning here, as having to do with profound changes in one's character and personal identity. In our example, as we have developed an international practice of fostering workplace teamwork, we may have come to shift our sense of self in the world from solely a specific cultural identity with the country of our birth to wider identification with humanity. We may have come to appreciate the vast differences across cultures and, at the same time, the core common qualities of the human experience and our interdependence. Our travels around the globe may have also given us an appreciation of our planet and its inhabitants, its wonders, and its frailties. Bateson describes this as "personal identity, which merges in to all the processes of relationship in some vast ecology or aesthetics of cosmic interaction. . . . Every detail of the universe is seen as proposing a view of the whole" (p. 306). We get the "big picture," a new perspective of our world, and we come to understand our own life as meaningful in a different way.

Torbert's Experiential Learning and Consciousness

The same year that Bateson published *Steps to an Ecology of Mind*, William Torbert (1972) published *Learning from Experience toward Consciousness*, in which he described a similar triple-layered perspective of "attention, feedback and consciousness" that parallels Bateson's orders of learning. The first, like Bateson's, is the specific level of behavior and perception, the world of empirical fact. Learning occurs through single-loop feedback—"change of specific behaviour or operation" (Torbert and Fisher, 1992). In our illustration of translating a conversation about teamwork into Spanish, one maintains a "focal awareness" on specific speech behavior, the operational task of implementing the conventions of language and by using Spanish vocabulary instead of English. The second level, attention and learning, learning through "double-loop feedback," is structural, that is, a "subsidiary awareness" of thoughts and implicit meanings generated through cross-cultural communication, including one's emotional responses, and possibly physical sensations arising in the experience. In this case, one experiences the differences in the Mexican cultural perspective and practices regarding teamwork, encountering the more complex challenge of how to communicate effectively while taking into account different cultural meanings underlying the spoken word. In speaking, one holds a "subsidiary presence" (Torbert, 1972, p. 22), an awareness of how one affects and is affected by the other person and his or her understanding of teamwork. "Double-loop learning" (Torbert, 1972, p. 194) through feedback reveals what one did not know—the norms and values associated with teamwork. This second-level preoccupation is adapting one's strategy toward the accomplishment of a goal. Typically, this experience generates not only thoughts regarding strategy and approach, but also emotions and sensations arising from confronting an ambiguous and important challenge. Finally, the third level of experience and learning Torbert (1972) describes is that of shifting one's "consciousness," developing of an awareness of the "thread of intentional meaning" in one's actions as connected to one's underlying "life-aim" (p. 22), learning through "triple-loop feedback." In our example, one's engagement with teamwork in the context of a different culture may generate a transformation in one's overall sense of self and life purpose. Continuous engagement in cross-cultural workplaces and communities may lead one to understand one's life as contributing to a broader international purpose. "Triple-loop learning" is associated with an "autobiographical awareness" through which one examines one's "taken for granted purposes, principles or paradigm" (Torbert and Fisher, 1992, p. 195). While framed very differently from Bateson's broader systemic awareness, we can recognize a similar depth of contemplation and understanding in both third level experiences. For Torbert, these levels of experience, attention, and learning are "distinct but interpenetrating levels of organization in human beings" (1972, p. 34); that is, they are potentially simultaneously occurring—one can, for example, be working on getting spoken Spanish right in working with Mexican colleagues to foster great teamwork in a community, and be, at the same time, developing an awareness of one's life purpose in fostering a worldwide sense of community and collaboration.

The significance of Bateson's and Torbert's work on learning is that both highlight the more complex levels of learning that are our challenges as we think about our twenty-first-century learning agenda. They frame the confrontation with ambiguity and complexity as *opportunities to learn.* They invite us to think about ourselves as learners in these experiences in which learning arises in our relationship with a context and its constituents (we are embedded) in relation to a real-world challenge in which we must act (we are embodied). These conceptualizations recognize the common twenty-first-century experience that we do not know enough about our learning challenge yet to be able to plan detailed learning activities, or even set specific objectives to be accomplished through our actions. Instead, learning about the challenge emerges as we move through the experience. Robert Quinn (2004) aptly named this demanding new approach to moving forward through an uncertain world "building the bridge as you walk on it."

Bateson and Torbert described forms of learning as they observed them occurring in various contexts. Several others who shared this layered perspective on learning, Chris Argyris and Donald Schön at Harvard and MIT, and Paulo Freire in Brazil, were at the same time exploring the application of this perspective in professional education and literacy education, respectively.

Argyris and Schön: Single- and Double-Loop Learning

During the same period, Chris Argyris and Donald Schön (1974) developed a research-based discussion about the first two layers of learning—single- and double-loop learning. They developed highly specific language for elements of the task of double-loop learning that they hoped professionals would be able to use if they looked carefully at the difference between what they believe and what they actually do.

That is, these educators attempted to maximize professional learning through an invitation to proactively power themselves into situations and open themselves to information from their environments that they might not anticipate. In order to foster professional effectiveness, Argyris and Schön believed multiple orders of learning were necessary.

> In single-loop learning, we learn to maintain the field of constancy by learning to design actions that satisfy existing governing variables. In the double-loop learning, we learned to change the field of constancy itself. . . . Double-loop learning changes the governing variables [the "settings"] of one's programs and causes ripples of change to fan out over one's whole system of theories-in-use. (p. 19)

They highlighted especially the struggle that people in formal educational settings and work organizations experience in the latter process, that of acknowledging that their assumptions, beliefs, goals, and/or action strategies no longer lead to expected and desirable consequences. Their work drew a great deal of attention; it signaled the growing recognition in the Western workplace that in a context of accelerating change, not only is learning beyond the technical a clear and present requirement, but also that most of us are unprepared for it.

Freire: Conscientização (Critical Consciousness)

Brazilian adult educator and writer Paulo Freire had been discovering, articulating, and developing groundbreaking educational strategies to foster similar breakthrough learning among disenfranchised and illiterate adults in South America. Freire (1973) amplified the debilitating and disempowering effects for learners of the traditional "banking concept" approach to education.

> Magic consciousness . . . simply apprehends the facts and attributes them to a superior power by which it is controlled and to which it must therefore submit. Magic consciousness is characterised by fatalism, which leads men to fold their arms, resigned to the impossibility of resisting the power of facts. (Freire, 1973, p. 44)

He developed an educational approach, which he called "problem posing" in the practice of literacy education, expressly to foster formation of "critical consciousness"—"*development* of the awakening of critical awareness" (p. 19). Freire elaborated critical consciousness in a way that seems consonant with a person able to engage in what others earlier in this text called "double-loop learning":

> The critically transitive consciousness is characterized by depth in the interpretation of problems; by the substitution of causal principles for magical explanations; by the testing of one's "findings" and by openness to revision; by the attempt to avoid distortion when perceiving problems and to avoid preconceived notions when analyzing them; by refusing to transfer responsibility; by rejecting passive positions; by soundness of argumentation; by the practice of dialogue rather than polemics; by receptivity to the new for reasons beyond mere novelty and by the good sense not to reject the old just because it is old—by accepting what is valid in both old and new. (p. 18)

The "problem posing" approach reconfigured the teacher-learner relationship in the process of literacy learning so as to empower learners, that is, experience themselves as naming their world, rather than receiving and committing to memory the language conventions from an authority. The form of communication in "problem posing" education is that of dialogue.

> The educator's role is fundamentally to enter into dialogue with the illiterate about concrete situations and simply to offer him the instruments with which he can teach himself to read and write. This teaching cannot be done from the top down, but only from the inside out, by the illiterate himself [sic], with the collaboration of the educator. (p. 48)

It was this reconfiguration of power relationships that generated a shift in consciousness for the learner; the educational setting became a microcosm for the democratic society that Freire saw as an essential counterpart to critically conscious citizens. He stated: "Responsibility cannot be acquired intellectually, but only through experience" (p. 16).

Freire's focus on the sociopolitical context as part of his educational practice featured the third-order learning that Bateson and Torbert articulated. Freire, who struggled with authoritarian political regimes, saw his work as oriented toward third-order learning, in the sense that his intent was to enable learners to be critically aware of their wider context away from compliance and toward understanding themselves as responsible actors in their communities and as cocreators of history.

Schön: Professionals as Reflective Practitioners

Argyris and Schön (1974) did not directly address the broader cultural and biographical contexts of their research participants, which would have influenced the course of their single- and double-loop learning challenges. However, Donald Schön (1983) later highlighted the Western cultural environment and the prevailing approach to professional practice, education, and research that would have been the distinctive context of the learning professionals with whom he and Argyris had worked. Though not expressed in this way, Schön addressed the need for double- and triple-loop learning on a grand scale, namely, on the order of educational, social, and research institutions to transcend the reasons for a growing "crisis of confidence in the professions" and "scepticism" (p. 4) that was beginning to emerge in the 1960s. He used the term "Technical Rationality" to characterize the traditional culture of the professions as it had become based on the fundamental belief that "professional activity consists in instrumental problem-solving made rigorous by the application of scientific theory and critique" (p. 21). "Technical Rationality" is essentially "Learning I" (Bateson, 1972) or a single-loop learning approach (Torbert, 1972; Argyris and Schön, 1974). He provided evidence that it was not working. Though speaking of the American context, the following observation applies more broadly to Western cultures:

> Government-sponsored "wars" against such crises [as deteriorating cities, poverty, the pollution of the environment, the shortage of energy] seemed not to produce the expected results; indeed, they often seem to exacerbate the crisis. The success of the space program seemed not to be replicable when the problems to be solved were the tangled socio-techno-politico-economic predicaments of public life. The concept of the "technological fix" came into bad odor. Indeed, some of the solutions advocated by professional experts were seen as having created problems as bad or worse than those they had been designed to solve. . . . They were ineffective, they created new problems, they were derived from theories which had been shown to be fragile and incomplete. (pp. 9–10)

Schön (1983) challenged the fundamental assumptions of "Technical Rationality" for professional practice, particularly the assumption that practice should be based on general principles and standardized knowledge generated by positivist science and passed *down* to practitioners for application. He questioned the supremacy of scientifically derived theory in the context of professional practice, as well as its relevance to such practice. He cited Russell Ackoff's (1979) redefinition of the professional's task as managing "complex systems of changing problems that interact with each other," which he called "*messes*," distinct from problems that are "abstractions extracted from messes by analysis" (Ackoff cited in Schön, 1983, p. 16). Indeed, Schön named a radically different image of professional knowledge and learning:

> When someone reflects-in-action, he becomes a researcher in the practice context. He is not dependent on the categories of established theory and technique, but constructs a new theory of the unique case. His inquiry is not limited to a deliberation about means which depend on a prior agreement about ends. He does not keep means and ends separate, but defines them interactively as he frames a problematic situation. He does not separate thinking from doing, ratiocinating his way to a decision which he must later convert to action. Because his experimenting is a kind of action, implementation is built into his inquiry. Thus reflection-in-action can proceed, even the situations of uncertainty or uniqueness, because it is not bound by the dichotomies of Technical Rationality. (pp. 68, 69)

Had Argyris and Schön (1974) fostered reflection on the source of their tremendous difficulties as professionals in openly examining and shifting their assumptions and beliefs about their goals and action strategies in relation to their own professional effectiveness, a triple-loop layer in their learning may well have emerged. If they had been able to reconfigure their learning and working contexts, even within narrow boundaries, they may have been able to advance their success as learners and professionals.

Kegan: Evolution of Consciousness through "the Hidden Curriculum"

Robert Kegan (1994), who explored knowledge from a range of disciplines on this theme, made the following observation:

> [T]he expectations upon us . . . demand something more than mere behavior, the acquisition of specific skills, or the mastery of particular knowledge. They make demands on our minds, on how we know, on the complexity of our consciousness. . . . No additional amount of information coming into our minds will enable us to assume this kind of authority; only a qualitative change in the complexity of our minds will. (pp. 3–4)

Like Raelin, Kegan invited us to think about our everyday world as a learning setting, about our entire cultural environment as having a "hidden curriculum" for us. As our environment changes, it provokes "an evolution of consciousness, the personal unfolding of ways of organizing experience that are not simply replaced as we grow but subsumed into more complex systems of mind" (p. 9). Like Torbert, Kegan highlighted the simultaneous dual-level attention we have at a given time, namely, "objective" (for Torbert, "focal") and "subjective" (for Torbert, "subsidiary"), that play in the shift of consciousness.

Kegan's work helped us frame the significance of global transformations as they ripple through layers of cultural and social organization to impact the experience and the lives of individuals—citizens, neighbors, leaders, and employees. In what is implicitly a systems perspective, he suggested that the dynamics of social developmental change are understood by inquiring into "the fit or lack of fit between what the culture demands of our minds and our mental capacity to meet these demands" (p. 9). While his analysis was an examination of psychocultural dynamics in an American context, his carefully constructed conceptualization of the relationship between culture and individual learning illuminated the impact of global social and cultural transformations for the learning challenges of each of us, at least in Western cultures, in this new era of turbulence, unpredictability, and uncertainty. Kegan overviewed the kind of late-twentieth-century learning similarly to the twenty-first-century learning agenda in the previous chapter, including:

a. in the workplace, the demand for increasing autonomy and responsibility in one's work and, for organizational leaders, a shift from the author of direction to the provider of a vision-driven context for work;
b. in schools, the demand for learner self-direction, and recognition of knowledge continuously evolving through critical examination and reconstruction; and
c. in communities, recognition of a post-traditional, heterogeneous, pluralistic, socially constructed world where conflict is reframed as redefining relationships.

EVOLVING PERSPECTIVES AND TWENTY-FIRST-CENTURY LEARNING CHALLENGES

New Value-Perspectives for an Unpredictable World

All of us grow up with a "map" to our world that has been provided for us by our parents, our community, and our school. It tells us what our experiences mean, what is important, what is right and wrong, and what to expect and believe. This is our value-perspective that provides us not only with values and what is important, but also with a guide to what is real. The more culturally homogenous our community is, the more likely that first "map" is to be invisible to us because everyone else's "map" is the same as ours. As Robert Kegan cited earlier in this chapter, and our twenty-first-century learning agenda implies, we are being challenged to recognize that conceptual maps of our world are only proximate and they may vary from those of others that are not "less correct," plus, from time to time, we find out that our "map" is out of date—the terrain has changed. Second-order or double-loop learning is the result of having examined and revised our assumptions, beliefs, and expectations that are often tacit, those to which we have been acculturated. Everyday occurrences are interpreted within a culturally provided value-perspective. A cross-cultural instance is the astonishment of North Americans when they discover in fact that, in France, businesses they may have counted on using are closed during the lunch hour and that *déjeuner* is a major meal occurring over several hours, not one. This "surface" difference in practice is linked to the more profound difference in the cultural priorities of business and social life. Another temporal instance is our tacit expectation that the price of gas for vehicles 40 years ago would remain constant at under $.40 per U.S. gallon and our assumption that use of fossil fuel was a benign practice unrelated to the air we breathe and our climate. We now know that the cost of gasoline has, and will, continue to spiral upward and that our dependence on it has a destructive impact on the natural environment.

We now live in an age in which *it is necessary to live among different coexisting value-perspectives and to shift and evolve those value-perspectives that have been problematic to our survival.* Ultimately, our twenty-first-century learning agenda is likely to call for third-order or triple-loop learning, in which we understand ourselves and our life purposes differently. We may come to see ourselves as global citizens who automatically *expect and appreciate* different daily practices in every part of the world. We may have to come to hold sustainability as a cherished priority, an ethical imperative such that travel, for example, is automatically undertaken in ways that minimize or offset our environmental footprint.

Value-perspectives are pervasive and profound. They imply a complete way of being—our tacit structures of meaning and value; our ways of seeing and knowing; our deeply held beliefs about living, relating, and working; our assumptions and expectations regarding environments, including communities, organizations, society, and the natural world. The term "value-perspective" is one coined by Max Weber, who connected the evolution of culture and individual development. David Owen (1994) explains:

> The value-perspective expresses itself in the form of a "world image" which is constitutive of the ground of social life—it constructs the *structures of recognition* through which our cultural identities are articulated and thus the form in which our material and ideal interests manifest themselves. (p. 95)

> A value-perspective . . . manifests itself as an attempt to provide a complete and coherent explanation of the place of the individual within the world. In so far as it is successful, this value-perspective facilitates the individual's experience of himself as a goal directed agent. (p. 97)

Writing at the beginning of the past century, Weber saw value-perspectives changing when individuals encounter conflict between "life-spheres" or "modes of human activity" (e.g., economic, political, religious) within a given culture. Characteristic of the very different world we now inhabit, we are examining value-perspective change arising not only from within a culture but also in the meeting of diverse cultures in a dynamic and unpredictable global context. Another difference over the past century is that while value-perspective change could occur in the relatively more culturally homogeneous traditional societies that Weber observed, a world of accelerating change generates challenges to our taken-for-granted assumptions at an unprecedented rate. Robert Kegan (1994) has invited us to consider "contemporary culture as a kind of a 'school' and the complex set of tasks and expectations placed on us in modern life as the 'curriculum' of that school . . ." (p. 3) to trigger the development of "qualitatively different orders of mental complexity" (p. 187).

Before we can learn to evolve our value-perspectives, we have to recognize that we have them! This is no simple task, since they are the lens or "glasses" we wear daily to see our world. In our culture, over the past 40 years, rich research literature on different value-perspectives has emerged that are quite widely read. These have come from many developmental theorists and authors from diverse fields of theory and practice—psychology, education, and theology, to name a few—who have documented aspects of developmental shifts of mind and consciousness (Erikson, 1950; Graves, 1970; Loevinger and Blasi, 1976; Gould, 1978; Levinson, 1978; Fowler, 1981; Gilligan, 1982; Belenky et al., 1986; Mezirow, 1990; Beck and Cowan 1996;

Barrett, 1998; Perry, 1999; Freire, 2000; Wilber, 2000a; Torbert, 2004).[1] See endnote for elaboration.

Evolving to Meet Our Twenty-First-Century Learning Challenges

In looking back over the emerging new perspective on "learning," it is striking that there is a remarkable consonance between the more profound practice and understanding of embodied and emergent learning we have seen developing over the past 40 years, on the one hand, and the enormous twenty-first-century challenges that do not have simple solutions, on the other. It is as if we are preparing ourselves for the critical conditions we are discovering in our new millennium environment. In another, more systemic perspective, we are, at the same time, creating and being shaped by this new, unpredictable, turbulent world. "Everything we do is a structural dance in the choreography of existence," observed Humberto Maturana and Franciso Varela (1987, p. 248). These researchers explained that environment triggers, but does not direct, change in living entities and that the entities, on the other hand, can generate changes in the environment (p. 75).

Accelerating technological innovation has contributed to creating a world of continual flux and momentous challenges that, if we see ourselves as helpless to influence our future, spawn fear and a sense of being overwhelmed. The twentieth century supplied some horrifying examples of how individual fears and insecurity can be coalesced into unimaginable socially sanctioned brutality. Arun Appadurai (2006) reminded us that this phenomenon continues in the twenty-first century in different, but equally brutal, forms. The alternative is to greet uncertainty with the sense of agency in creating our future, an openness to novelty, the capacity to be creative and innovative, and an appreciation of cultural diversity. Ken Wilber (2000a) in his encyclopedic work on the Human Consciousness Project has comprehensively reviewed the developmental schemas cited earlier in this text, in addition to the contributions of philosophers, anthropologists, psychiatrists, and psychologists that articulated changing value-perspectives. Wilber (2000b) observes, "One of the striking things about the present states is how similar, in broad outline, most of its models are. . . . [T]hey all tell a similar tale of the growth and development of the mind *as a series of unfolding stages or waves*" (p. 5). Second, there appears to be a similar or, at least, complementary direction of the change among developmental schemas that reflects "*decreasing* narcissism and *increasing* consciousness, or the ability to take other

people, places, and things into account and thus increasingly extend
care to each" (p. 18).

> As a rule, thinking and the capacity to take the roles of others emerge,
> *egocentric* gives way to *sociocentric*, with its initially conformist and
> conventional roles, mythic-absolutist beliefs, and often authoritarian
> ways. A further growth of consciousness differentiates itself from its
> embeddedness in sociocentric and ethnocentric modes, and opens it
> to formal, universal, world centric, postconventional awareness, which
> is an extraordinary expansion of consciousness in two modes that are
> beginning to become truly global. (Wilber, 2000a, pp. 43, 44)

The escalating complexity that defies the wisdom of a few calls for
distributed knowledgeable action. Robert Kegan (1994) described a
key dimension demanded by the "hidden [cultural] curriculum": "The
transformation is one of self-authorship, of becoming the definer of
one's acceptability" (p. 301) and "guided by [our] own vision" (p. 173).
We become psychologically self-supporting, self-assessing, and self-
directing. We could say that at this level we become capable leaders of
ourselves, authors of our own stories. In describing the "Autonomous
Stage" of human development, Jane Loevinger spoke of "seeing reality
as complex and multifaceted," "high toleration for ambiguity," "the
courage to acknowledge and deal with conflict rather than ignoring it
or projecting it onto the environment," "self-fulfillment . . . supplant-
ing achievement," "a broad view of life as a whole," and "broad . . .
social ideals" (Loevinger and Blasi, 1976, pp. 23, 26). The more
complex levels of the Beck and Cowan (1996) spiral dynamics schema
are characterized by freedom "from greed, dogma, and divisiveness";
distribution of "resources and opportunities equally among all"; "decisions through reconciliation and consensus processes"; "existence is
valued over material possessions"; "flexibility, spontaneity, and func-
tionality have the highest priority"; and "differences can be integrated
into interdependent, natural flows." Torbert's (2004) description of
leaders is as strategists who, among other things, exercise judgment
beyond rules, recognize mutuality and autonomy, and deal with conflict creatively; he also views leaders as alchemists who have evolved a
"reframing spirit" that attends to continuously changing contexts.

EMERGENT LEARNING: PATHWAY TO A NEW VALUE-PERSPECTIVE

Emergent learning, or second- and third-order learning, is the experience of the journey between developmental stages that represent
different ways of seeing, acting, and, indeed, being in the world. As

presented in the next chapter, the emergent learning process experience can be seen to retrace some elements of prior developmental stages, as well as to enact new elements of the next developmental stage. It is a bridge. Therefore, the nature of the process is both shaped by, and shapes, the qualities of the successive stages between which we are traveling. As such, the qualities of the learning process through which we evolve our perspective may be expected to vary to some degree, depending on the stage of origin and of destination. The emergent learning process presented in this book will be particularly relevant as a representation of the learning journey from what Loevinger and Blasi (1976) described as the "conscientious stage" to the "autonomous stage," and what Kegan (1982) called the "institutional" to the "interindividual," or what Maslow (1943) named "esteem and self-esteem orientation" to "self-actualization." In broad terms, this is the journey from a stage in which we successfully participate in and identify ourselves within a conventional culture to a stage in which we discover the world "within," our capacity to learn and change ourselves and to accept personal responsibility for actions and decisions.

While reflecting a similar trajectory of development, Richard Barrett's (1998, 2006, 2010) seven levels of consciousness, in my view, highlight the critical place of emergent learning most clearly. It is *the bridge between the world of conventionally oriented self-interest to openness and consciously values-guided engagement in the wider world*, described as the fourth level, or transformation.

Adapted from Abraham Maslow's (1954) hierarchy of needs, Barrett's first three levels of consciousness are survival consciousness (a reasonable level of physical safety and economic security), relationship consciousness ("meaningful attachments to those with whom we share a common identity" [p. 57]), and self-esteem consciousness (social respect and sense of self-worth). In these first three levels, our sense of ourselves is contingent on the opinions of others and "the greater our fears, the more deeply we are attached to these opinions" (p. 58). We are, in this way, enormously susceptible to provocations to becoming fearful. Our twenty-first-century world of unpredictable change and high levels of uncertainty is fraught with opportunities to be fearful. We are called upon to negotiate culture differences and relate to people who do not conform to own taken-for-granted conventions and who change our neighborhoods and workplaces. Our temptation to act out of fear and denial is ever present, but instead we need to invest fully in our future in a context of global economic flux and environmental threat.

It is in the fourth level of consciousness that Barrett called "transformational consciousness" (self-actualizing in Maslow's terms) that we "take full responsibility for the way things are" (Barrett, 1998, p. 64). Arising from discomforting or devastating events, we become ready to "re-examine our beliefs" and enter a state of "profound reflection." We "stop blaming others for [our] misfortunes and pain" and make "a conscious choice—from living in fear to living in truth." We "become aware of the importance of values to guide [us] in [our] daily decisions" (p. 64).

This level of consciousness is the one that the emergent learning process, described in the next chapter, addresses directly. It is a necessary human experience that enables us to move beyond self-concern and compulsive self-protection. The remaining three levels of consciousness constitute constructive, creatively driven engagement in successively wider circles of our world. If we are able to transcend our self-preoccupations through getting ourselves authentically in the driver's seat and establishing an inside-out perspective for which we take responsibility, we can engage constructively, effectively, and generously in our world. Our focus becomes the common good. Barrett, who is concerned with organizational and national cultures as well as individual values, formulated the descriptions of these three levels of consciousness from the standpoint of a member of an organization: "organization consciousness" in which "self-interest [is interpreted] as best served by supporting the good of the whole" (Barrett, 1998, p. 64); "community consciousness" in which we are concerned at this level with "making a difference in the world" (p. 65), and likely to see ourselves as "stewards of the planet and a humanitarian outlook" (p. 65); and "society consciousness" in which we have a "world outlook and keep abreast of international developments," seeing "the world as a complex web of interconnectedness" (p. 65), so that we are likely to have "an unshakeable sense of commitment, and a frequent sense of joy and contentment" (p. 66).

These qualities represent states of being that relatively few of us experience as a center of gravity, so our task in this dynamic and challenging millennium is to catalyze transformation in ourselves, and in each other, and to enhance our capacity to meet the challenges in our twenty-first-century learning agenda outlined in Chapter 1. Emergent learning is the experience that presents us with the learning challenge of saying "yes" to engaging the unknown. It simultaneously provides us with ways to strengthen specific competencies for thriving in our ever-changing and unfolding world. The next chapter describes that process.

CHAPTER 3

EMERGENT LEARNING FROM AN
INSIDE-OUT PERSPECTIVE

We shall not cease from exploration
And the end of all our exploring
Will be to arrive where we started
And know the place for the first time.

T. S. Eliot, (1959) Four Quartets, *No. 4*

Each time we are confronted with the unfamiliar, we make a profound choice. We either engage in exploring and learning from what we have encountered, or try to secure ourselves inside familiar territory. The option we choose at one point in time tends to predispose us to repeat it the next time. As we accumulate a preponderance of one of these choices over the other, we define our lives and who we become in essential ways. Our actions are shaped by how we understand ourselves and our world, so how we *learn*, or not, very significantly shapes our own and others' lives. These choices and actions also ultimately contribute to the texture of our world, which, in turn, presents us with further challenges.

This chapter is an "inside-out" summary description of the emergent learning process pattern *from the perspective of the person experiencing it*. It is a *generic narrative* of a person's experience as it unfolds through the whole process. Chapter 4 is an examination of similarities and differences between this pattern and other conceptual formulations of emergent change as described in the literature over the past 30 years.

THE "INSIDE-OUT" PERSPECTIVE

The emergent learning process patterns described in this chapter are constructed from the vantage point of the person experiencing them. There are three advantages to the "inside-out" perspective. First, we move forward on the basis of our own vantage point, navigating our way through the tumult of life in a turbulent and uncertain environment. As such, the emergent learning process provides a practical map through the complexity. By observantly stepping into and identifying common patterns in the experience of second-order or double-loop learning, we can develop a high level of expertise that we can rely on in navigating our way at the edge of chaos. The second advantage of the "inside-out" perspective is that it *renders visible to us all the dimensions of the learning process—not only patterns of thought but also patterns in what we sense and feel, how we relate to others, and who are significant in our change experience, and to the context of our immediate experience.* It provides us with a more complete picture of what it means to create a new perspective. Finally, the inside-out viewpoint situates us *within,* rather than outside, an evolving world. The consequences of this positioning of ourselves, while subtle, are profound, as we contemplate our twenty-first-century learning agenda. It represents a momentous step away from the Enlightenment notion of detachment as a means of control and predictability (Tarnas, 1991). It invites us into a new relationship with our environment—one of engaging responsibly without the need for certainty.

Origin of the "Inside-Out" Perspective on Emergent Learning

The emergent learning description has been formulated based on three related inquiry processes outlined by Bateson and Bateson (1987).

> The mental world is vastly bigger than we are, but we do have various "tricks" that enable us to grasp something of its vastness and detail. Of these tricks the best known are *induction, generalization,* and *abduction.* [emphases added] We gather information about details, we fit the pieces of information together to make pictures or configurations, we summarize them in statements of structure. We then compare our configurations to show how they can be classified as falling under the same or related rules. It is this last step, for which I have used the term *abduction,* that is the glue that holds all science . . . together. (pp. 174–175)

Induction

The process model of emergent learning was first identified in an intensive, comparative inductive study (Taylor, 1979, 1986) of the experiences of eight people[1] who were challenged with taking personal responsibility for their own learning in a formal educational setting, that is, setting their learning goals, organizing their learning activities, and assessing their progress. (This work is referred to as "the original study" throughout this book.) They described their experiences, each week, of a 13-week course in completely open-ended weekly interviews prompted by the question, "Tell me about your experience this week in relation to the course." As such, the interview set contained detailed, chronological, "inside-out" (from the learners' perspectives) descriptions at regular and frequent intervals throughout this experience.

Generalization

My profession as an educator has been in leadership education settings, where the first challenge is to lead one's self, and a pivotal element of this is fostering one's own learning, both planned and emergent. Mid-career adults encountering the challenge of taking responsibility for their own learning in a graduate education context have found that their experience of shifting to a self-managing perspective maps closely to the emergent process pattern presented here; their commentaries are similar to those of the original study.

Using the example of engaging and managing one's self in an educational setting, it was not the task demands of planning, conducting, and assessing one's own learning that created a significant second-order learning moment for these people, but the fact that doing so profoundly challenged their assumptions about learning, knowledge, teachers, and themselves. These learners were social professionals (in health, education, social and public service), all of whom had spent considerable time in educational institutions as students, and some of whom had continued as teachers and educational administrators. The shift to a self-directed learning approach may be seen as a simple matter of learning how to do things differently. However, it represents a fundamental change in what C. Murray Parkes (1971) called "an assumptive world." For the people in this setting, it contradicted their traditional Western perspective on what learning means, as summarized in the previous chapter. According to Parkes, we orient ourselves in relation to "familiar objects" and, ostensibly, recognizable behavior and events. The momentous underlying shift is located, initially, in the loss of these familiar "objects," which signals loss of that orientation. Since the particulars of an educational environment organized for learner self-direction diverges greatly from a traditional formal learning environment—the role of the teacher, the role of learners, the approaches to selecting learning objectives and organizing learning activities, and assessing learning—a state of disorientation is triggered. Robert Kegan's (1994) explanation is similar:

> Educators seeking "self-direction" from their adult students are not merely asking them to take on new skills, modify their learning style, or increase their self confidence. They are asking many of them to change the whole way they understand themselves, their world and the relation between the two . . . We acquire "personal authority," after all, only by relativizing—that is, only by fundamentally altering—our relationship to public authority. This is a long, often painful voyage, and one that, for much of the time, may feel more like mutiny than a merely exhilarating (and less self-conflicted) expedition to discover new lands. (p. 275)

Engagement in self-directed learning in an educational setting provides us with an example, one that can be observed in minute detail of the kind of emergent learning that we are challenged to do in the wider arena of our twenty-first-century challenges. The pattern of second-order learning identified in this setting can be considered a "fractal," that is, a microcosmic version of this process in the broader contexts of life and work. "Fractal" is a term coined by Benoit Mandelbrot as a fractional dimension, a "self-similar" configuration that repeats itself through both small and larger scales of that in which it is embedded, ". . . symmetry across scale. It implies recursion, that is, pattern inside pattern" (Gleick, 1987, p. 103). The patterns that characterize emergent learning in this limited setting suggest the shape of the challenge on a larger scale. It is not a "part" as in "part of an assemblage," but a scaled example of the whole. The specific learning outcomes of the process are changes in ourselves as learners that can either enhance or diminish our capacity to engage the larger challenges.

The twenty-first-century learning challenges described in Chapter 1, all call for personal and cultural shifts toward participation with responsibility, self-initiated collaborative action, and the capacity to engage the unexpected as opportunities to learn and adapt. As an example, the challenge posed to students in this learning setting *simulated the demands embedded in many workplaces where authority, responsibility, and accountability are being lateralized in organizations attempting to remain responsive to turbulent change of the twenty-first century.* Cultures around the world have barely begun to adapt to the need to lateralize and distribute authority.[2] At best we might say that we have "one foot in each of two worlds"; our civilization is very much in the midst of sorting out the dance of centralized positional authority and distributed personal responsibility. This is reflected in my leadership education practice: more than 30 years have elapsed since the original study, but graduate learners still struggle in the same way with educational programs that are designed according to participative organizational principles.

Abduction

The third step of inquiry, as Bateson and Bateson (1987) highlighted, is that of comparing one configuration to others generated in logically similar contexts. Whenever I have presented this emergent learning process pattern, people have recognized it in the wider context of their lives. We encounter experiences that restructure our lives and, in doing so, challenge us to engage unfamiliarity, uncertainty, and creative and responsible action. In the workplace, we may suddenly find ourselves trying to catch up to the vision of new management that changes policies and structures, distributing responsibility and accountability throughout the organization (de Guerre and Taylor, 2004). As a manager, if I am not making the decisions about how the work is to be done, what is my role? Do I have a role? In our personal lives, a first marriage or partnership ends, and with it our beliefs about the life-long nature of marriage and family. We are suddenly responsible for matters in our lives that we had unconsciously relied upon others to handle. In addition to learning to cope with losses and new tasks, we are also challenged to reformulate our identity and perspective on significant aspects of our lives that events have redefined. Who are we without a marriage or primary partnership? What and who do we want in our lives? However heavy the losses, it is the way in which we reformulate our perspectives or new "assumptive worlds" through these life events that shapes our personal and collective futures. The relevance of the emergent learning process sequence to the wider context of our lives is supported by other change process formulations reviewed in Chapter 4. Most importantly, I invite *you* to consider how the generic pattern of emergent learning may illuminate your own experience.

EMERGENT LEARNING PROCESS NARRATIVE

The term "emergent" implies "rising out of a surrounding medium" (*Oxford English Dictionary*); in this case, emergent learning arises from a previously quiescent period, a state of equilibrium, in which our perspective on the world is adequate in comprehending and navigating our practical experience. Some unexpected events can be accommodated (i.e., meaningfully explained, accounted for, or adapted to) with our perspective on our world. However, occasionally an event will occur that cannot be accommodated and it is important enough to challenge the nature of perspective itself. The emergent learning sequence is what we experience when we encounter something that renders our current perspective inadequate. It comprises four phases and four transitions between phases, depicted in figure 3.1. These phases, transitions, and the constitutive features of the sequence are discussed below.

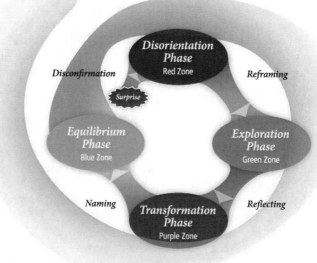

Figure 3.1   Emergent learning process overview.

The emergent learning process summary is represented as a *generic narrative* optimizing its relevance in a range of individual change experiences that challenge us with second- and third-order learning. Typical comments from the original study are included here in boxes to illustrate features of the sequence. The sequence will undoubtedly vary with the sociocultural context, the nature of the particular challenge, and the psychosocial strengths and prior experience of the person. In the original study, it was possible to cycle through the sequence within a three-month period in a formal educational setting, while the developmental significance of restructuring relationships, families, and careers is likely to be accomplished over a period of years. Additionally, the emergent learning sequence is presented here in its optimal form. It does not describe, for example, the experiences of people who get stuck in confusion. Rather, it represents a pattern that directs our attention at how to navigate emergent learning challenges successfully, a theme that will be picked up in Chapter 5.

You are invited as a reader to test the relevance of the sequence to your own experience and, in doing so, to notice how the features of the sequence may vary and what contextual features and conditions fostered or inhibited the process. I have included illustrative commentary from the original study as indicative of how discourse changes throughout the process; it is likely to be mild compared with our experience in more intense challenges that we experience.

Equilibrium Phase (Blue Zone): Anticipatory

In the normal course of our experience, we make sense of our world and anticipate events using cognitive structures—constructs (Kelly, 1963) and mental models (Senge, 2006)—that help us navigate our experience. When the constructs match experience in a new setting, we may note it briefly. Our map fits the territory—all is well. We experience equilibrium, the relevant definition of which in this context is "well-balanced condition of mind and feeling" (*Oxford English Dictionary*). The color that distinguishes the Equilibrium Phase is blue. Culturally, darker blue tones can be associated with conservativism understood as in the sense of stability and sophistication. According to the same dictionary, blue is "often taken as the colour of consistency and unchangingness."

> "Within half an hour from the time I came into the room, I had identified I don't know how many things that would match what, for me, would be a successful workshop."

First Transition: Disconfirmation

Emergent (second-order) learning begins with disconfirmation of expectations based on an existing set of beliefs and assumptions. The reality we have constructed in our minds has lost its currency with the reality we are experiencing.

Surprise

Whether experienced and expressed as a sudden shock or as gradually intensifying unease, the beginning of learning is marked by a challenging surprise, triggered by an unexpected event. Sometimes the event is as obvious as it is overwhelming, such as the death of a loved one or the sudden loss of employment. In

> "It hit to the core, the core about what I believe in terms of the nature of people and the nature of change. Not only in teaching but really . . . me as person, the whole shebang."

other circumstances, the event can be very subtle but equally consequential. I remember vividly the day I received a phone call from my mother, whose voice sounded very different than ever before. My mouth went dry—somehow I knew, tacitly, not consciously, the importance of this moment. It marked my preconscious awareness of the beginning of my mother's dementia, and a journey for me in coming to understand decline and death of people in my life. It may seem to have been a minor event, but that symbolized a fundamental assumption on which a whole series of other assumptions and beliefs depend. Most of us can remember a particular moment when we sensed something was "seriously wrong," even if we did not know what it was at first. The news comes to us often in what Eugene Gendlin calls "felt sense." Distinct from emotion, felt sense is "a bodily sense," "a layer of the unconscious that is likely to come up next . . . not yet open up, not yet preconscious" (Gendlin, 1996, p. 19). It becomes our task over the next three emergent learning phases to wrestle the full meaning of the experience to consciousness.

Assumptions, Expectations, and Beliefs Challenged

Our lives are rooted in relationships, places, and practices, and our possessions; changes in these extrinsic elements of our life space (Parkes, 1971), whether they occur as consequences to our own initiatives or whether we experience them as devastating occurrences that happen to us, are losses. What we often do not recognize is that loss of currency of our ideas, beliefs, and assumptions is also, in and of itself, enormously distressing. They are integral and highly *valued* elements to our lives and to our tacit understanding about the way things are. Indeed, the substantive losses are also underpinned by our value-perspective through which our loss has meaning. Peter Marris (1974) observed that even positive changes in our lives imply losses— for example, geographical moves to a better job and neighborhood mean loss of, at least, regular contact with friends and possibly, family. And while some losses will definitely feel like they *happened to us*, we are still participants through the way we attribute meaning; at the very least, we exercise choice in how we interpret losses into our lives. In the depth of grief from a profound loss, it will not be possible for us to consider the experience with potential for learning. Nevertheless, it is our life challenge over long periods of time to arrive at a perspective that is more life enhancing than life diminishing.

First Phase: Disorientation (Red Zone)

Before we can identify what has happened, a significant unexpected and challenging event can leave us in disorientation and mental confusion. From the inside-out perspective, the Red Zone is a season of disconnection, triggered by high contact with unfamiliar conditions for which we do not feel prepared. Second-order learning is, by definition, the discovery that our conceptual map does not relate to the current territory. This essential feature of the process is typically accompanied by loss of an inner connection, and presents in the form of negative self-judgment; "I" becomes dissociated from "me." We simultaneously become disconnected from others, as evident in a reduced quality in communication (withholding information, misunderstanding) and a tendency to compete with others. We may also be inclined to gravitate toward others who are also similarly disaffected; we can create a social surrounding that provides support and justification for our complaints against another or others. We consolidate ourselves in discontent.

Confusion

Disorientation is "the condition of having lost one's bearings; uncertainty as to direction" (*Oxford English Dictionary*). The more significant is the loss or shock, the more profound is our state of disorientation, and the more likely it is

> "Since I didn't come *armed* with any knowledge, presuppositions, or any assumptions. I was just sort of *there* on my own not knowing what was going on.... I could feel myself tensing up and getting anxious at a lot of moments."

to manifest, not only psychologically but also physically, with pain and tension, sleeplessness, and the like. At the very least, when we have the sense of something gone wrong, we become anxious and fearful. We immediately feel helpless and vulnerable, unable to even know where to begin to remedy the situation. In my own experience of the ending of what I thought was a life partnership, there was a month of intense mental confusion that culminated in one night going to bed knowing that I would either wake up the next day having completely "lost my mind" or be "coming out if it." In a work or educational setting where professional competence is important, when we encounter something that we did not know, it is frequently shocking to us because we realize that *we did not know what we did not know.* We become aware of our unconscious incompetence,[3] a lack of awareness of a radically new experience in which we know little about how to conduct ourselves. The ancient Greek word *metánoia* meant "change of mind." It endures in English as "the act or process of changing one's mind" (*Oxford English Dictionary*). We have just stepped onto the bridge, losing our footing on one side and not yet having planted ourselves on the other.

Crisis of Confidence, Anxiety

We are likely to experience a crisis of self-confidence; we are confused, distressed, and, at least temporarily, unable. The state of not knowing, even in an unfamiliar context, is often interpreted as a personal flaw or shortcoming—one should know. It is typical that we most often take the role of the critical authority and judge ourselves harshly. We question ourselves and frequently generalize our sense of inadequacy to other domains of life—our capacity to perform at many things can be affected. We are more likely to engage in negative self-talk and to be self-critical. It is often the case that a crisis in one domain of our life can affect our self-confidence and our performance in others as well.

> "In some ways it's my own stupidity. . . . You dumb-dumb, my colleague picked up on it and you didn't." "If these philosophies are being accounted for in this theoretical model and I didn't recognize it, how dumb could I be?"

Vulnerability, combined with a diminished sense of self-confidence, generates anxiety for us. We are entering an unfamiliar experience in which we cannot predict what will happen. Martin (2009) notes, "anxiety is a universal emotion experienced by everyone everywhere . . . We need our anxiety." He goes on to describe it as the "flight" side of the "flight-or-fight" response, a healthy mechanism that, in many situations, is protective. It is normative for us to experience anxiety in the face of uncertainty. A disproportionately anxious reaction to the experience is also within the range of normal behavior. "Almost everyone misinterprets events from time to time, so it's perfectly normal to experience unrealistic fear and anxiety on occasion" (p. 11).

Deteriorating Relationships

Withdrawal of Authentic Interaction with Others

In our culture, confusion and disarray are usually not positively regarded in public settings such as workplaces and educational environments, so we withdraw from others, if not literally, then by attempting to present ourselves to others in ways that mask our real state of distress. In feeling lost and confused, we transit into coping mode. We typically try to manage extreme discom-

> "There were some jarring points in it for me in terms of relating to people. . . . I wasn't getting on with people."

fort by pretending that nothing is wrong. We present ourselves as we expect others expect us to be. We become disconnected.

Diminished Communication Capacity

As we become self-preoccupied, we lose our presence in the moment and our full attention to others; we reduce the level of awareness about what is going on around us, and our communication to those around us loses its directness and flow. As the distress intensifies, over time, we become more guarded in our relationships, disconnected and fearful, less supported, less capable,

> "I realized that when I'm in a bad mood I totally misinterpret what people are feeling and what is going on."

and more likely to generate uncontested negative interpretations of events. We may also become so preoccupied with ourselves that we miss what is occurring entirely.

Comparison and Competition

We are more likely at this point in the process to compare ourselves with others, and compete in unhelpful ways that either reinforce our negative self-appraisal or serve to assuage our self-doubt. As the experience intensifies,

> "I got a little aggravated at times because other people seem to be pulling it together better than I am."

competition emerges, not for one's personal best, but as an attempt to fortify one's sense of self by being better than others. Social comparisons have been found to be associated with esteem-related issues (e.g., Myers and Crowther, 2009) and negatively related to self-compassion (Neff, 2009) as well openness to experience (Buunk et al., 2005). Competing and comparing pave the way for further reduced communication and erodes the quality of our relationships with others. In a wider perspective, a pattern of response to change and uncertainty may contribute to dangerous trends of antipathy between social groups and ethnic communities.

Relation to Authority

A key relationship that defines the Disorientation Phase is our relationship to those we see as authorities. Particularly in a setting where the structure and culture call for a different kind of participation, where people in positions of authority take a facilitative rather than directive approach to leadership, designated authorities are blamed for the confusion experienced. In offering this emergent learning sequence to participants as a way of "normalizing" their Red

> "I have a very clear-cut idea of what I see as the role of a leader. . . . And *I think* as I'm seeing it now—it demands greater input of energy and thinking through the procedures. . . . I'm getting the information they are giving, I'm not getting it in ways that I want. . . . I think my problem is that I can't seem to get a handle on what they're doing and it seems as if they are not doing anything."

Zone experience, I learned from one student at the end of the program that he thought I had engineered his distress purposefully to confuse him!

We may respond with helplessness (dependence) or opposition (counterdependence) or a combination of the two. We may choose to withdraw from the setting as a means of maintaining some control, or collect critical comments about the authority to whom we attribute our duress, and look for ways to oppose the authority.

Protracted Red Zone

The consequences of communication breakdowns, mutual misunderstanding, and acrimonious interactions among peers and with authorities can grow and intensify. The tendency is to commiserate with peers who are similarly disaffected. In a workplace or a community, this can become institutionalized as factions that endure, thus also fostering a permanent Red Zone. We can unintentionally exacerbate our distressing experience and create a downward spiral. As we remain disconnected from others, we are more likely to give prominence to our negative interpretations and act out of them. This pattern contributes to strain in relationships, which, in turn, is likely to create responses that may put us even more on the defensive. And so we have a spiral downward.

Psychological Defenses

As our discomfort increases with the strain of the uncertainty and distress and our first efforts to "making it go away," such as denial, minimization, and rationalization fail, we resort to more extreme defenses, such as projection of our own states and perceptions on others, and passive-aggressive behavior, or

> "I'm lousy at a whole lot of things that I really wanted to learn. . . . It was a very heavy suit of armor I was clunking around in. I found it hard to take it off."

indirect aggression. Anxiety turns to anger. We tend to project blame on others, often while still blaming ourselves. In a learning or work setting especially, we are likely to resent being made to feel embarrassed and in some way lacking competence.

Defenses are like pain killers; they have their place in assisting us to recover from a challenge or a wound that is nearly overwhelming, but they are significant liabilities if we get locked into them permanently. In one of the most intensive longitudinal studies of psychological defense patterns over a lifetime, the Grant Study, George Vaillant (1977) highlighted the impact of defenses like projection and passive-aggressive behavior on overall career, social, psychological, and medical adjustment. For example, he observed that "the use of [these kinds of] mechanisms could be shown to precede rather than follow the development of chronic physical illness" (p. 86). Those of us who get locked into Red Zones also become more problematic for and therefore less attractive to others, which can foster further Red Zones and contribute to a spiral downward.

Negatively Focused Alliances

Finally, it is at this point in the journey that we may be tempted to merge our discontent with that of others. Negatively focused alliances with others often create justification of our blaming behavior through solidarity in our complaints. The common ground is opposition to the same person(s) and/or practice(s). In ongoing community and work settings, these groups can become pockets of chronic dissent that have a destructive impact not only on the system in which they occur but also on our own progress in dealing with the realities we encounter. The choices we make in these moments are formative not only at the time but, potentially, in the future too, as we deal with other challenges.

The color red has many different meanings, most of which can be seen as symbolic qualities of the disorientation phase. In the color spectrum, red has the longest wavelength observable by the human eye; it is a color that extends the capability to see in the dark! This phase of emergent learning is the period in which tendency toward negativity is most likely to be present, and in which there is potential for destructiveness. In North America, red frequently signifies "stop" or "danger." In football, the "red zone" is the last 20 yards before the goal line—the area in which the battle is the fiercest and the score of the game is often decided. It is in the Disorientation Phase that one struggles with critical choices that will determine whether the outcomes of the process will enhance or diminish a person's capacity to learn and to engage constructively in the world. Chinese and Japanese traditions associate red with courage and heroism, respectively, and, of course, the symbol for "crisis" in Chinese includes both symbols for "danger" and "opportunity." Certainly, the challenges of the Disorientation Phase require personal courage in wrestling a constructive outcome from distress and discomfort.

Second Transition: Reframing

One real possibility is that we remain stuck in the Red Zone and opt out of the emergent learning process. We can continue to project blame for our discomfort and fortify this perspective with alliances with others who also remain discontented. We can become focused on our expectations that are not met and our negative assessments of those whom we hold responsible. We may become in some way locked into hopelessness about being able to do anything to change things for the better. We may maintain inner and interpersonal disconnection from significant others indeterminately; we may create a closed circle of interpretation and generate continuously negative and self-sealing explanations of events. To the extent these patterns are replicated more and more widely in a social context, it becomes the foundation of a culture of fear and suspicion, which, in turn, socializes its members to a diminished interpretation of life. The implications of these patterns as influential in a global context are enormous.

Affirmation by a Credible Other

The way out of the Red Zone comes first in a moment of reconnection, specifically a moment of affirmation by a person significant to us in the setting because we have attributed credibility and authority to him or her. An implicit condition is that we are willing to open ourselves to an affirmation; we may have been affirmed many times by such a

> "I think I felt very anxious right at the beginning but then talking it over with a couple of other people and with the teaching assistant, I realized that I was *pleased* that I was confused about it!"

"credible other" in this process, but we are not yet ready to "hear" it. When we feel in some way inadequate, we gravitate away from the potentially affirming others, fearing that they will instead confirm our worst fears. It is, perhaps, the greatest risk to open ourselves to a person whose opinions we hold in high esteem when we feel particularly vulnerable.

The affirmation event is often very subtle. As a professor, when I am approached by students about something that seems functionally unnecessary, I assume it is the more important moment for the person to make contact with me and, perhaps, unconsciously to assure themselves that I am interested in and care about them and their work. Conversely, if, as leaders, we withhold affirmation, we can maintain anxiety and a sense of instability. This perpetuates fear-based authority and control instead of amplifying our opportunities to contribute to others' capacity to succeed and develop.

Reframing as Learning

It is at this point that we are able to reframe the experience that has been distressing as an acceptable state, and ourselves as being acceptable without having mastery, but rather as being in a process of learning or finding our way through the challenge. This moment in the sequence is the watershed between being stuck in psychic discomfort and moving forward into a domain of new possibilities. The decision to

> "I'm strongest when I show my weakness or when I allow myself to not know. . . . What I'm feeling is *unlocked*. I really feel I've broken out of my chains."

move forward changes the landscape radically from the glass half empty to the glass half full.

Second Phase: Exploration (Green Zone)

Passage into the Exploration Phase of the emergent learning process in a Western cultural context can represent, in itself, a significant shift of mind for us. We expect ourselves to know what comes next, to know our goals and objectives, and to have well-defined plans and strategies; these are marks of competence in our civilization. It is the accomplishment of the Red Zone to acknowledge that we do not know, and that it is acceptable to not know. Stepping into the Green Zone is a radically new experience, especially in a formal setting, and by doing so we enact emergence. It is here that the reach beyond the known begins.

> "Where I come from a lot of the stuff I took as being factual— . . . science. I see it very differently now—they're just theories and they're different today from what they are going to be in ten years' time. Looking back when I went to university, I just accepted truths."

The word green derives from the Old English word "groen," meaning to grow. We associate *green* light with "go," or moving forward. The word green has been used to mean novice, someone beginning something new.

The Green Zone represents the shift from an analytical, deductive mind to an intuitive, inductive mind, from an emphasis on left-brain thinking to an emphasis on right-brain thinking. We begin with our experience, primary knowledge, knowledge from experience, "knowledge that arises in action" (Macmurray, 1957, p. 101). There is an inward turn, with primary attention on our experience through reflection. "Contemplation dissolves . . . the conceptual framework by which we observe and manipulate things . . . stops our movement through experience and pours us straight into experience; we cease to handle things and become immersed in them" (Polanyi, 1967, p. 197). From a Buddhist perspective, Eleanor Rosch speaks of "primary knowing" in a similar way: "Such knowing is open rather than determinate, and a sense of unconditional value, rather than conditional usefulness" (cited in Senge et al., 2004, p. 99). What we come to know is embodied through our experience; we prepare to take responsibility for what we know that has been tacit. New perspectives "can be constructed only by relying on prior tacit knowing, which consists in our attending from it to the previously established experience on which it bears" (Polanyi, 1967, p. 21). In this sense, "all cognition is recognition" (Macmurray, 1961, p. 76).

Coincidently and, perhaps, necessarily, when entering an indeterminate world, we also engage directly with people who have complementary interests and questions. We simultaneously join with a new circle of intention and inquiry. We engage the process of socially constructing knowledge (Berger and Luckmann, 1966); we make sense of our novel shared territory together.

Relaxation without Resolution

When we are able to relax without knowing the answers, without resolving the issue that precipitated the Red Zone experience, we know we have shifted into a different season of inquiry. Charles Hampden-Turner (1971) described the "temporary suspension of [our] syntheses so that new meanings can enter the 'open' mind" (p. 48). He noted that in doing so, it is an act of "building trust," a "mature trust . . . not only a determination to create and maintain trust with others but . . . a trust in one's own powers of resynthesis" (p. 50).

> "I still don't know what's going to happen. . . . I'm more interested than anxious, more excited than tense."

In being able to leave our anxiety and defensive routines behind, we are now able to turn our attention more fully to others and to explore new possibilities. There is a confidence that, while we still do not understand, we will eventually; we can let go of our worries about the future and find ourselves more confident that things will evolve in a positive direction.

Present Oriented, Intuitively Guided

We become much more present oriented. We engage more directly with immediate experience unmediated by expectations and explicit, specific goals. Since we do not know our destination exactly, the journey in this phase is intuitively guided. We encounter and gravitate toward people and activities that seem relevant to our interests, though we may not know exactly why. Intuition is defined as "the immediate apprehension of an object by the mind without the intervention of any reasoning process" (*Oxford English Dictionary*). We discover one step at a time. In this sense, the Exploration Phase is the beginning of the specifically *emergent* aspect of learning.

Analogical Thinking

Petrie and Oshlag (1993) pose the question, "how is radically new knowledge possible?" They suggest that "metaphor can provide a *rational* bridge from the known to the radically unknown, from a given context of understanding to a changed context of understanding" (p. 584). Marshak (2009) calls them "an essential bridge between literal and symbolic, between cognition and affect, and between the conscious and unconscious" (p. 126). In using analogies and metaphors, we draw on the images from our past experience in such ways as to represent fundamentally new experiences before we are able to define them. Analogies that occur to us as we move through an uncharted territory help us to communicate to ourselves, as well as to others, about the nature of the experience. Our analogies contain a great deal of information we have been able to "apprehend," but are unable to define in didactic language.

> "I clicked into being in the middle of things—swimming but not being frightened. A lot of stuff . . . isn't quite under control but it's manageable . . . It struck me that the analogies I used in the beginning of the course where it was something that was outside me where I might be able to stretch it or I might be able to look at it—manipulate it. . . . This one that came out of me last week—I was swimming right in the middle of it."

Collaborative Inquiry

A defining feature of this phase is finding others who have similar or complementary interests with whom we pursue mutual interests and questions. If we listen to the quality of our conversation with them, it is likely to be one of dialogue in which we all bring themes and questions to the exchange, and we may well come out with ways of seeing things that none of us had done in the beginning. William Isaacs' (1999) definition of dialogue is "a conversation in which people think together in relationship . . . [and in which] you relax your grip on certainty and listen to the possibilities that result from being in relationship with others . . ." (p. 19). In this season of

> "There were really strong bonds that formed in an hour among the six of us. It was really interesting to watch that. . . . People were saying fantastic things. Some people said things that just summed up for me a lot of what I had been thinking and not been able to verbalize."

reduced anxiety, the likelihood of real *listening* is enhanced. Also, the recovery of an adequate level of our positive self-regard in the setting enables us to recognize the strengths of others as well; living in the *respect* of others becomes our tendency. The shift from a concern for knowing what the results should be and the need for certainty to a more present-oriented engagement in exploration favors the condition of *suspending* what we think we know and stepping into what we do not know. David Bohm (1996) saw it as important "to suspend . . . assumptions, so that you neither carry them out nor suppress them. You don't believe them, nor do you disbelieve them; you don't judge them as good or bad" (p. 20).

> "The small group is both supportive and confronting and illuminating."

We are likely to establish strong connections with new people in the course of exploring personally meaningful questions; we are likely to be deeply appreciative of our fellow travelers who provide both support and challenge in our quest.

Generative Use of Ideas

We may well find fellow travelers in print. We may explore new ideas in the form of reading, in film, or online in articles and online discussions. New concepts and ideas help us to construct parts of a new map of our experience. Our relationship to text within books, movies, or online is interpretive rather than definitive. We are not assimilating information, but rather exploring new ideas with which to understand our experience as it unfolds.

> "When I read an article now I can connect into it from experiences I have. That flash of recognition is really a sense that I've learned something from an experience and here it is sort of codified in front of me . . . So I can really use books a lot more. I've already learned it but seeing it there in black and white just establishes my learning more."

The site of the original study in a university setting highlighted the significance of an available rich and relevant literature. The importance of the world of ideas in our unpredictable environment is further suggested by the fact that there were more than 140,000 titles on the theme of "change" on Amazon.com in April, 2010.

Series of Insight Episodes

Insight episodes are, in a sense, small previews of the next phase in emergent learning. Even while generating a quality of completeness in a moment in time, they did not constitute a new phase of the inquiry. They were embedded in an ongoing phase of exploration. Occurring typically in a series, the apparent effect is that of building momentum in the inquiry. Insight episodes occur when we are able to connect our experiences to ideas that explain or help us understand them.

> "We got out three or four real 'ah ha's.' They tended to center on how one or another of us felt about how something had been done or something like that—but we'd been able . . . conceptualize them . . . They hit me as really significant little bits and pieces kind of thing . . . that probably don't right now fit together and make a whole, but, you know—kind of little gems of thoughts you want to register away."

This is the process of creating primary knowledge of the new territory (Macmurray, 1957). The accumulating insights become the material that our minds use in creating a new coherent perspective.

Growing Confidence and Satisfaction

Our capability to relax with uncertainty that marks the beginning of the Exploration Phase is a statement of confidence. That confidence is amplified by experiences of collegial engagement in discovery that gradually enhance clarity through moments of insight. A typical comment is, "I was pleased with myself!" More profoundly, we are enacting our capability to "name the world . . . [through which we

> "There's a sense of satisfaction—not only have you read about it but you *have* experienced it. . . . You can build on top of the concrete experience."

constantly] recreate that world" (Freire, 2000, p. 90); we embody responsible participation by articulating our own interpretations. "I feel like a powerhouse!" one person exclaimed.

Third Transition: Reflecting

A saturation point is reached in interactive exploration and there is a shift to more intensive reflection; we are drawn intuitively to solitary reflection even when we might feel it socially awkward to do so.

While the task in the Exploration Phase is generating insights that meaningfully connect new experiences and concepts, the focus at this transition point is on a retrospective review of the journey and the creation of meaningful connections among the insights that have been accumulated. Movement through this transition is not a foregone conclusion, however. We have to be able to have confidence in the value of our own thoughts, maintain our concentration sufficiently, and be willing to take responsibility

> "I think my head has stopped being blown apart . . ." "I have perceptions about this now, perceptions about that. I can conceptualize such and such that I couldn't have before."

for our ideas. Momentum generated through reflection can propel us into the next phase of learning.

The process of generating a new perspective is an act of creation in the same way as accomplished by innovators and artists, as most beautifully described by Edmund Sinnott (1959):

> In science, [we] must be laboring to find the answer to a problem or to bring a mass of apparently unrelated facts to [our] mind into a unity; in art [we] must be dreaming and pondering about a painting or a piece of music which [we feel] is there but cannot quite be brought into existence; in poetry, [we have] an intense preoccupation with something beautiful but still vague which [we] are trying to express. [We are] wrestling to bring into actuality these cloudy, half-formed products of the imagination. Often along the way [we] will jot down notes on sketches or snatches of music or single lines of [our] still inchoate theme. Then, in a time of relaxation or when something else is occupying [our] mind, the answer which [we seek], or at least the creative hub of it, will come into [our] mind as if spontaneously. (p. 24)

Third Phase: Transformation (Purple Zone)

It is out of the intensive reflection that there suddenly emerges a powerful major insight that reveals a fundamentally new perspective. It emerges suddenly as a synthesis of insights that have been generated throughout the exploration phase. An orientation that was lost with the Red Zone is succeeded by a new one. From the former orientation, new experiences seem to be scrambled—unfamiliar, even nonsensical. Suddenly, we become reoriented to a new intellectual position; the "repositioning" makes it possible for one to apprehend the new pattern that makes sense of the particulars. The meaning of "insight" here is captured by the following definition (*Oxford English Dictionary*): "The fact of penetrating with the eyes of the understanding into the inner character or hidden nature of things; a glimpse or view beneath the surface."

Heightened Consciousness

This phase is characterized by a heightened consciousness, hyperalertness, and an awakening. There is simultaneous participation and observation in the moment; we are fully engaged in the experience and, at the same time, are fully aware of ourselves. This experience can be so intense that we can be physically shaken. Senge et al. (2004) spoke of this experience as "presence," "a state of 'letting come,' of consciously participating in the larger field of change" (pp. 13–14). My first experience of this extraordinary insight occasion was at the close of a week-long intensive group learning event through which I had transcended an egocentric sense of myself and understood my significance as being an integral part of the world—not at its center, but a part without which the world would not be the same. A sense of peace that accompanied that major insight lasted for weeks and became an image to live up to. In Zen Buddhism, this extraordinary experience is called "satori," or enlightenment:

> "I get a physical reaction to it. . . . I don't think my heart is thumping—it's an expansion in the chest area. When I'm talking right now is how I feel at the moment and that is very— 'hyped' is the word. . . . It is a different kind of 'hype' than I have been experiencing."

> Satori is defined as an intuitive looking into the nature of things in contradistinction to the analytical or logical understanding of it. Practically, it means the unfolding of a new world hitherto unperceived in the confusion of a dualistically trained mind. Or we may say that with satori our entire surroundings are viewed from an unexpected angle of perception. Whatever this is, the world for those who have gained a satori is no more the old world as it used to be; . . . it is never the same one again. (Barrett and Suzuki, 1996, pp. 98, 99)

This domain of human experience is not a common feature in our public discourse, and is often greeted with skepticism in Western culture. It is perhaps even more difficult to discuss our moments of synthesis than it is to publicly acknowledge our disarray. Mihály Csíkszentmihályi (1990, 1992) contributed greatly to "normalizing" what he calls "flow":

> In flow the self is fully functioning, but not aware of itself doing it, and it can use all the attention for the task at hand. At the most challenging levels, people actually report the *transcendence* of self, caused by an unusually high involvement with a system of action so

much more complex than what one usually encounters in everyday life. The climber feels at one with the mountain . . . When all these elements are present, consciousness is in harmony—and the self, indivisible during the flow episode—emerges strengthened. (1992, p. 33)

Synthesis

The outcome of the Transformation Phase is a synthesis that makes sense out of the experiences and insights to this point in the sequence; it is the revelation of a new perspective. The Mezirow (1978) term "perspective transformation" applies as the outcome of this phase. There is a focus on values, purpose,

> "My values have changed. My values are decreasingly concerned about being efficient, getting it totally organized, structured and beautifully arranged having exactly the right words to describe it, allowing no ambiguity. . . . The old system, if I'm honest about it I didn't even listen to people I didn't think of as being very smart . . . Now all people who have ideas and their ideas are very valuable to me. I may not agree with them . . . but I want to hear them."

and ideals that exemplify the new perspective.

This transformation we experience opens up a new approach (second-order learning) in a significant aspect of our lives. It may pave the way for a new understanding of ourselves and our life purpose (third-order learning). It may be one of a series of similar major insights that represent what Eleanor Rosch (2007) calls "many interdependent synergistic facets which are simultaneously ways of entering the whole and themselves part of the enlightened awareness itself" (p. 261). However, we take the transformation experience forward; it does provide a synthesis of the exploration that was set in motion by the original disorienting experience.

Immense Confidence and Satisfaction
There is a sense of wholeness and resolution, an experience of immense satisfaction and self-confidence. The experience brings elation, extraordinary depth, and richness about the culmination of this process. It is an extremely positive, affirming experience. "[Flow] obtains when all the contents of consciousness are in harmony with each other and with the goals that define the person's self. These are subjective conditions we call pleasure, happiness, satisfaction, enjoyment" (Csíkszentmihályi, 1992, p. 24).

Purple as a color has been associated with royalty and, therefore, power. The *Oxford English Dictionary* has it figuratively "characterized by richness or abundance; splendid, glorious; (of emotion) deeply felt or extravagantly expressed" These are all apt adjectives, in poetic terms, for the experience of the Transformation Phase.

Fourth Transition: Naming

Communicating the Synthesis to Relevant Others
When we name the new perspective to others who would be expected to appreciate it, a complete sense of closure is accomplished through the recognition by these others of the sense and significance of the new synthesis. We know what we know, so it is not a reconsideration of the major insight, but rather affirmation that it is intelligible and meaningful to others. We need to know if there is a circle of shared understanding to which we belong *with* our new perspective. We also take responsibility, that is, "own" our new perspective in a social context. Naming our insight requires us to have conceptualized it, making it less likely that our experience will dissolve into the flow of our experience. When we are able to name such an experience and its significance to us, we make it noticeable, not only to others but also in our own

> "I didn't know if they'd understand what I was trying to say but they got it very well. . . . People understood where I was coming from."

memories as a turning point. The conceptualization becomes a framework to which earlier insights and later refinements can be meaningfully integrated.

This transition point is similar in many respects to the one through which learners passed between the Red and Green Zones—out of disorientation into exploration. Both initial phases involve a strong element of solitude and intensity, though the first tends toward agony and the second toward ecstasy. Both phases close with an affirmation from credible others, though the movement out of the Red Zone appears to require an affirmation of self that permits one to let go of self-blame, while movement out of the Purple Zone is associated with affirmation of the major insight as significant and intelligible. Both transitions involve the learner naming something, though the first is the renaming of an experience in a way that reframes it from necessarily negative and a deficit to a positive potential, while this second instance is constituted by naming the new conceptualization or part of it for the first time to significant others. Finally, the first transition is the beginning of inquiry ushering one into a season of interdependent, open-ended inquiry, and the second is the closing of an inquiry in a season of independent consolidation of a new perspective.

Fourth Phase: Equilibrium (Blue Zone)

Another palpable shift is that from the intense Transformation Phase to the detachment of the Equilibrium Phase. The emotional intensity of earlier phases in the sequence has subsided; there is relative quiescence. The core elements of the conceptual map of a new and more expansive perspective are in place. We begin again to relate to our world through this new perspective, now with a new set of related beliefs, assumptions, and expectations. We become preoccupied with applying and elaborating a new perspective.

Analytical Thinking
Navigating through our world with a new conceptual framework draws us into logical analysis contrasting with the analogical thinking of the Green Zone. We are now refining our conceptual framework rather than generating concepts from our experience. Through the major insight that constitutes the overall synthesis, we return to a conceptually mediated approach to our world. We have a viable map for the territory we are experiencing. If there are changes to our conceptual framework with which we interpret our experience, they are minor tune-ups. More structured logical thinking now plays a role in elaborating, generalizing, and applying the new perspective. The beginning of the Equilibrium Phase is marked by a shift from insight to concept, from interpretation to definition with a center of gravity moving from direct experience to conceptualization.

> "There's a distinction . . . Before, it was far more exploratory, far more open, far more experiential . . . more interior, relying more on my own subjective experience than now [which] is more in my head [than] my gut."

The color blue represents calm and coolness. Culturally, darker blue tones can be associated with conservativism (in the sense of stability) and sophistication. According to the *Oxford English Dictionary*, blue is "often taken as the colour of consistency and unchangingness."

> "I'm operating now from a position of strength—of inner strength."

Self-Confidence
The surge of confidence that came with the Transformation Phase continues, but in a less dramatic way; we feel personally strengthened through this experience. Attention is focused outside ourselves to a great extent; we are less aware of our interior world with respect to the emergent learning theme that has now come "full circle."

Independent and Instrumental Relationships
As we become clear conceptually, there is a simultaneous shift away from intensive involvement with others. The Equilibrium Phase is a season of independence. We know what we need to do, and proceed on our own. What involvement with others does occur in this phase is medi-

> "This is what I want to go after in the course. And if there's anybody else interested in doing it, that's great. But if not, I'm doing it on my own."

ated by predetermined, conscious, and instrumental purposes. In contrast to Green Zone, gravitation toward others without knowing consciously quite why, we now have specific reasons for approaching others that relate to our own conscious purposes.

We have returned to a period of psychic quiescence with a new and more expansive perspective with which to understand our world, at least until we meet our next perspective challenge.

SUMMARY OF THE EMERGENT LEARNING PROCESS

We have followed a generic "inside-out" story of emergent learning through four distinctive phases and four phase transitions with the defining features configured in dimensions of mental, emotional, and social relationship processes. Figure 3.2 is a visual summary of these patterns.

Variations on the Emergent Learning Sequence

Emergent learning has been presented here in its optimal, most straightforward form. The intention is to present a map of emergent learning that can be used to navigate effectively through the experience. There are, however, at least three ways in which emergent learning opportunities are often more complex.

We do not always complete the entire sequence. At any transition point, we may opt out of the process, or stall. Two examples have

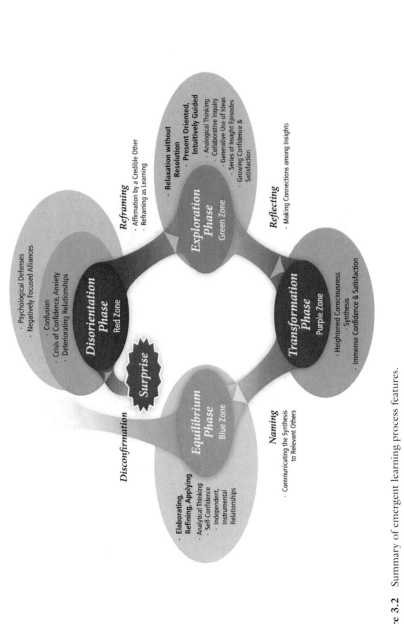

Figure 3.2 Summary of emergent learning process features.

been highlighted—one as being stuck in the distress of the Red Zone and the other of being unable to draw our thoughts together enough to generate a synthesis that brings the process to a conclusion. There was also an instance in the original study of a person having broken out of the Red Zone but then collapsing back into it as a result of returning self-doubt and recurring anxieties.

The description of the emergent learning process is situated in a limited time frame. It is possible that an experience at a particular slice in time is only a temporary setback and that the process will later resume when conditions are more favorable.

Cycles within Cycles

A close examination of emergent learning suggests a layered structure to the experience in which an iteration of the process comprises smaller self-similar versions of itself. Its significance is also understood in a wider context of challenges and changes.

Within an emergent learning sequence there are also events that resemble the process as a whole. A series of experiences in the Disorientation Phase (Red Zone) leave us more and more confused because they are "outside" our understanding and expectation. These moments add to an overall confusion, anxiety, and sense of disconnection. The series of "insight episodes" that begin in the transition from the Disorientation Phase into the Exploration Phase (Green Zone) that culminates in the major reorientating insight have a similar structure. We are able to make sense of an experience or to solve a puzzle or problem. These moments add to our confidence, satisfaction, and a sense of connection. These mini-sequences are similar to the structure of the process as a whole. While there can be an occasional moment of illumination in the Disorientation Phase or a moment of confusion in the Exploration Phase, the predominance of experiences, disconnection or connection, combines to create the character of a phase. They seem to accumulate in a phase to a kind of tipping point, "the prevalence of a social phenomenon sufficient to set in motion a process of rapid change" (*Oxford English Dictionary*). The phase change is distinguished from an episode by the sense that there is a shift in the quality of overall experience, the sense that we have turned a corner. Nevertheless, the mapping of the phase change in a process is most reliably determined in retrospect where we can see the significance of a particular experience to what has preceded, and follow it.

The Instance of Second-Order Learning into Third-Order Learning

In the Disorientation and Exploration Phases, we are grappling with the second-order process unleashed by the recognition that our perspective, or "map" of our world, is inadequate to interpret an unfamiliar experience. We enact an exploratory intuitively guided approach in developing a new understanding and orientation to meeting the challenge, a different approach to learning (Bateson, 1972; Torbert and Fisher, 1992). We change how we engage the unfamiliar, informed by a different set of assumptions and expectations. In the Transformation Phase we suddenly grasp a new perspective on how we are learning differently. However, the momentum generated in this process has the possibility to "jump" the learning to third-order learning if, in addition to developing a consciousness of how we are doing things differently, we also begin to have deeper insight into how *we* have changed, how we understand ourselves and our purpose differently—"actions as connected to one's underlying 'life-aim'" (Torbert and Fisher, 1992, p. 22) or even "personal identity which merges in to all the processes of relationship in some vast ecology or aesthetics of cosmic interaction" (Bateson, 1972, p. 306).

Emergent Learning in a Life Context

A given experience of emergent learning is nested at a particular point within a flow of a person's life experience. Its significance and progression will be influenced in part by the history of experience leading up to it (e.g., a history of success, positive identity, and self-efficacy), the co-occurring change events in the person's life (e.g., desirable or undesirable changes), and the sociocultural strengths that can be accessed (e.g., a rich, accessible reservoir of ideas and imagery, trusted relationships). These influences are considered in detail in Chapter 5, but here we consider some of the significant features of a life context—historical and current.

Complex and Simple Contexts of Emergent Learning

An emergent learning process is a cyclical (or helical) sequence of experience in association with a particular challenge and learning theme. The theme is most easily discernable in retrospect when it has become a whole at the point of the major insight and we can name the theme clearly. Our lives are complex and we can encounter multiple concurrent challenges that provoke emergent learning. Typically, the same challenge will be experienced differently if, on the one hand, it occurs in the context of relative quiescence and stability in our overall life situation, or if, on the other hand, it occurs in the midst of several events that open up several domains of uncertainty and challenge simultaneously. Our job suddenly seems to spin out of control, with our authority eroding, while at home we are more frequently getting into arguments with our adolescent children who are losing interest in school, associating with the "wrong crowd," and unwilling to take our advice; the tension from one setting seems to wear us down for dealing with the other. Progress in one domain augments our strength to deal with the other. On the other hand, getting stuck in the Red Zone in one emergent learning challenge can diminish our capacity to meet other demanding experiences.

Viewed from an historical perspective, progress in emergent learning processes is influenced by our personal history of life experience. In Chapter 5, we observe initial strengths and limitations that both shape and are shaped by the process. One such influential quality is our level of self-esteem. A number of learners in the original study lacked the confidence to open themselves to the unknown; they were unable to let go of their expectations and beliefs enough to enter the Exploration Phase with the confidence they would eventually be able to understand the new territory they had encountered. All participants in the original study experienced the Red Zone. However, those who came into the emergent learning experience with strong self-esteem were able to name their challenge as something they did not know and enter exploration more quickly. This and other qualities influence the shape and pace of emergent learning.

As we step back from a specific cycle of emergent learning into the wider context of our lives, it is possible to see a complex pattern of cycles within cycles that combine to foster growth or decline and to generate resilience or resignation.

Shifting Value-Perspectives Implies a New Community

As we review the sequence, the inside-out perspective reveals a "set of players" that all have a role in our emergent learning process. We begin with those who are associated with the disconfirming event; those who may have supported us through the Red Zone, culminating with the affirmation by the credible "other," continuing with fellow travelers through the Exploration Phase including those in print; and finally, those who confirmed the meaning and value of the final synthesis. As we shift our perspective, we simultaneously become a part of a new circle of interpretation, which includes those for whom our new understanding is meaningful and relevant to their value-perspective—whether new or longstanding. There is a social dimension to emergent learning. A new value-perspective is constructed both socially and as a profound individual experience.

Environmental Influences
The triggers for individual change are typically relevant events in our sociocultural, economic, political, and natural environments. It is no coincidence that emergent learning—reexamining and reconstructing our "assumptive world" (Parkes, 1971)—is now more critical to our survival at this point in history than ever before. We are part of a rapidly evolving global context that presents us with the unexpected at a pace and intensity never imagined by our grandparents. In the Western world we are now, within a lifetime, able to witness several iterations of change that have shaped our lives. Some of us could have witnessed both the advent of air travel in the 1930s and its evolution into rapid global transit; both the rise and fall of world political regimes such as Soviet Communism; the transition from the predominance of extended family to the nuclear family now to the blended family; and the world both without and with the threat of nuclear warfare. Many of us have known the world prior to apparent environmental deterioration; the rise of the global economy, the knowledge worker, and automation; and the decline of many forms of institutionalized religion.

Individual emergent learning processes can be seen as integral to an evolving cultural change process, which now has global proportions and a planetary environmental context. Each time we are willing to work through the Red Zones of our lives to a point of being open to the unknown and to connecting with fellow travellers, we are accomplishing two crucial things. First, we are opening ourselves to an expanded perspective within which we can understand more of our world and our potential to contribute to the common good. Second, we are building the specific personal strengths required to engage in subsequent challenges as opportunities for emergent learning; we are developing resilience in the face of change.

The First Time Around as Breakthrough

The first time we are faced with reexamining our fundamental assumptions, the reality to which we have been socialized—the nature of knowledge, learning, authority, relationships—we are breaking new ground into a world of continuous change. We are, for the first time, questioning our reality as given and known. We are stepping into a different horizon of interpretation, a different value-perspective— knowledge as evolving, emergent learning as a way of life, authority as influence, relationships as integral to learning, and an openness to the wider world and ourselves as responsible, continuous learners. We have entered what Richard Barrett called the "transformation" level of consciousness (Barrett, 1998). We are likely to experience many iterations of this emergent learning process related to different themes as we "consolidate" this shift, but the first time we *enact* second-order learning, we are stepping into a fundamentally different way of seeing the world. These are the individual learning challenges implied by the continuously changing and unpredictable twenty-first century. We are confronted with a pace of change that demands constant knowledge creation *as we go*. This means that neither we nor anyone else can be an *established* authority once and for all. We can expect only the unexpected along with its conflicts, complexity, and periods of confusion. We can catalyze ourselves through change if we are able to trust ourselves in the face of the unknown, if we can trust those whom we believe are the credible authorities for now, and trust others enough to collaborate in a context of uncertainty. We have to become comfortable with the idea that knowledge is not "out there" in a complete form for us to acquire, but that we live in an emerging reality, which we comprehend and create as we go. This shift of mind comes only through enacting it, *embodying* it. This is astonishing for those of us who were socialized into a rational empirical world.

Becoming accomplished at emergent learning enables us to move beyond a preoccupation with what Maslow called "deficit needs" of our own to realizing our potential, including making a difference to the survival and well-being of others (Barrett, 1998). It generates not only new knowledge but also practical wisdom that enables us to act with confidence and good judgment. It is of paramount significance in the context of our twenty-first-century learning agenda.

CHAPTER 4

CONVERGING PERSPECTIVES
ON EMERGENT LEARNING

[The] spontaneous emergence of order at critical points of instability is one of the most important concepts of the new understanding of life. It is technically known as self-organization and is often referred to simply as "emergence." It has been recognized as the dynamic origin of development, learning and evolution.

Fritjof Capra (2002, p. 37)

Coincident with increasing global turbulence over the past three or four decades, the accumulation of a rich source of scholarship and practice related to second- and third-order learning in diverse contexts and theoretical domains has occurred. The existence of multiple models enables us to conduct an abductive phase of inquiry—"comparison of configurations"—that Bateson and Bateson (1987) suggested is "the glue that holds all science together"; it is where "we look for contrasts that develop and differentiate as sophistication increases" (p. 175).

In our quest to understand and develop our capabilities for the twenty-first-century learning agenda, this chapter is concerned with models that draw our attention to our underlying assumptions and beliefs as they relate to new conditions that are experienced. In short, process configurations that are selected are those that represent *emergent* learning and change. Six formulations represented here are based on the following: decades of practice as a scholar-practitioner in group and organizational change (Edgar Schein); organizational change practice combined with extensive reviews of existing research and other literature (Charles Hampden-Turner and David Kolb), pattern identification in a multiplicity of life transition stories (William Bridges), a study of women entering a program of higher education mapped into and refined by further studies of learning in adult education settings and life challenge contexts (Jack Mezirow, Victoria Marsick, and a large group of professionals and scholars who applied their work in a vast range of contexts); the observations of senior consultants who chose to tackle intense organizational and broad-based social problems (Don Beck, Christopher Cowan, and Otto Scharmer); and the study of adaptive processes in nature and social organization (C. S. Holling and Lance Gunderson). Each brings distinctive contributions, and taken as a whole, they point to a common basic syntax of change in value-perspectives (described in Chapter 2) concerning how we understand our opportunities, responsibilities, approaches to action, and ourselves. As independently generated, their similarities offer confirmatory evidence of emergent learning process patterns. Their differences shed light on the influence of the qualities of the context and the participants, and the vantage point from which they are described.

The conceptual configurations of emergent learning that I have selected are naturally occurring processes in the course of life as it unfolds in the face of challenge. Therapeutically assisted processes depicted in clinical models, though they contribute from other perspectives and especially to the dynamics of the Red Zone, have not been included here.

CONFIGURATIONS OF INDIVIDUAL EMERGENT LEARNING PROCESSES

The selected process models of second- and third-order learning are sequenced chronologically below according to publication date. We will note and appreciate the difficulty in separating, even for purposes of examination, individual and social emergent processes.

Kurt Lewin and Edgar Schein: Unfreezing, Changing, and Refreezing

In the 1930s and 1940s, distinguished social science and field theorist Kurt Lewin placed the challenge of individual and organizational change in a dynamic systems perspective and drew our attention to the significance of states of equilibrium and disequilibrium. Lewin named three phases in change: "unfreezing," "changing," and "refreezing."

However, it was Edgar Schein (1995a) who highlighted the importance of Lewin's formulation of change for its recognition of the pain of unlearning, and for its appreciation of the "difficult relearning as one cognitively attempted to restructure one's thoughts, perceptions, feelings, and attitudes" (para 2). Schein summarized Lewin's unfreezing stage of the change formulation as involving "data that disconfirm our expectations or hopes" and the arousal of "survival guilt" in that we are not living up to our own standards and expectations. Through his extensive work as a scholar, educator, and consulting practitioner in organizational change, Schein noted that, over his long career, his "thinking has evolved from theorizing about 'planned change' to thinking about such processes more as 'managed *learning*'" [italics added] (p. 1).

Building on Lewin's work, Schein identified seven elements necessary for personal and organizational change. The first affirms the beginning of change through disconfirmation. "It is my belief that *all* forms of learning and change start with some form of dissatisfaction or frustration generated by data that disconfirm our expectations or hopes" (Schein, 1995a, p. 2). A dimension of disconfirmation is the necessary presence of "survival anxiety" arising from the belief that if we do not change, we will "fail to achieve some goals or ideals we have set for ourselves" (p. 2), similar to the "relevant unknown" of emergent learning. The second critical element for change is a second kind of anxiety, namely, "learning anxiety," which generates defensive routines, "the feeling that if we allow ourselves to enter into a learning or change process, if we admit to ourselves or others that something is wrong or imperfect, we will lose our effectiveness, our self-esteem, and maybe even our identity" (p. 2). These are the patterns of experience observed in the Red Zone. The third essential component Schein saw as necessary for successful change is "enough psychological safety to allow [the person] to accept the [disconfirming] information . . . and become motivated to change" (p. 3), the alternative being in some way to reject the information. "The true artistry of change management lies in the various kinds of tactics that change agents employ to create psychological safety" (p. 3) as a release from "learning anxiety." This is the core struggle of the Red Zone, where the affirmation from a credible authority contributed to relaxation without the answer or solution. Schein identifies the fourth critical component as "cognitive redefinition" (p. 3) or reframing, that is, "broadening" of the meaning of a concept and possibly the development of "new standards of judgment or evaluation" (p. 3). This event in the sequence parallels the "reframing" moment that is the second feature of the transition out of the Red Zone. However, Schein associates this event with the conclusion of the sequence after what is described in Chapter 3 as the Exploration Phase. Cognitive restructuring derives from either the fifth critical component, "modeling," or the sixth critical component, "learning through a trial and error process based on scanning the environment for new concepts" (p. 4). It was the second of these two learning paths that was the prevailing theme of the Green Zone and, ultimately, the quantum shift in perspective that occurred in the Purple Zone among learners in the original study. The final component Schein thought was essential for change was "personal or relational refreezing." This begins following the Transformation Phase with the transition activity of communicating the new synthesis to people we expect would understand it, and then continues throughout the Equilibrium Phase while expanding upon and applying it.

Lewin's model, elaborated and carried forth by prominent scholars and practitioners such as Edgar Schein, is the simplest and one of the most widely known formulations of individual change; it not only has been applied at the level of individuals, but has also been used to represent change in social systems, large and small. Undoubtedly, it has been one of the most influential elements of our cultural reservoir of change constructs.

Charles Hampden-Turner: The Process of Psychosocial Development

Hampden-Turner constructed an idealized meta-model of the emergent learning process, based on diverse similar formulations, to provide a picture of the developmental cycle, as well as a contrasting theoretical composite of the failure of development. These two process configurations (as described below) are helpful in highlighting the elements of emergent learning that appear commonly across a great number of contexts. Hampden-Turner (1971) concluded that while we should not expect to predict individual behavior, we can look for process regularities: "The capacity to synthesize, symbolize and explore, though leading to unique results, is still a lawful process containing measurable uniformities" (p. 31). This supports the practical intention of this book to foster proficiency in second-order learning.

Charles Hampden-Turner published *Radical Man* in 1971, which was based on his prodigious review of over 45 psychology and social theorists, and philosophers. He then synthesized these wide-ranging perspectives into a developmental sequence comprised of eight "segments" or essential elements. The sequence is ultimately configured as a helix depicting successive iterations in a larger developmental pattern. Hampden-Turner depicted a double helix representing change in a relationship between two persons, with the intersection with "the other" with one point in each of the respective change sequences.

Hampden-Turner emphasized our capacity as human beings to choose the existential perspective through which we create meaning that shapes our action. He defined "radical man [sic]" as one who is able "to rebel against the absurdity of atrophying cultures, empty forms, and repressive banality of physical coercion, in such a way that it permits him to create new meaning and renew himself and his environment" (p. 41).

This particular work of Hampden-Turner's was published within several decades of the end of the holocaust in Europe in an era in which existentialism was a salient response to the horrifying events of those times. "Existential" for him referred to its Latin root, "to stand out," especially against meaningless or destructive social conventions and cultures. It also implied the "inside-out" perspective, which is the emergent learning process configuration in this book. The psycho-social development process for Hampden-Turner is simultaneously about social change—"radical man . . . strains every nerve to bridge the distance to those who are deviant or despised"—"the individual fulfills his potentiality and becomes extended and actualized through entering into the perceived reality of others" (p. 53). The inherent contingency between the quality of individual learning, on the one hand, and the quality of the conditions and dynamics in the wider social context, on the other, is a central proposition of this book.

Hampden-Turner's model of psychosocial development also explicitly emphasizes the experience of differences *between persons* as the trigger for change and, as such, the embodiment of beliefs and assumptions in relationships. The description of the emergent learning sequence in Chapter 3 highlights the nature of different assumptions, beliefs, and practices that trigger change as "figure" and the relationship patterns as "ground."

As drawn from an enormous volume of literature, Hampden-Turner's two idealized process extremes, first in their positive and then in negative form, both consisting of the helical developmental forms, each with nine segments are as follows:

Man [sic] exists freely:
   a. through the quality of his PERCEPTION
   b. the strength of his IDENTITY

c. and the synthesis of these into his anticipated and experienced COMPETENCE

d. He INVESTS this with intensity and authenticity in his human environment

e. by periodically SUSPENDING his cognitive structures and RISKING himself

f. in trying to BRIDGE THE GAP to the other(s)

g. He seeks to make a SELF-CONFIRMING, SELF-TRANSCENDING IMPACT upon the other(s)

h. and through a dialectic achieve a HIGHER SYNERGY

i. Each will attempt to INTEGRATE the FEEDBACK from this process into mental matrices of developing COMPLEXITY. (p. 37)

Hampden-Turner saw this helical process in the experience of one person necessarily intersecting that of another person through segments "g" and "h". The segments in the psychosocial development process model are similar to the common patterns of learners in the emergent learning study reported in Chapter 3. Hampden-Turner helpfully distinguished the dimensions of Blue Zone (Equilibrium Phase) that we bring to any challenge—how we see the world ("the quality of perception"), how we see ourselves ("the strength of identity"), and how we see what we are able to do ("experienced competence"). He highlighted investment "authentically or intensely," the "suspending cognitive structures," and as "suspension of personal syntheses and the acceptance of risk is the building of *trust*" (p. 50), but did not describe the struggle and intense emotionality represented in the inside-out learning commentaries of the Red Zone. "Bridging the distance to the other(s)" begins at the close of the Red Zone, beginning with credible authorities, and continues with peers throughout the Green Zone (Exploration Phase). Learners in the original study experienced a "self-confirming, self-transcending impact upon the other" through insight episodes in the Green Zone, and as they named their major synthesis to others and put closure on the creative inquiry and transited out of the Purple Zone into a new state of equilibrium, the Blue Zone. Hampden-Turner described the qualities of relationships in the Exploration Phase as did the learners in the original study: "direct, mutual, present, sharing rather than possessing, value in the relationship for itself, not imposing on the other but in helping them unfold" (p. 52). The last two segments of Hampden-Turner's psychosocial development process model address particularly the Transformation Phase of emergent learning, "through dialectic achieve a higher synergy" and "integrate the feedback from this process into mental matrices of developing complexity." He did not use the language of second-order or double-loop learning (this discourse was published after his work featured here), but spoke of "an effective and intellectual synthesis which is *more* than the sum of its parts, so that each party to the integration can win a 'return on investment' that is greater than the competence risked" (p. 55). Hampden-Turner agreed with William James that the drive toward more enhancing perspectives is at the heart of choice and value-based living: "He knows he must vote always for the richer universe, for the good which seems most organizable, most fit to enter into complex combinations, most apt to be a member of more inclusive whole" (James, 1949, p. 83, cited in Hampden-Turner, 1971, p. 56).

Hampden-Turner associated his optimal psychosocial development process with maturity and the following representation of the opposite extreme as "a severe state of underdevelopment" (p. 79).

Segments in the negative cycle are:
- "PERCEPTION is *narrow* and *impoverished*";
- "identity is '*locked in*' and *stagnant*";
- "leading to an overall sense of *in*COMPETENCE and anticipated *loss*";
- failure "to INVEST authentically and intensely";
- "non-SUSPENDING, RISK-reducing strategies";
- "avoids trying to BRIDGE (wider) DISTANCES to others";
- "often unable to make a SELF-CONFIRMING, SELF-TRANSCENDING IMPACT (even over shorter distances)";
- seeks domination over, or submission to, others' perspectives in a non-dialectical, negantropic failure of SYNERGY"; and
- "accepts little or no *responsibility* for FEEDBACK, which leads to *disintegration* and lack of COMPLEXITY" in self and other. (p. 79)

The negative cycle process framed above highlights the challenges and accomplishments of people describing their experience of emergent learning, as well as the consequences of chronic failure in making use of opportunities for growth and learning. Considered in populations on a large scale, we can see the implications for life on the planet in the face of our twenty-first-century learning challenges.

David Kolb's Process of Experiential Learning

Lewin, along with John Dewey (1916, 1967) and Jean Piaget (1951), also informed the thinking of David Kolb (1984), who described a process of experiential learning. In particular, Kolb identified similarities in structure among Lewin's action research and laboratory learning models, Dewey's articulation of learning from experience, and Piaget's cognitive development theory, and synthesized them into a theoretically based model of experiential learning. Kolb argued for recognition of learning as a process, and constructed a cyclical model incorporating the key structural features of his four sources: concrete experience, reflection and observation, development abstract concepts, and testing of the concepts (see figure 4.1). According to Kolb, learning is rooted in concrete here-and-now experience, which connects to abstract conceptualization through reflective observation and inductive thinking. This compares generally with the Green Zone (Exploration Phase), reflective transition, and the Purple Zone (Transformation Phase). In the Kolb model, abstract conceptualization is then connected back to concrete experience through active experimentation, which compares to the Blue Zone (Equilibrium Phase) in which a new perspective is elaborated and applied.

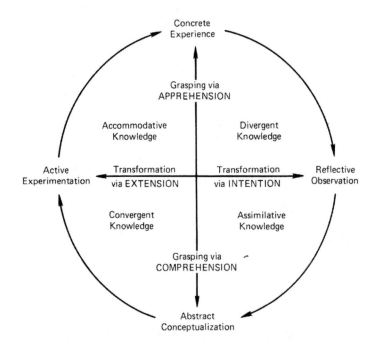

Figure 4.1 David Kolb's Experiential Learning Cycle.
Source: Kolb, David A., *Experimental Learning: Experience as a Source of Learning and Development*, 1st edition, ©1984. Printed and electronically reproduced by permission of Pearson Education, Inc., Upper Saddle River, New Jersey.

As a theoretical model constructed from the observations and conceptualizations of other theorists, Kolb's experiential learning process model is in itself an abstract conceptualization. The very considerable strength of the Kolb model is that it is generic; it is rooted in observations and formulations from diverse domains of thought and scholarship. Kolb's model is based on other theoretical models all constructed from an outside observer's vantage point, while the emergent learning process sequence is *constructed from the point of view of the person experiencing* it. As such, the emergent learning process described from the learner's point of view affirms the basic cognitive-action structure of the Kolb model. What is not evident, however, is the essential weave of patterns of relationship, emotionality, and thought that actually construct the emergence of a fundamentally new understanding. The emergent learning process sequence is a *composite story* that affords the identification of specific points of intervention and initiatives that could catalyze the process (see Chapter 5).

There are at least two points in the emergent learning sequence on which Kolb's theoretical model is especially helpful. First, the generic structure highlighting the constructive tensions between opposites on the cycle model—between the concrete and abstract, reflection and action—invites us to think of what happens when opposites are connected and when they are disconnected. Disorientation of the Red Zone can be understood as temporary suspension of the ability to connect experience and concept—encountering an experience for which one has no adequate map, or concept. Managing to reframe "not knowing" from being an indication of incompetence to being a learning challenge launches a journey comprised of insight. Insight is the reconnection of experience and concept; these insight episodes generate momentum through the exploration of the Green Zone. They culminate in the reorienting major insight experience of the Purple Zone, where there is simultaneity of experience and concept—connections occurring at a rapid rate. Viewed in this way, we can appreciate the experiential learning process depicted by Kolb as a fractal within the process whose dynamics (slow to rapid connection) are constitutive of the overall phase patterns in second-order learning. The more popularly known practical contribution from this model is Kolb's Learning Styles Inventory instrument based on the generic model, which has become widely used.

A dimension of David Kolb's work that has received less attention is what he called "the experiential learning theory of growth and development" (p. 141). Kolb saw a process of maturation in three stages in a life span—acquisition, specialization, and integration (see figure 4.2). Kolb distinguishes three levels of integration: absolutistic (good/bad), simple contingency thinking governed by fixed rules (if A then it's option 1), complex contingency thinking based on "determining the perspective taken on experience" (p. 135), and a higher level of integration that "allows great flexibility in integration and organization of experience, making it possible to cope with change and environmental uncertainty by developing complex alternative constructions of reality" (p. 136). He reasoned that each of the "four learning modes" of the experiential learning cycle evolves through integrative complexity.

Affective complexity in concrete experience results in higher-order sentiments, perceptual complexity in reflective observation results in

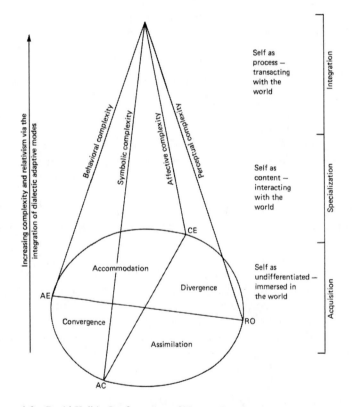

Figure 4.2   David Kolb's Configuration of Human Development.
Source: Kolb, David A., *Experimental Learning: Experience as a Source of Learning and Development*, 1st edition, ©1984. Printed and electronically reproduced by permission of Pearson Education, Inc., Upper Saddle River, New Jersey.

higher-order observations, symbolic complexity in abstract conceptualization results in higher-order concepts, and behavioural complexity in
active experimentation results in higher order actions. (p. 140)

Kolb saw each domain of complexity contributing to the development of the others in a maturation process of three stages—acquisition
("undifferentiated, immersed in the world"), specialization ("self as
content, interacting with the world"), and integration ("self as process—transacting with the world"). He proposed that the transition
between stages two and three "is marked by the individual's personal,
existential confrontation of . . . the conflict between social demands
and personal fulfillment needs" (p. 145). He traced the experience
of development through this process of maturation through "a state of
embeddedness, defensiveness, dependence, and reaction to a state of
self-actualization, independence, proaction and self-direction" (p. 140).
We return to David Kolb's work with respect to the dialectic of opposites in Chapter 5, where we consider the notion of complementarity as
an important element for the progression through emergent learning.

Transformational Learning and Adult Educationists
The study from which this book on emergent learning originated was
a doctoral dissertation in the Adult Education Department of the
Ontario Institute for Studies in Education during a period of excite-
ment and innovation in adult learning in the 1970s. Enhanced by social
and political upheavals of the 1960s, there was a renewed appetite for
looking at many things differently. In adult education, where there had
always been an emancipatory focus, there was a growing interest in self-
directed learning (Knowles, 1975) and independent learning (Tough,
1971). At the same time as this original study of emergent learning
was being conducted, Jack Mezirow and Victoria Marsick (1978)
conducted a study of women reentering colleges after an absence
from the formal system. They documented patterns of this experience in relation to the wider social context of "rapidly changing social
norms relating to women's potentialities for self-fulfillment" (p. 10).
Both studies independently generated similar second- and third-order
learning processes. They observed 10 stages in the process:

1. a disorienting dilemma;
2. self-examination;
3. a critical assessment of sex role assumptions and a sense of alien-
   ation from taken-for-granted social roles and expectations;
4. relating to one's discontent to a current public issue;

5. exploring options for new ways of living;
6. building competence and self-confidence in new roles;
7. planning a course of action and acquiring new knowledge and skills for implementing one's plans;
9. provisional efforts to try new roles; and
10. a reintegration into society on the basis of conditions dictated by the new perspective. (p. 15)

As compared to the emergent learning process sequence, there are some clear similarities—disorientation, increasing confidence with increasing competence, and perspective transformation. The differences derive first from the description being largely from an observer's point of view, thus focusing on activities rather than the "inside-out" experience, and, second, from the incorporation of the content (steps 3 and 4) within the process.

Instead of further exploring and articulating the *process* of perspective transformation as a chronological pattern, Mezirow constructed a strong literature about the *result* of such a process, namely, the "transformation of meaning perspectives." As a consequence, Mezirow has been widely credited with coining the term "transformational learning." His focus was primarily on the cognitive and epistemic dimension ("habit of mind and resulting point of view" [2000, p. 17]) of perspective transformation, though in his most recent publication (2000), Mezirow discusses the social and affective dimensions, but without linking these dimensions in any regularized way to the transformation process itself. Edward Taylor (1997) conducted a study and critical review of other research on perspective transformation that derived from Mezirow's work. The following features are differences reported from the Mezirow/Marsick sequence, which are consistent with what has been described here as the emergent learning process: "more recursive, evolving, and spiralling in nature" (Coffman, 1989; Elias, 1993; Holt, 1994; Laswell, 1994; Taylor, 1994, p. 4); a stronger role of "surprise, intensity and processing of feelings" (Coffman, 1989, p. 4); "without the expression and recognition of feelings, [people] will not engage in the new reality" (Coffman, 1989, p. 4); the importance of anger—"anger had to be resolved before the [person] could move on in the transition process" (Morgan, 1987, p. 5); the presence of "blind faith in order to switch"; and people "temporarily suspended their critical faculties to make behavioural changes they did not fully understand" (Hunter, 1980, p. 5). The Taylor review (1997) also reported that work that found the onset of confusion and disarray (onset of the Red Zone experience) in the broader life context tends to occur more gradually as often as the sudden "response to a crisis" (Courtney, Merriam, and Reeves, 1996; Pope, 1996). Taylor concluded that his review of transformational learning studies "sheds a great deal of light on the intricacies involved in the process of perspective transformation and at the same time reveals that only the surface has been scratched in understanding its nature and relationship to adult learning" (p. 10).

In a subsequent review of the research literature from 1999 to 2005, Taylor observed that most of the published work was concerned with how to foster transformative learning in formal learning situations. More recently, Taylor and Mezirow and associates (2009) have drawn together a compendium of a wider range of practices that has evolved out of this scholarship (see Chapter 6).

Jack Mezirow has been a major contributor to the theory and practice of adult education, namely, in the development of a critical perspective or consciousness about often-taken-for-granted traditional cultural assumptions and beliefs. Carrying forward from the original emphasis on the facilitation of perspective change, Mezirow and his associates have contributed immensely to what we know about the facilitation of transformative learning in adult education and workplace settings, and to our recognition of its significance to the development of autonomous and critical thinking vital for democracy.

William Bridges: Transitions

Also in 1978, William Bridges (2004) first published the original edition of *Transitions: Making Sense of Life's Changes*. Bridges observed that we most frequently associate change with publicly observable events. He wanted to bring to light the psychological process we do not usually talk about, "the inter-reorientation and self-definition that you have to go through in order to incorporate any of those changes in your life" (p. xii). His succinct presentation of three phases of change, "endings," "the neutral zone" ("a period of confusion and distress"), and "beginnings," are reminiscent of Kurt Lewin's unfreezing, changing, and refreezing. Bridges's phases were generated in a seminar, "Being in Transition," in which participants reflected on the changes in their lives. Based on their stories of life transitions supported by anthropological, philosophical, and autobiographical writing as well as ancient spiritual texts, he developed rich descriptions of each of the phases.

Bridges identified "five aspects of 'Endings': "disengagement, dismantling, disidentification, disenchantment, and disorientation" (p. 109). The first two of these aspects are external: disengagement (loss of the familiar context and the "break up of the old queue system that serves to reinforce our roles and to pattern our behaviour") (p. 113) and dismantling (changing one's surroundings). The final three, disidentification, disenchantment, and disorientation, are internal. Disidentification is the "inside" version of disengagement in which we "loosen the bonds of the person we think we are so we can go through a transition toward a new identity" (p. 118). Describing disenchantment, Bridges draws attention to the volitional nature of transitions: "The disenchantment experience is the signal that the time has come to look below the surface of what has been thought to be so italicized out. It is a sign that you are ready to see and understand *more* now." The "disorientation" aspect of "endings" is especially similar to that of the emergent learning sequence: "We recognize the lost, confused, don't-know-where-I-am feeling that deepens as we become disengaged, disidentified and disenchanted" (p. 122). "Endings are . . . experiences of *dying*. They are ordeals, and sometimes they challenge so basically our sense of who we are that we believe they will be the end of *us*" (p. 131). Citing Mircea Eliade (1967), "the trial indispensable of regeneration; that is, to the beginning of a new life" (p. 224). Bridges underlines that, paradoxically, endings are beginnings.

What Bridges has called the "neutral zone" is the period of giving ourselves over to emptiness and formlessness. We are between stories: the old one having been left behind and the new one not having yet been formulated.

> Chaos is not simply "a mess." Rather, it is the primal state of pure energy to which a person (or an organization, society, or anything else in transition) must return for every new beginning. It is only from the perspective of the old form that chaos looks fearful. From any other perspective, it looks like life itself, as yet unshaped by purpose and identification. (p. 141)

Bridges did not highlight exploration, but instead the critical need for the "gap" of the Neutral Zone in which discovery can take place.

> the Neutral Zone is a time when the real business of transition takes place. It is a time when an inner reorientation and realignment is occurring, a time when we are making the all-but-imperceptible shift from one season of life to the next. (p. 154)

He especially cautioned against our cultural impulse toward the quick fix, noting that our civilization has lost the rituals that both affirm the need for and provide the symbolic tools for moving in Neutral Zones. Representing one of the defining features of emergent learning, Exploration Phase as advice, he recommended solitude, reflection (experience logs, autobiography, journal), and present-oriented attention.

The final transition phase is "the new beginning." Bridges qualified a *real* new beginning as an "inner realignment"; he cautioned us to "distinguish between a new beginning and a defensive reaction to an ending. . . . The defensive reaction is simply a way of perpetuating the old situation" (p. 167).

> Genuine beginnings begin within us, even when they are brought to our attention by external opportunities. It is out of the formlessness of the neutral zone, that new form emerges as out of the barrenness of the fallow time that new life springs. We can support and even enhance the process, but we cannot produce the results. Once those results begin to take shape, however, there are several things that can be done. (p. 169)

Bridges' language about emergence captured the quality of the Green Zone (Exploration) and especially the Purple Zone (Reorientation) in the emergent learning process sequence.

He observed that we have lost many of the "social mores that once structured new beginnings" (p. 172) but underlines the importance of reconnecting and "translating insight and idea into action and form" (p. 174). That said, he did not designate a phase of the process for these activities.

As described by Bridges with remarkable similarities in pattern and language, life transitions *are* very significant experiences of emergent learning. It seems understandable that retrospective stories of life transitions would have a more deeply emotional quality and would be of a more generalized nature, thereby having fewer detailed *common* features. While the phases reflect a similar flow of experience, they are demarcated differently. Bridges' Neutral Zone incorporated the reframing transition out of the Red Zone in which there is an acceptance of a gap between a lost form and the creation of a new one, and included the accomplishments of the Green Zone, and the reflecting transition to the Purple Zone. The "New Beginning" combines the Purple Zone, the "Naming" phase transition, and the Blue Zone. Additionally, while Bridges provided several examples of the presence of other people in a person's transition experiences, he did not describe a continuous weave of social relationship patterns as they vary across the three phases. Similarly, the continuous pattern of mental processes characteristic of each phase and phase transition in the emergent learning sequence is not found in his description of transitions.

Is it possible that most, if not all, of the features of the emergent learning process could be found in life transitions? Yes, it is possible, especially where those life transitions involve an inner realignment of self-identity as a capably responsible agent, and change as continuous and unpredictable. The difficulty is that life transitions take place in complex naturalistic settings over longer periods of time than the setting in which the emergent learning process schema was generated. It is very difficult to gather the detailed observations that could establish *common detailed* patterns.

SIMULTANEOUS INDIVIDUAL / SYSTEM LEARNING AND CHANGE

It is especially evident from the inside-out vantage point that the emergent learning process as experienced by individuals occurs in a social context and that a system of social relationships is integral to the process of learning (Chapter 3) and as featured in Hampden-Turner's model (1971). While the process frameworks reviewed above feature the individual process of learning primarily, if not exclusively, as *figure* and the social processes as *ground*, two value-perspective shift configurations treat the two simultaneously. What we lose in the detail of the individual experience, we gain in witnessing the nexus of these two interdependent orders of change. This is also the focus of Chapter 6.

Beck and Cowan: Worldview Transitions

Donald Beck and Christopher Cowan (1996) originated the term "spiral dynamics" in extending the groundbreaking work of Clare Graves' (1966, 1970) on what he called "levels of existence."

> . . . the psychology of the mature human being is an unfolding, emer-
> gent, oscillating, spiraling process marked by progressive subordination
> of older, lower-order behaviour systems to newer, higher-order systems
> as man's existential problems change. (Graves, 1974)

Beck and Cowan (1996) refined and elaborated Graves's eight "levels of existence" into [v]MEMEs[1] ("value memes") and configured them as a helix, or spiral, each ᵛMEME situated at different points on the spiral. The spiral was a double helix, but unlike the Hampden-Turner self-other helix described above, the helix consisted of the person in relation to their life conditions. Graves proposed that the life conditions and the person co-created one another and that as life conditions change, they trigger changes in the person. They described progression on this spiral as a "pendulum-like shift between a focus on 'me' and concerns of 'we,' orientations somewhat akin to *ying* and *yang*" (p. 56). However, it is the change process from one ᵛMEME to another that is articulated as an emergent learning process. It consists of four, possibly five, phases. ALPHA is the phase in which "human systems are in a state of equilibrium, homeostasis, integration," that is, where a "person has it together" or a "company is doing well in its niche" and "society is meeting the needs of its citizens" (p. 86). BETA and GAMMA are both aspects of the disconfirmation transition and Disorientation Phase; they "represent conditions of instability, and turbulence, and chaos" (pp. 86, 87). BETA is the phase in which

> problems are better felt and then told. We experienced the frustration and discomfort in our hearts more than our minds. Things feel shaky. We sense the turmoil but cannot get a handle on its causes. We know something is amiss. We can see it, touch it, taste it, and smell it but not explain it. And we can't explain why we cannot. . . . We try to do more of what we are doing only better; we have "failed to recognize that aspects of *Life Conditions* ALPHA has been handling have changed, making the operating systems incongruent or irrelevant" (pp. 87, 88).

In the GAMMA phase "the denial and foggy thinking of BETA give way to stark reality. There is now a clear vision of how bad things are" (p. 89). The authors observed that the intense and locked-in GAMMA phase can be avoided if we progress proactively rather than simply react, requiring an open stance in a challenge (as opposed to an arrested or blocked stance). However, they noted that "few people see the light before all hell breaks loose" (p. 100). GAMMA is described vividly with the analogy of "being locked in the trunk of an automobile, unable to get free. No one can hear your desperate pleas for help. No more breathing space" (p. 89). "The emotions of frustration and confusion at BETA give way to deep anger and hostility of GAMMA" and "Even the past does not fit any more" (p. 89). The phase shifts from patience in BETA to action, which may be undertaken with a sense of "nothing left to lose." Beck and Cowan pointed to extreme conditions that produce the dramatic dimensions of GAMMA. "The GAMMA trap spawns psychopathic rather than neurotic behaviours, ranging from forms of self-destructiveness . . . to morbid anti-social acts . . . Riots break out, post offices are shot-up, and airplanes are bombed from the GAMMA Trap" (p. 91). The authors refer to the replacement of Martin Luther King, Jr., in the United States with Malcolm X, and nonviolent marches with GAMMA rebellions like the violent confrontations in cities such as Los Angeles. If GAMMA's constraints can be overcome, "a DELTA surge is ignited" (p. 91). When emerging from GAMMA, the DELTA phase is depicted as breaking free, "a rocket of change" (p. 92) against the past—revolution. From the DELTA phase the new ALPHA emerges. The new ALPHA is described as a "consolidation of ideas and insights from BETA and GAMMA through the DELTA Surge" (p. 92). The authors describe, from an observer's standpoint, the behavior exhibited throughout the process and helpfully distinguish variations characteristic of different value-perspectives, or ᵛMEMEs.

The authors reflect the complexity of change in documenting seven variations they have observed, of which the "optimal version" of individual emergent learning as described in Chapter 3 addresses only one—an "evolutionary change." "Evolutionary" is compared to "shifting gears [where] a different power ratio is engaged" (p. 101) (second-order learning). As contrasted with revolutionary change, "there is no need to destroy what was in order to shift toward what will be" (p. 101). Interestingly, Beck and Cowan point out that this kind of change variation is associated with initiatives that foster *contextual change* in contrast to attempting to change something about the person directly.

Beck and Cowan (1996) describe an emergent learning process on a macrosocial scale in their identification of "Five Steps in the Pathway of ᵛMEME Change" (p. 85), combined with their "conditions for ᵛMEME change" (p. 75). The "condition" of "dissonance" ("awareness of a gap," "enough turbulence to create a sense of 'something is wrong,'" and/or "abject failure of old solutions to solve problems" [p. 83]) is the inherent phase transition in the emergent learning sequence in Chapter 3. However, both mark the shift from ALPHA or Equilibrium and BETA or Disorientation. The "condition" of "barriers" that includes "excuses and rationalizations" is an inherent element in the Disorientation Phase, or Red Zone. "INSIGHT" is situated in the model as a condition for change, rather than as a feature in the sequence at one or several points. It is described with an "outside-in" logic, in contrast to an "inside-out" perspective that illuminates the *emergence* of insight. "By 'insight' we mean there is an understanding of (1) what went wrong with the previous system and why, as well as (2) what resources are now available for handling the problems better" (p. 84). And finally "consolidation" is a condition for Beck and Cowan, while it is a phase of applying and elaborating the new perspective in the emergent learning sequence described here. "Exciting discoveries have not yet become mature expressions and so appear half-baked and clumsy. It takes awhile for the new systems to blend into a profile" (Beck and Cowan, 1996, p. 84).

Some of the differences in the "spiral dynamics" description arise because it simultaneously describes individual and change processes in social systems, inspired by Clare Graves' early work, and as observed and informed by the work of the authors in organizational and community settings, some of which involved work with people in embattled situations, such as South Africa under apartheid.

A distinctive strength of the formulation of a "spiral change," based on observations of large-scale social dynamics in turbulent contexts, highlights the dangers and the destructive potential of change. Beck and Cowan helpfully describe a wide range of variations on change that does not lead to second-order learning. They have also represented, in more detail than others, how the emergent learning process itself varies, depending on the ^{v}MEMEs or value-perspectives that the person is moving from and toward. Beck and Cowan remind us that precipitating conditions do not always lead to a fundamentally new perspective that can position us for a more constructive and effective approach to our world. Their scenarios based on work with social issues such as those highlighted in Chapter 1 underscore the fact that the challenges are as daunting as they are essential.

Otto Scharmer: Theory U

More recently, Otto Scharmer (2007), senior lecturer at MIT and organizational consultant, constructed a model of "learning from the *future* as it emerges" (p. 7). Scharmer's conceptualization is based on his own experience and work, with both global companies and grassroots organizations around the world, as well as the work of over 150 leading practitioners and thinkers around the world. His schema, Theory U, is a series of five distinctive "movements" configured in a U-shape (see figure 4.3) across three of four "field structures of attention," which are as follows:

1. *I-in-me*: what I perceive based on my habitual habits of seeing and thinking,

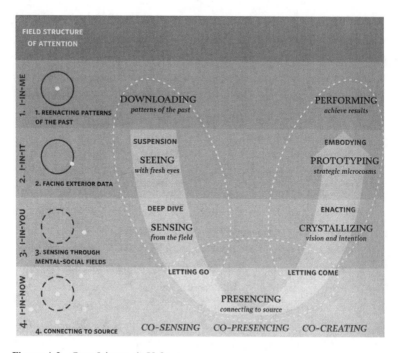

Figure 4.3 Otto Scharmer's U-Space.
Source: Scharmer, O., *Theory U: Leading from the Future as It Emerges.* 2007, p. 244. Reproduced by permission of Society for Organizational Learning, Cambridge, MA.

2. *I-in-it*: what I perceive with my senses and mind wide open,
3. *I-in-you*: when I tune in to and sense from within my heart wide open,
4. *I-in-now*: what I understand from the source or bottom of my being, that is, from attending with my open will. (p. 1)

In the first of these modes of attention, we can recognize the Blue Zone qualities of having and operating from a map that we are confident fits the territory. On the left hand side of the "U," operating from this mode of attention, Scharmer calls "downloading"; our attention is on past patterns. As we move down the U on the left hand side to the second field of attention, "I-in-it," the first "movement" is called "Seeing," that is, what Francisco Varela called "suspension of habitual patterns" (cited in Scharmer, 2007, p. 36). This is similar to the beginning of the Green Zone, relaxing without a map of the territory, having let go of the old one and yet to replace it with a new one. A major difference between Scharmer's model and other emergent learning process schemas is that there is no Red Zone, no period of disorientation, no falling apart—an inherent feature of the process.

Instead, his representation of this aspect of experience in the face of the unexpected is a mirror opposite process—five mirror opposite moments in what he calls "Anti-Space of Social Pathology" in contrast to the "U-Space of Social Emergence"—"Not Seeing," "De-Sensing," "Absencing," "Self-Deluding," "Aborting," and "Destroying" (p. 266). The model depicting the "anti-space" as an inverted U assumes steady movement toward destruction; that is, there are no explicit paths of return to the positive process.

Continuing with the positive process "the U space of social emergence" (p. 266), the shift is from "Seeing" to "Sensing" on the "I-in-you" mode of attention. Scharmer described this moment as conversing with others, "not just talking together, [but] . . . thinking together" (p. 146), as dialogue—"the art of *seeing together*" (p. 135). This is the pattern of the Green Zone—collaborative inquiry.

The shift to the deepest mode of attention, "I-in-now," at the bottom of the U is "Presencing," "a blending of the words, 'presence' and 'sensing.' It means to sense, tune in, and act from one's highest future potential—the future that depends on us to bring it into being" (p. 8). Scharmer explained that presencing "happens when our perception begins to connect to the source of our emerging future." While described somewhat differently than the Transformation Phase, there is an obvious similarity as an extraordinarily penetrating awareness, multiple points of awareness, "*both inside and outside*" (Theory U), and "simultaneous participating and observing" in the Transformation Phase. Many in the series of examples of this experience provided occurred in a group context, while this phase in the process described in Chapter 3 has been presented as one undertaken in solitude. This is an intense, intrapersonal moment whether in a social context or in a solitary space.

The next U moment is "Crystallizing," that is, "sustaining [the] connection [of the Presencing moment] and beginning to operate from it." Taking the moment of deep insight forward from the Transformation Phase is the naming of the deep insight to others; this appears consistent with this Theory U moment as a return to the "I-in-you" mode of attention.

Moving back up to the "I-in-it" level, Scharmer sees the next moment as "Prototyping living microcosms in order to explore the future by doing and experimenting" (p. 203). This means "acting from the future" (p. 207), which is "highly connected to the inspirational spark of the future 'that stands in need of you' (Buber, 1970)" (p. 206). It is a meditation on intention and mindfulness of just the right opportunities required to fulfill it and "to deliver it into reality" (p. 208). This moment of Theory U was not highlighted in the narratives that led to describing the transition out of the Transformation Phase, possibly due to the context in an educational setting where ongoing action is not a part of the context. It is an important extension of the inner journey that more often concludes with the shift of mind.

The return to the "I-in-me" mode of attention involves introducing the prototype into a larger arena of action and influence. The question becomes "how to embed it in an institutional infrastructure . . . places, practices, peers, processes, and rhythms that allow it to be developed and sustained" (p. 218). The detached language of the Equilibrium Phase is not represented in Theory U; the work of the Blue Zone equivalent in Theory U is creativity continues on the "prototype" in a practical context.

In a culture that shies away from matters deeply personal, Scharmer's great gift is his intense detail and emphasis on the inner dimension of emergent learning. As a narrator, his viewpoint is "from-within" throughout the journey, with an emphasis on the perspective of the practitioner who has personal experience of the process and who has also fostered unfolding of the process for others in working with groups and organizations. However, his careful and continuous attention to the link between inner world and outer context is not situated in a specific setting. His observations are drawn from a wide range of experiences and many scales of context, including wider cultural and political scenarios. His thoughtful contributions are connected to practical ways to foster emergent learning.

COMMON THEMES AND CONTRAST ACROSS PROCESS CONFIGURATIONS

Similarities among process models of second- and third-order learning generated in diverse contexts—from simplest to the most detailed—point to a common flow of experience. Each of the configurations has increased our understanding through additions and amplifications. However, as Bateson and Bateson (1987) reminded us, we are attempting to comprehend complex phenomena; we cannot expect any one conception of emergent learning to be "complete." Each is also a reflection of the context and perspective from which it was derived, and offers a unique set of strengths.

There is a significant structural difference in two of the models. Hampden-Turner and Scharmer do not include Red Zone experience as an inherent feature of emergent learning; instead it is elaborated as part of a complete decremental spiral, beginning with disconnection and the ensuing distress, in an uninterrupted trajectory toward the destructive—a mirror opposite of the emergent learning experience. Scharmer (2007) describes his experience, while he was still a school boy, of witnessing the complete destruction by fire of their family home of generations with its contents: "at that moment I realized there was a whole other dimension of myself that I hadn't previously been aware of, a dimension that related not to my past—the world that had dissolved in front of my eyes—but to my future, a world that *I* could bring into reality in my life" (p. 24). This is a remarkable shift toward a new value-perspective that apparently occurred almost instantly illustrating that it is possible to leap whole phases of the emergent learning process, that is, "skipping" the disorientation and exploration, to the transformative moment. This experience, however, is very rare. It is important to envision and strive toward the possibility of developing the same level of resilience in the face of such a shocking and unpredictable event. More usually though, "all forms of learning and change start with some form of dissatisfaction or frustration" (Schein, 1995a, p. 2). Mezirow's colleagues and students recommended that their "disorienting dilemma" be represented with a stronger role for "surprise, intensity and the processing of feelings" (Coffman, 1989, p. 4). For several reasons, I believe it is important to retain "falling apart" as an integral element of the sequence. First, especially for those of us in Western cultures for whom confusion, vulnerability, and disarray are a social embarrassment, our tendency to deny these aspects of our experience is often at the heart of what consolidates and exacerbates our distress toward destructive outcomes. People have found recognition of the Red Zone, as part of the learning process, to be valuable and even liberating; it gives us "permission" to be visibly in disarray rather than feeling that we have to hide our actual emotional state. Second, in our extraverted culture it is often distressing or devastating moments that provoke us to turn "inside" and become aware of what is going on within ourselves, which later becomes the ground for our shift of mind. Third, recognizing breakdowns as inherent features of emergent learning highlights the importance of our resilience, as well as our creativity as essential twenty-first-century strengths.

Another significant dimension of difference among the second-order learning formulations is how *explicit* attention is distributed across mental, affective, and social streams of the process and the wider social context. Schein emphasized the mental and, to a lesser extent, the affective and social dimensions. Bridges combined the mental and affective and, to a lesser extent, the social stream. Hampden-Turner focused on mental and, to a lesser extent, the social dynamics. Kolb described largely mental processes. Mezirow, Beck and Cowan, and Scharmer featured primarily mental processes in the context of group and/or wider social processes.

A third dimension of difference is what aspects of the sequence are emphasized. Formulations of second- and third-order learning were selected because they represent, for the most part, a full cycle process, that is, touching on all or most aspects of falling apart and coming together. However, these authors concentrated their attention on different points in the process. For example, Schein contributed critical distinctions between different types of anxiety in the Red Zone, and highlighted the critical release from "learning anxiety" through well-designed support from leaders or "change agents." Hampden-Turner contributed the double helix formation of the process (dialectic), emphasizing the equivalence of the Exploration and Transformation Phases of the sequence. Otto Scharmer provided an intensely inside-out version of the same territory, extending into the commitment to action leading into equivalence of the Equilibrium Phase. Bridges and Mezirow both spoke to the flow of events in all phases of the emergent learning process as described in Chapter 3, but marked their phases or steps differently. Beck and Cowan emphasized the dialectic between the person and the context and configured the process similarly to the process featured here, but located some of the elements in a separate description of "variations." They contributed narrative that amplifies our awareness of the potential for profound destruction that can evolve from the intensified Red Zone or GAMMA phase. These can then align with a larger process of social deterioration—"psychopathic rather than neurotic behaviours, ranging from forms of self-destructiveness . . . to morbid anti-social acts" (p. 91) that can arise.

The description of emergent learning process presented in Chapter 3 is the most inclusive and detailed *inside-out* version of the configurations reviewed, but rather is limited by its source in one context. It is helpfully supplemented by features contributed by other models. However, what it strongly represents is the vantage point of the learner. A map constructed from the perspective of the traveler is most helpful to the traveler—the markers are in the "terrain of our experience." Remarkably, there is a common structure to that "inside-out" experience that endures, even when the "outside" terrain changes; indeed it enfolds them. The fundamental challenge for those of us from traditional Western culture is to penetrate beyond the limits of conscious, empirical-rational thought. There is mounting evidence that this shift is critical.

LESSONS FROM THE NATURAL WORLD

The natural world *is* transformation, change, and renewal—from the grand scale of evolving planetary eras to micro-miracles like the transformation of the caterpillar to chrysalis, and ultimately to the emerging butterfly. As environmental threats mount, more intensive attention has been paid to these processes in recent years, due to their deeper significance as sources of resilience and their messages about sustainability. Planetary sustainability depends on a global shift of mind from seeing ourselves somehow separate from the natural world to being an integral part of it. The patterns of *emergent* learning engage us as whole and sentient beings, emphasizing that consciousness itself evolves as an *embodied* phenomenon and *because of* a relationship with our context (*embedded*). Understanding ourselves as emergent learners provides us with *a giant step inside creation* and, perhaps, a major advance in meeting our challenge of reversing the trend toward accelerating environmental deterioration. Tarnas (1991) suggests that such an "evolution of world view" is critical not only to the planet but also to humankind.

> Nature pervades everything, and the human mind in all its fullness is itself an expression of nature's essential being. And it is only when the human mind actively brings forth from within itself the full powers of a disciplined imagination and saturates its empirical observation with archetypal insight that the deeper reality of the world emerges. A developed inner life is therefore indispensable for cognition. In its most profound an authentic expression, the intellectual imagination does not merely project its ideas into nature from its isolated brain corner. Rather, from within its own depths of imagination directly contacts the creative process within nature, realizes that process within itself, and brings nature's reality the conscious expression. . . . The human imagination is itself part of the world's intrinsic truth; without it the world is in some sense incomplete. (p. 434)

The adaptation processes of the natural world are also a source of wisdom for our own conscious unfolding.

Holling and Gunderson: Panarchy—Cross-Scale Adaptive Change Process in Human and Natural Systems

As members of the Resilience Network, C. S. Holling and Lance Gunderson (2002) have advanced a "heuristic model of change" that is a crossover theory, based on their observations of "adaptive change and learning" in both natural and social worlds. Their model is an integrative theory of adaptation that serves as a conceptual framework to understand complex global change, comprised of human and natural dimensions; they called their theory "panarchy." Their intention was to understand the failures of regional resource and ecosystem management, and this required comprehensive perspective on change across interacting domains—economic, ecological, and social institutional.

> The cross-scale interdisciplinary, and dynamic nature of the theory has led us to coin the term *panarchy* for it. Its essential focus is to rationalize the interplay between change and persistence, between predictable and unpredictable. Thus, we drew on the Greek god Pan to capture the image of unpredictable change and upon notions of hierarchies across scales to represent structures that sustain experiments, test results, and allow adaptive evolution. (p. 5)

The authors highlight two approaches to defining stability. The traditional approach, "*engineering resilience . . .* focuses on efficiency, control, constancy, and predictability" (p. 27). The second approach, "*ecological resilience*" (p. 28), "focuses on persistence, adaptiveness, variability, and unpredictability" (p. 27). The former "concentrates on stability near an equilibrium steady state, where resistance to disturbance and speed of return to the equilibrium are used to measure the property" (p. 27); in other words, equilibrium is the primary state or defining point of reference. The latter "emphasizes conditions far from any equilibrium steady state, where instabilities can flip a system into another regime of behaviour, that is, another stability domain" (p. 27). The second type invites us to consider change as the primary state, or defining point of reference. This distinction parallels the difference between first-order learning where we expect and are able to assimilate new experience and information, to an existing perspective and assumptive world, and second-order learning where the new experience, instead of being accommodated, uproots the perspective itself. The authors note that knowledge of this more complex ecological resilience is "rooted in inductive rather than deductive theory formation" (p. 30).

Holling and Gunderson articulated what they call a metaphor for "interpreting events and causes" of adaptive change for "productive temperate ecosystems and possible similarities in human organizations and economies" (p. 33). The process comprises four phases configured in the form of a mobius strip on a grid of two axes as depicted in figure 4.4. The *y*-axis represents potential—the availability of resources for the regeneration process. The *x*-axis represents the degree of connectedness and control. The four phases are: *"exploitation, conservation, creative destruction or release, and reorganization"* [italics added].

Described in the same sequence as the emergent learning process, we can see similarities between the creative destruction that leads to "release," the Ω "release" phase, and disconfirmation transition that leads to the Disorientation Phase. In both cases, a highly developed and tightly organized synthesis collapses. There is a sudden loss of form and structure. Organization becomes disorganization.

In the cases of extreme in growing rigidity, all systems become accidents waiting to happen. The trigger might be entirely random and external—a transient dry spell for a forest, a new critic appointed to a board of directors for a company, an election of a new minister of government responsible for an agency. Such events previously would

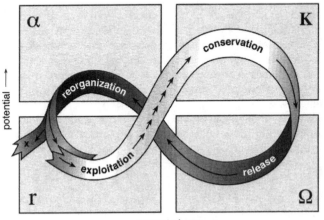

Figure 4.4 C. S. Holling and Lance Gunderson's Panarchy Model of Change and Adaptation.
Source: Panarchy, edited by Lance H. Gunderson and C. S. Holling. 2002, p. 34. Copyright@ 2002 Island Press. Reproduced by permission of Island Press, Washington, DC.

cause scarcely a ripple, but now the structural vulnerability provokes crisis and transformation because ecological resilience is low. . . . A gale of creative destruction can be released in the resulting Ω phase. (p. 45)

The creative destruction phase is "triggered by agents of disturbance such as wind, fire, disease, insect outbreak, or drought, or a combination of these," preceded by a conservation phase in nature where "the accumulating nutrient and biomass resources become more and more tightly bound within existing vegetation, preventing other competitors from utilizing them . . ." to the point of becoming "overconnected and increasingly rigid in its overcontrol" (p. 35).

Though the structure has been lost—as in the case of a forest destroyed by fire—its elements nevertheless remain in the system in a disaggregated state. These become the resources that become reorganized into new forms. The authors describe it as a "diversity that 'lies in waiting' to allow the system to respond adaptively to unexpected future external changes . . .," "in tree trunks not consumed by fire and insects; in nutrients released by decomposing material; in the seed banks established in the soil" (p. 45), and so on.

The α phase is identified as "a process of reorganization to provide the potential for subsequent growth, resource accumulation, and storage" (p. 41). The reorganization α phase in a natural environment "involves the transient appearance or expansions of organisms that begin to capture opportunity—pioneer species," and the social institutional world "is essentially equivalent to one of innovation and restructuring in an industry or in a society—the kinds of economic processes and policies that come to practical attention at times of economic recession or social transformation" (p. 35). This is a period in the sequence when there is "low connectedness among variables" (p. 41). This simultaneously fosters the emergence of new elements, but it also presents the risk of losing elements of the system that could be important to regeneration of new forms. It is a state of both potential and vulnerability. As such, the reorganization reflects features of the Red Zone at the choice point between the unfolding of a growth cycle toward new synthesis, or one of stagnation and decline.

The shift into growth, r to K, "exploitation" to "conservation," that in the natural world combines regeneration from "residual vegetation in physical structures [that] represent biotic legacies from the previous cycle" with a "template on which seeds from distant sources germinate" (p. 43). Species that thrive do so by coupling with others.

a subset of species begins to develop close into relations that are mutually supportive—i.e., they form self-organized clusters of relationships. . . . the trust needed for effective cooperation increases and becomes more dependable. In short, the actors whether species—or people, develop systems of relationships that control external variability and, by doing so, reinforce their own expansion. That is, connectedness increases. (p. 44)

The description of the exploitation phase points to patterns similar to those that constitute the Exploration Phase of the emergent learning sequence. A new ecology of mind (to borrow Gregory Bateson's [1972] term) is like a new biological ecology, which is generated from the emergence of particulars (insights or plants, respectively) that are supported by mutually beneficial relationships (collaboration). Holling and Gunderson speak of the shift from "exploitation" (r phase) to "conservation" (K phase) noting that the "diversity of species peaks just as intense competition and control began to squeeze out those less able to adapt to changing circumstances." From the "inside-out" perspective there is no exact equivalent to this dynamic in the emergent learning process, but there is the emergence of a preeminent and organizing theme, the major insight. Also, in a wider context, just as we become more akin to others within a new circle of interpretation implied by a new perspective, our relationship may change with those who remain in a value-perspective that we are leaving behind.

The "conservation" (K phase) is most similar to the Equilibrium Phase in the emergent learning sequence, where the predominant form is elaborated and consolidated. Over time, paradoxically, the very synthesis that leads to success is ultimately vulnerable to the vicissitudes of a changing context.

The governing dimensions of the Panarchy model discussed to this point have been the potential on the vertical axis, or y-axis (r and Ω phases as low potential with K and α phases as high potential), and the connectedness on the horizontal axis or x-axis (α and r phases as low connectedness and K and Ω phases). "Potential" is understood to be the following: in environmental terms as "biomass, physical structure, and accumulated nutrients" (p. 49); in social terms as cultural capital, such as "networks of relationships—friendships, mutual respect, and trust among people and between people and institutions of governance"; and in economic terms as "accumulated useable knowledge, inventions and skills that are available and accessible" as well as "the unique self-awareness and cognitive abilities of people" (p. 50).

Connectedness is defined as "the strength of internal connections that mediate and regulate the influences between inside processes and the outside world—essentially the degree of internal control that a system can exert over external variability" (p. 50).

The authors and their colleagues depict *resilience* as a third dimension in the Panarchy model, defined as "the capacity of a system to experience disturbance and still maintain its own ongoing functions and controls" (p. 50). In two dimensions, resilience on the third dimension can be shown to decrease as the system reaches its conservation peak and initial release segment (K and Ω phases), but immediately begins to rise as the release and reorganization phases (Ω to α phases) progress and peak in the transition between (α and r phases).

> The essential requirement is to recognize that conditions are needed that occasionally foster novelty and experiment. Those become possible during periods when connectedness is low and resilience is high. The low connectedness permits novel reassortments of elements that were previously tightly connected to one another. The high resilience allows tests of those novel combinations because the system-wide costs of failure are low. These are the conditions needed for creative experimentation. This recognition of resilience varying within the cycle is the first element added that provides a way to reconcile the delicious paradoxes of conservative nature versus creative nature, of sustainability versus creative change. (p. 40)

Anticipating our discussion in Chapter 6 concerning environments for emergent learning, it is helpful to consider the authors' extension of this change pattern as it relates to both contexts. Holling and Gunderson recognize this change process as a pattern nested in different orders of change (see figure 4.5) that are occurring at different paces, typically, the order that comprises multiple constituent smaller change processes evolves at a slower pace than those within it. "Semiautonomous levels are formed from interactions among a set of variables that share similar speeds" and "each level communicates a small set of information or quantity of material to the next higher [slower and coarser] level" (p.72).

> As long as the transfer from one level to the other is maintained, the interactions within the levels themselves can be transformed or variables changed without the whole system losing its integrity. As a consequence, the structure allows wide latitude for experimentation within levels, thereby greatly increasing the speed of evolution. (p. 72)

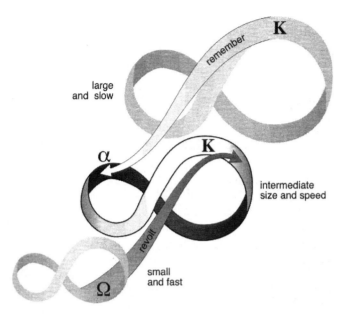

Figure 4.5 C. S. Holling and Lance Gunderson's Cross-Scale Panarchy Processes.
Source: Panarchy, edited by Lance H. Gunderson and C. S. Holling. 2002, p. 75. Copyright@ 2002 Island Press. Reproduced by permission of Island Press, Washington, DC.

However, Holling and Gunderson point out that the Ω phase in one level may "cascade up to the next larger and slower level by triggering a crisis, particularly if that level is at the **K** phase, where resilience is low" (p. 75). An example would be a campfire triggering a forest fire when its trees are particularly dry. The more mature and densely forested the area, the greater the destruction. The converse occurs as influence from the wider context on its "constituents": after a forest fire, the "nutrients have been mobilized and released into the soil" as a "biotic legacy" (p. 76). They call these cross-scale Panarchy processes, Revolt and Remembering, respectively. The nested Panarchy processes constitute, for Holling and Gunderson and their Resilience Network partners, "the heart of what we define as sustainability" (p. 76).

> The fast levels invent, experiment, and test; the slower levels stabilize and conserve accumulated memory of past successful, surviving experiences. The whole panarchy is both creative and conserving. The interactions between cycles in a panarchy combine learning with continuity. That clarifies the meaning of sustainable development. Sustainability is

the capacity to create, test, and maintain adaptive capability. Development is the process of creating, testing, and maintaining opportunity. The phase that combines the two, sustainable development, is therefore not an oxymoron but represents a logical partnership. (p. 76)

We observe nested change processes in the human experience of emergent learning as well. As specific, longstanding sets of assumptions about knowledge, learning, and authority were interlinked in a pattern similar to "Revolution," the Red Zone or Disorientation Phase was generated from a series of moments in which present experience disconnected from tacit expectations or assumptions—thus specific new interpretations and practices arose that contradicted current beliefs. Conversely, once in the Red Zone, we begin to question everything that we have believed and assumed, or lose confidence in our ability to act in even slightly challenging situations. Further, the implications of new syntheses about learning and knowledge as emerging from experience challenge current conceptions of authorities as the only legitimate source of knowledge. This, in turn, leads to rethinking the nature of authority in organizations and institutions. In a similar pattern to "Remembering," the Exploration Phase, or Green Zone, is constructed of insight episodes in which a reservoir of ideas (longstanding and novel) are combined in new ways leading to a new perspective that better accounts for the experiences that contributed to breaking through the old perspective. New perspectives that emerge also become resources to reassembling constructs in a more encompassing paradigm, or shift of mind. Michael Polanyi (1967), in exploring the nature of tacit knowing, drew our attention to the contingency between levels of consciousness, namely, that "the universe is filled with strata of realities, joined together meaningfully in pairs of higher and lower strata" (p. 35) such that the level of the particular and the more general level that provides "comprehensive meaning" (p. 34) are linked logically. By implication, change in one is likely to generate change in the other. It is in this sense that we might entertain the possibility that a shift of understanding about ourselves and our learning holds the promise of seeing ourselves as influential contributors to the shape of the world we inhabit and cultures we create, and as responsible agents in meeting critical twenty-first-century challenges. One of our most pressing challenges is that of reversing the trends of environmental deterioration.

The Resilience Network authors, Frances Wesley, Stephen Carpenter, William Brock, C. S. Holling, and Lance Gunderson (2002), underline the importance of our structures of meaning in relation to their impact on ecological systems. While ecological systems operate in the context of time and space, social systems have a third governing dimension, namely, our capacity to create and recreate meaning using symbolic forms, particularly language. As meaning becomes a cultural feature, the power of value-perspectives becomes a force that can both negatively and positively influence resource management and sustainability. On the negative side, "our meaning systems have the ability to insulate us and separate us from the physical ground of our being . . . meaning that systems absorb large amounts of uncertainty" (p. 108); thus we are able to minimize the significance of ecological provocations for change. By acting to mitigate events that lead to renewal, we can predispose the environment to larger, more devastating change events. Forest fire prevention can, paradoxically, foster greater vulnerability of the natural environment. Further, the same consciousness that serves technological innovation can encourage "a command and control kind of system," which is inspired by a mode of thinking that is contrary to that needed for dealing with complexity.

> Human technology has a tendency to be built on a linear logic, as opposed to cyclical process; it often represents single-variable interventions in complex or imbricate [that is, overlapping] systems. Technological solutions focus on the limited scales of a particular problem. In consequence, they often create new problems and other timescales. (p. 117)

The Resilience Network's examination of human and natural change processes highlights the power of our value-perspectives, our ways of thinking and seeing the world, and the importance of fostering the evolution of systems of thought that enable us to engage the complex challenges of our era. It is to the question of how we might catalyze and enhance our capacity to foster relevant shifts of mind that we now turn to in the next chapter.

CHAPTER 5

LEADING OURSELVES: CULTIVATING
PERSONAL PRACTICES FOR
EMERGENT LEARNING

. . . every act of knowing brings forth a world . . .

Humberto Maturana and Francisco Varela (1987, p. 25)

The challenges of living with unpredictability can be seen as over-whelming, or they can be embraced as a call to make a difference. "If there are meaningful choices, there is uncertainty" (Langer, 1997, p. 130). In the context of our twenty-first-century learning chal-lenges, our task is to embrace the uncertainty as an opportunity to influence the future, by meeting the unexpected in conscious and capable ways.

The purpose of this chapter is to review effective ways of develop-ing personal "fitness" for lives of continuous surprises. The experi-ence of emergent learning *itself* develops our abilities as we gather momentum in iterative encounters with the unknown. Strengths generated in one cycle of the process are brought to the next chal-lenge. However, just as high-performance athletes spend much more time preparing than competing, we can also foster habits in the course of living and working that build our strength to navigate this process with fluidity and with maximum learning benefits.

Here, we consider some of the *practices* that can enhance our ability to sustain ourselves through challenging times and that enable us to seize those extraordinary opportunities for breakthrough learning. The notion of "practice" here goes beyond repetition; it points to habits of mind, heart, and relationship that support emergent learning. It is important to observe that volumes could be written, and in some cases have been written, about most of these practices. The intent is to draw connections to relevant domains of theory and practice that can be explored in a quest to build expertise in emergent learning. In order to provide a range of entry points, some of these practices will be framed from a more transactional or methodological "doing" and "thinking" perspective, while others derive from the ontological orientation—the "sensing," "feeling," "being" perspective.

DISCONFIRMATION (TRANSITION) AND DISORIENTATION PHASE

Do one thing every day that scares you.

Eleanor Roosevelt[1]

Our world is disrupted unexpectedly by an event—something goes wrong. Our expectations have been vanquished; we are lost and confused. We experience this moment as "happening to us," though later we may recognize that we chose our way into the situation. Confusion is a logical result of thinking we are in one kind of experience and actually finding ourselves in another. Confusion is a necessary consequence of finding that our mental "map" does not fit the territory. Encountering the unexpected provides us with the opportunity to become aware of our assumptions; they are the opportunity to transcend their limits. However, there are a series of consequences to this confusion that, although theoretically are not a "given," are common especially when we encounter a contradiction of deeply held beliefs and expectations. The first is likely to be a loss of confidence and the onset of anxiety, followed by deteriorating relationships (withdrawal of authentic interaction, diminished relationship quality, comparisons, and competition) with peers, and a fight-or-flight response in the face of authorities. The Red Zone can be protracted by a more strenuous attempt to protect ourselves through psychological defenses, and the development of negatively focused relationships aimed at fortifying us against engaging directly with the distressing challenge. We saw in the work of Beck and Cowan (1996), and we know from our own observations, that psychological distress from a life shock can reach astonishing proportions, especially as it coalesces with the distress of others into a social process. Martin (2009) reminded us that even disproportionate distress is "within the range of normal behaviour" (p. 11).

The Practice of Mindfulness (Part 1)

"Unease, anxiety, tension, stress, worry—all forms of fear—are caused by too much future, and not enough presence" (Tolle, 1999, p. 50). "Do not be anxious about tomorrow, for tomorrow will be anxious for itself" (Matthew 6:34, p. 762). For millennia, ancient wisdom traditions have pointed to the importance of living in the present in order to maintain our balance. Faith traditions across the world have provided opportunities to transcend the realm of fleeting thoughts and things, and move to a more enduring ground of being. Recently, in our everyday Western culture, meditation in general, and mindfulness meditation in particular, are becoming more practiced outside conventional religious settings, though they are still relatively infrequent, even eccentric, practices. Meditative practices such as yoga have increased exponentially over the past three decades (over 17 million Americans practice yoga[2]), and published health research on yoga and meditation have increased about fivefold and fourfold, respectively.[3] The recent appearance of "presence" in secular discourse attests, perhaps, to the need to anchor ourselves more deeply to achieve balance in increasingly turbulent times.

Jon Kabat-Zinn, founder and director of the Stress Reduction Clinic at the University of Massachusetts Medical Center, pioneered the "mainstreaming" of mindfulness meditation in the United States in clinical settings for chronic pain and stress disorders. "Mindfulness means paying attention in a particular way: on purpose, in the present moment, and nonjudgementally" (Kabat-Zinn, 1994, p. 4).

> Mindfulness provides a simple but powerful route for getting ourselves unstuck, back into touch with our wisdom and vitality. It is a way to take charge of the direction and quality of our lives, including our relationships within the family, our relationship to work and to the larger world and planet, and most fundamentally, our relationship to oneself as a person. (p. 5)

Ronald Siegel (2010) noted that, among other important benefits, "Mindfulness can help us embrace, rather than resist the inevitable ups and downs of life and equip us to handle our human predicament" (p. 25).

Mindfulness can enable emergent learning throughout the process; indeed, it *is* an emergent learning process in itself. Aspects of mindfulness are introduced throughout this chapter, based on relevance to different points in the emergent learning process. In the Red Zone, it reduces strain and conserves psychic energy for learning. Both

Kabat-Zinn (1994) and Tolle (1999) invoked the image of a turbulent river to represent thought-based experience. "Meditation means learning how to get out of this current, sit by its bank and listen to it, learn from it, and then use its energies to guide rather than tyrannize us" (Kabat-Zinn, 1994, p. 9).

> To stay present in everyday life, it helps to be deeply rooted within yourself; otherwise, the mind, which has incredible momentum, will drag you along like a wild river. . . . [Being rooted] means to inhabit your body fully. To always have some of your attention in the inner energy field of the body. To feel the body from within, so to speak. Body awareness keeps you present. It anchors you in the Now. (Tolle, 1999, p. 78)

Brown et al. (2007) have defined mindfulness as "a receptive attention to and awareness of present events and experience (awareness of present events and experience)" (p. 212).

> The basic capacities for awareness and attention permit the individual to "be present" to reality as it is rather than to react to it or habitually process it through conceptual filters. In this mode, even the usual psychological reactions that may occur when our attention is engaged—thoughts, images, verbalizations, emotions, impulses to act, and so on—can be observed as part of the ongoing stream of consciousness. (p. 212)

Ellen Langer (1997) identified mindfulness with five psychological states:

1. openness to novelty;
2. alertness to distinction;
3. sensitivity to different contexts;
4. implicit, if not explicit, awareness of multiple perspectives; and
5. orientation in the present. Each leads to the others and back to itself. (p. 23)

The role of mindfulness practice in fostering body awareness puts us in touch with "felt sense," that is, tacit knowledge of our context and challenges that are not yet accessible to our conscious attention. In the Red Zone, by anchoring us in the present, mindfulness practice replicates the experience of the present-oriented Green Zone Exploration, fostering a "forward reach." In particular, the reframing transition is a form of "suspension" practiced in mindfulness meditation; we let go of knowing, having the answers. So mindfulness meditation is not only a means of reducing pain; it releases us from being "stuck," and strengthens our ability to flow into the transition out of the Red Zone.

The Practice of Fostering Complementarity

Whether "hard wired" or acquired, a number of our strengths emphasize one side of a duality over another. An entire iteration of emergent learning calls for engagement of both sides of most polarities.

The binary system most central to learning, especially emergent learning, is our right and left hemispheric brain. Our right brain comes to the fore in the Red Zone when the expectations and assumptions *we have in mind* lose their currency with our experience. "The right brain, more than the left, expresses *being*—that complex meshing of competing emotions that constitutes our existential state at any given moment" (Shlain, 1998, p. 19). The right brain is associated with nonverbal, concrete, touch, feelings, and—as we see through the Exploration Phase or Green Zone—nonlinear, iconic, imagery, and intuitive thinking process. There is a simultaneity of thought and experience in the Transformation Phase or Purple Zone, leading to a switch in emphasis to left-brain qualities of mind—words, analysis, generalization, and action—into the Equilibrium Phase, or Blue Zone. It is an intriguing parallel that the sequence of emergent learning recapitulates the development of our brains.

> Of the twin human hemispheres, the right side is the elder sibling. In utero, the right lobe of a human fetus's brain is well on its way to maturation before the left side begins to develop. The old, wise, right side, more familiar with the needs and drives stemming from earlier stages of evolution, can be better relied upon to negotiate with them than the younger left side. (Shlain, 1998, p. 18)

We also see the sequence replicated generally in the childhood development of mental function, beginning with sensory-motor-based learning through to the capacity to think abstractly without reference to the particular (formal operational).

At its best, the mind "works in concert—two sections of an orchestra that sounds awful if one side packs up its instruments and goes home" (Pink, 2006, p. 25). Fluency in emergent learning both relies on and develops whole mind engagement. The practices identified in this chapter contribute in specific ways to both. Focusing on complementary opposites is especially important in the Red Zone, where in conditions of anxiety and other strains, we tend to favor our "strong suit" more than usual such that we lose even compensatory contact with its opposite, which may be a critical component necessary to moving through the challenge.

We consider here two widely known contributors to thinking about learning and development, Carl Jung and David Kolb. They associated the engagement of nondominant paired opposites with major shifts of value-perspective and life stage, and were selected not only for the quality and relevance of their thinking, but also because there are instruments based on their work that can be used to augment our awareness about our preferences as a basis for strengthening our capacity to navigate the Red Zone.

Carl Jung: Complementary Personality Types

Carl Jung, possibly influenced by the Principle of Complementarity in quantum physics (Mansfield and Spiegelman, 1991), advanced an understanding of the interplay of opposites in our psychological development. For Jung, psychic energy is generated by the tension of opposites. As cited in Progoff (1973), Jung stated:

> Everything human is relative because everything depends on a condition of inner antithesis; for everything subsists as a phenomenon of energy. . . . All life is energy, and therefore depends on forces held in opposition. (p. 52)[4]

Jung's contribution on polarities is probably best known through a widely used instrument, the Myers Briggs Type Indicator (MBTI) developed by Katherine Briggs and her daughter, Isabel Myers. MBTI assists us to identify our type preferences based on functions of the psyche. Before describing these, however, there are several more fundamental polarities that Jung highlighted for us.

Jung saw the basic process of developmental change over our lives. He called this process "individuation," as one through which we desire to understand ourselves more deeply. Individuation requires that we leave the comfort of our publicly known selves (Personae) and venture into the less tidy aspect of ourselves, our Shadow. The importance of this journey to our twenty-first-century learning agenda was expressed poignantly by Jung himself. If we have not "met" our own Shadow, we may be more inclined to align ourselves with the kind of tyranny that was witnessed in Nazi Europe—"the existence of a dictator allows us to point the finger away from ourselves and at the shadow" (Jung, 1958, p. 94).

Jung believed that an aspect of becoming more individuated in midlife is the integration of "Anima," the feminine (if we have lived the "Animus," the masculine principle), and "Animus" (if we have lived principally the "Anima"). "The anima and animus . . . are personifications of parts of the personality which are in some senses opposed to the conscious ego, and possess certain attributes of the opposite sex . . . the anima causing moods and animus causing opinions" (Storr, 1973, p. 53).

Jung also saw individuation as the engagement of opposites along dimensions of personality type, as mentioned above. In the first half of life we develop one-sidedness in our orientation to the whole that we balance with its complement as we mature. We tend to prefer the attitude of introversion, depicted by Jung as "a hesitant, reflective, retiring nature that keeps itself to itself . . ." or the attitude of extraversion that is "an outgoing, candid, accommodating nature that adapts easily to a given situation . . ." (p. 65).

Jung further proposed four different functions of the psyche configured in pairs of opposites: "The chief contrasts are between thinking and feeling, on one hand, and between sensation and intuition on the other" (Jung, 1969, p. 124).

> Consciousness is primarily an organ of orientation in a world of outer and inner facts. First and foremost, it establishes the fact that something is there. I call this faculty *sensation*. By this I do not mean the specific activity of any one of the senses, but perception in general. Another faculty interprets what is perceived; this I call *thinking*. By means of this function, the object perceived is assimilated and its transformation into a psychic content proceeds much further than sensation. A third faculty establishes the value of the object. This function of evaluation I call *feeling*. . . . These three functions would be quite sufficient for orientation if the object in question were isolated in space and time. . . . It is the fourth faculty of consciousness, *intuition,* that makes possible . . . the determination of space-time relationships. (p. 123)

> Intuition, as I conceive it, is one of the basic functions of the psyche, namely, *perception of the possibilities inherent in the situation.* (Jung, 1969, p. 141)

We all need to perform all these functions in order to live and act in the world, but we have what Jung thought to be an innate preference for one of the two poles of the pair—the preference is conscious and the paired opposite is unconscious—"archaic and underdeveloped" (p. 36). The unconscious function comes into play when the conscious partnered function is unable to deal with the experience adequately. "If thinking fails as an adapted function, because it is dealing with a situation to which one can adapt only by feeling, then the unconscious material activated by regression will contain the missing feeling function . . ." (p. 36). Jung believed that our preference for one function over another does not change over a lifetime, but that the unconscious side becomes more developed and accessible. If we are aware of our preferences, we can foster the development of their paired opposites.

In Red Zones, we tend to rely even more heavily than usual on our "strong suit," where we feel confident and tend not to risk engaging the less "competent" opposite in a time we feel vulnerable. Since all four functions are needed to understand a particular situation and to consider in making decisions about it, and we need awareness of both "inside" and "outside," our attitude (introverted or extraverted) and functions (sensing, intuiting, feeling, and thinking), what we are ignoring may well hold the key in getting "unstuck" and moving out of the Red Zone. For example, my preference is intuiting and I tend to focus solely on problem-solving forward. I then have to consciously ensure that I take the time to acquaint myself with the details of the current situation (sensing functioning) that may hold clues to my "way out" of an anxiety-producing challenge. Myers and Briggs (Myers, 1980) developed Jung's functions, further distinguishing sensing and intuiting as modes of perception and thinking and feeling as modes of judging, and including perceiving and judging (how long we spend gathering information for decisions) as a fourth pair of opposites that becomes part of the identification of personality type. The four functions, taken together, are sequenced in terms of preference, and the degree of consciousness and amount of energy attributed to these functions diminishes as we move though this series. How these functions manifest in our behavior is influenced by our preference for extraversion or introversion (our attitude); when combined with our attitude, there are, therefore, really eight different patterns. When combined with the fourth pair of options, perceiving and judging, to this configuration we have a total of 16 different personality types.

In circumstances of stress and transition, we can find ourselves acting out of our unconscious with a greater potential of driving us further into confusion, away from self-understanding and at odds with others.

Anything that individuals find stressful forces them to use all of their energies to combat whatever is causing the stress. This depletes conscious energy resources. When stress is ongoing, pervasive, and unrelieved, a person is likely to have little resistance to the expression of unconscious contents." (Quenk, 2000, p. 8)

Anger and loss of perspective accompany being "in the grip" of our unconscious (p. 48). Knowledge of our natural preferences and our typical "flat sides" enables us to consciously engage our "opposites" in order to develop them in times of quiescence. This helps to strengthen ourselves through better balance and to find our way out of being seized by our inferior function and the neglect of our tertiary function. As we take in the world through our senses in the present, we can consciously provoke ourselves to consider the future dimension and possibilities that exist in the present; if we are visionaries projecting our thoughts forward in the context of a big picture, we can discipline ourselves to get grounded in the details with our attention in the present. If we are most assured of our conclusions by exercising analytical logic, we can provoke ourselves to a more complete consideration by consciously asking the "why" questions in relation to consequences for people. A much more detailed picture of specific self-development options become evident when we look at each of the 16 personality types identified by the MBTI. Myers and Briggs and their colleagues have produced an extremely rich reservoir of thought and material we can use to foster complementarity. Also, David Kiersey (1998) has developed Jung's work a little differently, based on observations over time to distinguish four temperaments that also serve to assist our awareness of preferences, and their impact on our behavior. Jung's belief was that it was failure of the preferred function to enable us to adapt to a challenge and that the less conscious function will be "activated by regression"—" by activating an unconscious factor, regression confronts consciousness with the problem of the psyche" (Jung, 1958, p. 36). He spoke of resistance to this process. By developing awareness of our preferences, and by proactively nurturing our less developed functions, we can potentially reduce the dimension of struggle and foster our own movement forward.

David Kolb: Complementary Learning Styles
David Kolb's (1984) experiential learning model provides another perspective on sets of opposites, both of which are needed, but for which we have personal stylistic preferences. In Chapter 4 we reviewed Kolb's experiential learning model as a theory-based learning process model (see figure 4.1) that comprises two dimensions: (1) "prehension" on a vertical axis between "apprehension" of the concretely experienced world and "comprehension" of the abstract world of concepts and (2) "transformation" on the horizontal axis between

"intention" from the inner reflective world and "extension" toward the external world of action. Kolb's Learning Style Inventory (LSI) is designed to reflect our relative preference on each of the two dimensions. The schema yields four possible learning style preferences: diverger (concrete experience and reflective observation); assimilator (reflective observation and abstract conceptualization); converger (abstract conceptualization and active experimentation); and accommodator (active experimentation and concrete experimentation).

Each of the points on the experiential learning cycle is essential to the accomplishment of learning from experience, and in using that learning to influence our practice. If we are typically engaged in action, we are likely to have spent less time and attention in reflection and observation, and vice versa; if we are most comfortable with direct experience, we are less likely to spend time thinking and making sense out of experience, and vice versa. Accordingly, some of us readily engage in problem-solving and decision-making (convergers) and others of us enjoy exploring possibilities (divergers); some of us are naturals at implementation and making things work (accommodators), and others of us are more comfortable developing explanations and engaging in the world of ideas (assimilators). Kolb and his colleagues showed relationships between these learning styles and the Myers–Briggs personality types (1984, pp. 78–85).

Like Jung, Kolb saw strengthening the complementary side of our preferences as related to maturation and development. The third of his designated three life stages is of particular interest, as we are concerned about our capability to engage in emergent learning (second- and third-order learning), and in the Red Zone especially. As observed above, Kolb referred to Piaget's child development of intellectual functions, the acquisition phase of childhood, as setting the foundation for learning from concrete to abstract, or symbolic thinking. He saw the specialization phase as capitalizing on our strengths, "selecting [ourselves] into environments that are consistent with [our] personal characteristics" (Kolb, 1984, p. 143), which enables us to achieve our career, and our identity. Kolb referred to Jung's observations about personal fulfillment as deriving from a "higher level integration and expression of nondominant modes of dealing with the world" (p. 144). The third phase of development, integration, is achieved by integrating opposite learning orientations. This implies the development of complementarity.

We can imagine the difference between the experience of being strongly embedded in one side of these stylistic opposites in a period of high challenge and anxiety when the complements are needed to move forward, and then facing a similarly significant challenge while being able to consciously draw on both our strengths and their complements.

The Practice of Nurturing Self-Esteem and Self-Compassion

Especially important in our performance-oriented culture, the Red Zone places enormous demands on the quality of the "relationship we have with ourselves," and in particular the temptations to generate negative self-appraisals when confusion compromises our performance. It is therefore critical that we have a strong sense of positive self-regard as a backdrop for periods of intense flux. As adults, we build on the foundational self-regard inherited from our families, communities, and schools; the extent of the work in maintaining positive regard varies among us. Some of us will choose wisely, from time to time, to seek professional assistance in this work in order to catalyze the process of overcoming limits to facing challenges. However, we can each actively augment our reserve of a positive sense of ourselves in everyday living. We consider here self-esteem and self-compassion—two related, but somewhat distinctive, orientations to positive self-regard.

Self-Esteem
One of the most comprehensive and practical treatments of self-esteem is the work of Nathaniel Branden (1994), who calls it the "immune system of consciousness."

> When self esteem is low, our resilience in the face of life's adversities is diminished. We crumble before vicissitudes that a healthier sense of self could vanquish. We are more likely to succumb to a tragic sense of our existence and to feelings of impotence. We tend to be more influenced by the desire to avoid pain than to experience joy. Negatives have more power over us than positives. (p. 18)

Branden identified two essential aspects to self-esteem—self-efficacy and self-respect. Self-efficacy is "confidence in the function of my mind, in my ability to think, understand, learn, choose, and make decisions; confidence in my ability to understand the facts of reality that fall within the sphere of my interests and needs; self trust; self reliance" (p. 26). Self-respect is ". . . assurance of my value; an affirmative attitude toward my right to live and to be happy; comfort in appropriately asserting my thoughts, wants, and needs; the feeling that joy and fulfilment are my natural birthright" (p. 26). He observed that our level of self-esteem affects our capability to assess our experiences and capability to see ourselves realistically, exercise our intuitive and creative abilities, be independent and flexible, "admit mistakes," respect others and collaborate, and manage change (pp. 45–48). All of these abilities and dispositions will affect the course of emergent learning.

Branden noted that we do not work directly on self-esteem; we engage in six practices in the form of a number of very specific activities suggested for developing each of the following:

- *The practice of living consciously*—"to live consciously means to seek to be aware of everything that bears on our actions, purposes, values, and goals—to the best of our ability, whatever that may be— and to behave in accordance with that which we see and know" (p. 71). This meaning of "living consciously" relates to the practice of mindfulness, but is a contribution from a more transactional worldview. He drills down to 16 dimensions of the practice, including maintaining an active mind, "being 'in the moment,'" tracking successes and failures, being willing "to see and correct mistakes," aligning actions and purposes, "persevering . . . to understand in spite of difficulties," "commitment to learning," and "concern to be aware of values that move and guide me" (p. 72).

- *The practice of self-acceptance*—"my refusal to be in an adversarial relationship to myself" (p. 90). Branden described three dimensions of self acceptance:

  1. primordial "self-affirmation," "self-value" (p. 90);
  2. "our refusal to regard any part of ourselves—our bodies, our emotions, our thoughts, our actions, our dreams—as alien, as 'not me'" (p. 91); and
  3. having "compassion" for myself, "being a friend to myself" (p. 92). "To 'accept' is more than simply to 'acknowledge' or 'admit.' It is experience, to stand in the presence of, contemplate the reality of, absorb into my consciousness" (p. 92). It is also not to be confused with "liking" but to accepting the reality of my actions.

- *The practice of self-responsibility*—"I am responsible for the achievement of my desires; . . . for my choices and actions; . . . for the level of consciousness I bring to my work; . . . for the level of consciousness I bring to my relationships; . . . for my behaviour with other people; . . . for how I prioritize my time; . . . for the quality of my communications; . . . for my personal happiness; . . . for accepting and choosing the values by which I live; . . . for raising my self-esteem" (pp. 105, 106).

- *The practice of self-assertiveness*—"honouring my wants, needs and values and seeking appropriate forms of their expression in reality" (p. 118). It means representing ourselves, our needs and desires in a forthright respectful way.
- *The practice of living purposefully*—"to use our powers for the attainment of goals we have selected . . ." (p. 130). Branden made the point that what supports self-esteem over the long term is not our achievements, but *"those internally generated practices that, among other things, make it possible for us to achieve"* (p. 135).
- *The practice of personal integrity*—"the integration of ideals, convictions, standards, beliefs, and behaviour" (p. 143).

I find Branden's image of these practices as pillars very apt; when one practice deteriorates, the whole system of practices is affected. When, for example, I have not "walked my talk," I do feel weaker and more self-preoccupied until I "rebuild" a consistent practice of my values and commitments. The risk is, if I do not restore the strength in one practice, others will deteriorate as well. I draw on my own self-acceptance, for example, in working my way through restoring a level of congruence between values and actions I want to practice.

When we enhance each of these six contributing practices to self-esteem in periods of equilibrium, and in periods of relative quiescence, we will have enhanced a critical dimension of resilience in preparation for inevitable future challenges. This is a wise practice, since it is difficult to replenish our strength in a stressful context.

Self-Compassion

Self-esteem alone may not support resilience. Neff and Vonk (2009) noted that under some circumstances, likely related to protecting a positive sense of self, high self-esteem has also been associated with disregarding potentially corrective feedback and "trivializing failures," being less willing to "take personal responsibility for harmful actions," and this can cause us to "develop an inaccurate self concept," "engage in downward comparisons, a process that underlies prejudice and discrimination," and have a "closed mind-set that cannot tolerate alternative viewpoints" (p. 24). They cited others who have defined the quality of self-esteem—as being "self-determined and autonomous," rather than being contingent on the assessments of others, which can isolate healthy high self-esteem.

While it is helpful to work with other dimensions of genuine and healthy self-esteem described by Branden to strengthen our sense of ourselves, Neff (2009) has suggested the quality of self-compassion (for Branden, one of three forms of self-acceptance) "offers most of the benefits of high self-esteem, with fewer of its downsides" (p. 212). She described self-compassion as "(a) self-kindness versus self-judgement; (b) a sense of common humanity versus isolation; and (c) mindfulness versus over-identification" (p. 212). The emphasis on self-compassion takes us beyond thinking (e.g., assessing) and doing (e.g., asserting) to feeling (e.g., kindness) and connecting with others. In tumultuous moments it may bring a more penetrating positive force.

> Self-compassion is linked to many of the benefits typically attributed to high self-esteem in terms of positive emotions, while also providing stronger protection against the ego-defensive drawbacks sometimes associated with the pursuit and maintenance of high self-esteem. When compared to global self-esteem, self-compassion was associated with more stable feelings of self-worth that were less contingent on particular outcomes. It also had a stronger negative association with social comparison, self-evaluative anxiety, anger, and closed-mindedness. Self-compassion showed no association with narcissism, however, after accounting for the influence of self-esteem. (p. 44)

Self-esteem is widely recognized to be related to the quality of our relationships with others (e.g., Stinson et al., 2008; Knowles et al., 2010). Of particular concern is the deterioration of relationships (deficit-based competition and comparisons) and development of negatively focused alliances with others (us versus them) in the Red Zone. Buunk and Gibbons (2007) carefully reviewed the extensive body of research that has been done over the years on social comparisons, since its launch as a domain of inquiry by Leo Festinger over 55 years ago, and offered several conclusions relevant to relationships in the Red Zone. One is that when we do not perform to our own expectations, we "lower [our] comparison level, in part so [we] can avoid painful upward comparisons" (p. 10). And while there can be positive effects of social comparison, such as when coping with catastrophic injury or illness (Dewar, 2003), where people identify sources of learning about their common challenge, another pattern with a long history in the literature is one that was observed by Schachter (1959): "Misery doesn't love just any kind of company, it loves only miserable company" (p. 24, cited in Buunk and Gibbons, 2007, p. 5). "Schachter argued that social comparison was the main motive behind affiliation under stress and, in particular, was more important than the desire for cognitive clarity concerning the nature of the threat" (p. 5). More recently, White et al. (2006) found "Frequency of social comparison positively predicted feelings of envy, guilt, defensiveness, regret, having unmet cravings, and behaviors of lying to protect the self and lying to protect others" (pp. 39, 40). They further point out:

> [The] frequency of social comparisons has negative implications for personal well-being as well as for interpersonal and intergroup relations. It is possible that people who make frequent social comparisons choose their targets and dimensions of comparison in order to enhance well-being or to cope with a threat to self-esteem. (p. 42)

This use of social comparison is what occurs in the Red Zone; it leads to affiliations based on common complaint that further isolate us from our opportunities to learn, move forward, and create what we most value and desire. Social comparisons are ubiquitous. It makes sense to ask ourselves in a new situation, where do I stand among others here? However, when they are intensified into self-defense or self-rebuke, they distract us from moving forward toward a positive future. When we gravitate toward others in a context of considerable challenge, we can ask ourselves, in this group what are the most frequent themes in our conversations? Are they about what we want most for ourselves or are they about what we are against?

Shelley Carson and Ellen Langer (2006) highlighted the importance of self-acceptance (one of Branden's six elements of self-esteem) in combination with the theme of mindfulness that was touched upon earlier in this chapter. "The absence of ability to unconditionally accept oneself can lead to a variety of emotional difficulties, including uncontrolled anger and depression" (p. 29). Their meaning of mindfulness, in contrast to mindlessness, is being "actively engaged in the present and sensitive to both context and perspective" (p. 29); it "entails living daily life without pretense and without concern that others are judging one negatively" (p. 30). In emphasizing the importance of authenticity, Carson and Langer are urging us out of the Red Zone, which by definition is constituted by our withdrawal from people, in the sense of attempting to mask our real selves in a confused and "messy" state from being visible to others. They offer eight techniques of mindfulness "geared toward enhancing self-acceptance" (p. 40).

- "*Actively observe novel distinctions.* The act of observing new distinctions increases positive affect . . . Active exploration is judgment-free; as individuals continue to actively explore new aspects of self, they will enhance self-acceptance" (p. 40).

- "*Think of yourself as a 'work in progress'.* . . . replace rigid words with possibility words in their self-narratives. . . . This, in turn, creates a mindset open to personal change and acceptance" (p. 40).

- "*Contemplate puzzles and paradoxes.* . . . Actively thinking about paradoxes increases one's ability to tolerate ambiguity (and decreases the anxiety associated with uncertainty)" (pp. 40, 41).

- "*Add humor to the situation.* Humor itself relies on mindfulness by forcing people to see a new and unexpected side to a given situation. . . . When individuals notice humorous aspects of themselves or their situation, they are more likely to accept those aspects" (p. 41).

- "*View the situation from multiple perspectives.* When people are stuck in a rigid interpretation of their situation, they are less likely to be accepting of it" (p. 41).

- "*Consider alternative understandings of problematic aspects of yourself.* How many ways can a 'negative' aspect of self be viewed as useful? . . . beneficial? All problems can be seen as useful in some contexts" (p. 41).

- "*Keep a catalogue of moments of joy.* . . . A growing body of research indicates that an increase in positive mental state, even a mild increase such as one experiences from remembering positive events, markedly influences mental flexibility and creative problem solving" (p. 41).

- "*Start a 'mindfulness' journal.* . . . Look back on the events with the purpose of observing new things and new perspectives about them. . . . Keeping a journal also helps individuals to observe continuity and direction in their lives, enhancing self-acceptance" (p. 41).

As a final note on fostering self-esteem and self-compassion, the Positive Psychology Movement, beginning in this millennium with the work of Martin Seligman at the University of Pennsylvania, is both a reflection of and a resource for the growing recognition of the need for us to shift our perspective to the positive side of the human experience. The Appreciative Inquiry (AI) movement, reflecting this repositioning of perspective at an organizational level, began in 1987.

One of the first proponents of a positive, health-oriented discipline and practice of psychology was Abraham Maslow (1968)—he called it "a psychology of being." Underlining the experience of the Red Zone as a normative aspect of living, Maslow stated: "Not allowing people to go through their pain, and protecting them from it, may turn out to be a kind of over-protection, which in turn implies a certain lack of respect for the integrity and the intrinsic nature and future development of the individual" (p. 8).

The Practice of Emotional Intelligence

John Mayer (2004), one of the two people who first defined emotional intelligence about 20 years ago, did so as follows: "From a scientific (rather than a popular) standpoint, emotional intelligence is the ability to accurately perceive your own and others' emotions; to understand the signals that emotions send about relationships; and to manage your own and others' emotions" (p. 27). The word emotion derives from the Latin words that combine to mean "move" and "out"; emotions generate energy to get us into motion.

Definitions of emotional intelligence vary with some of them including more dimensions of our inner landscape than others. A prominent scholar on emotional intelligence, Richard Boyatzis (2009) of Case Western Reserve University, suggested that there are two basic dimensions of emotional intelligence. The first is "self-awareness," addressed in one competency, namely, "emotional self-awareness: recognizing one's emotions and their effects." The second is "self-management" addressed in four competencies—"emotional self-control: keeping disruptive emotions and impulses in check; adaptability: flexibility in handling change; achievement orientation: striving to improve or meeting a standard of excellence; and positive outlook: seeing the positive aspects of things and the future" (p. 754).

Daniel Goleman (1995), in describing the evolution and current structure of the human brain, noted that the amygdala is "the specialist in emotional matters" (p. 15). He explained that the amygdala "scans every experience for trouble" and if it finds something, it "reacts instantaneously, like a neural tripwire, telegraphing a message of crisis to all parts of the brain" (p. 16). Goleman compares it to an "alarm company" (p. 16); "it triggers the secretion of the body's fight-or-flight hormones, mobilizes the centers for movement, and activates the cardio-vascular system, the muscles, and the gut" (p. 16), and a series of other physiological processes. Importantly, "cortical memory systems are shuffled to retrieve any knowledge relevant to the emergency at hand taking precedence over other strands of thought" (p. 17). Goleman noted that a neuroscientist, Joseph LeDoux, established that signals from the senses simultaneously to the amygdala and the neocortex enables the "amygdala to respond before the neocortex" and "feelings that take the direct route through the amygdala include our most primitive and potent; this circuit does much to explain the power of emotion to overwhelm rationality" (p. 17).

In situations that create these emotional triggers, we react without deliberation. The Red Zone is an experiential context with an elevated level of anxiety that lowers our reaction threshold. Our responses, framed in anxiety and aggravation, can trigger similar responses from others, and generate a negative spiral in our interactions with others. Ultimately, managing our own and others' emotions can mean the difference between remaining stuck in Red Zones and learning our way to enhanced perspectives and experiences of our world.

Over the past several decades, evidence for the value of emotional intelligence has been gathering. Richard Boyatzis (2009) situated emotional intelligence as a competency, along with social intelligence and cognitive intelligence, which distinguished outstanding managers from others. Goleman (1998) cites a case of what he called "a billion-dollar mistake," concerning an insurance company whose sales process was guided by the injunction to sales personnel that "when a client displayed anxiety or uneasiness . . . the best response was not empathy but a rational argument. So the advisors were left trying to shut out the client's emotions as well as their own." (p. 236). The company lost an enormous amount of business—"A mountain of emotional negativity stood between our sales process and our bottom line" (p. 236), one planner reported to Goleman. Significant to our twenty-first-century learning agenda, Goleman et al. (2009) noted that leaders need the "emotional sources . . . to thrive in chaos and change" (p. 9) in order to "ignite our passion and inspire the best in us."

> The leader is the one whom others look to for assurance and clarity when facing uncertainty or threat, or when there's a job to be done. The leader acts as the group's emotional guide. Today, this primordial task remains foremost among the jobs of leadership: driving the collective emotions in a positive direction and clearing the smog created by toxic emotions. (p. 9)

Recognition of the importance of emotion in living, learning, and leadership is reflected in the frequency references in the literature, and "widespread application" (Boyatzis, 2009) in educational and training programs.

A number of measures of emotional intelligence have been developed, including the following: The Mayer Salovey Caruso Emotional Intelligence Test (MSCEIT) (Mayer et al, 2003); the Bar-On EQ-i (Bar-On, 1997); the Emotional and Social Competency Inventor 2.0, which is a 360 degree feedback instrument (Boyatzis and Goleman, 1996); and EQ in Action (Learning-in-Action Technologies online http://learninginaction.com/eq_in_action_profile.php).

The Practice of Social Choreography

A surprising event that seizes our attention and our concern has potential for shifting not only our minds but also our relationships. Every perspective, every set of ideas, every learning theme comes with a social system—people who embody or seek to embody it and for whom it has meaning. Emergent learning arises in a life context when we encounter an unexpected and highly relevant experience; it often takes time to figure out what the issue actually is and then how we will respond to it. If we engage the opportunity, we will be positioning ourselves as protégées of those with more experience in the new territory, and as fellow travelers with others who, like us, are facing a similar learning challenge. In some instances, our learning may require changes in our current relationships—changing value-perspectives may reposition us in social space more proximate to new friends and colleagues who share our perspective, and more distant from others who do not. A frequent example is first-generation citizens who adopt the perspective of their family's new country more readily than their parents, so there is the further challenge of managing these differences within their families, or losing these relationships. Also included in the emergent learning social system are those who embody resistance and opposition to the learning theme, as we have just observed.

In emergent learning, we have observed relationship dynamics as a stream of features that intersect with changes in thought and affect in optimal ways in the emergent learning process. We can catalyze that process by consciously taking opportunities to situate ourselves in such a way as to foster movement forward in relation to people who are significant to our learning theme. We need to associate with people who embody the practice or intention we want most for ourselves. Most of us do this intuitively, though perhaps not as readily as we might if we were conscious of our location in a process and its social implications. In the Red Zone, we may be unconsciously avoiding the person or people who would be most important in enabling us to move forward. It is helpful to be mindful when we are associating with others in opposition to a prevailing social direction. If this is our choice, it should be conscious and considered for its implications for our learning. Additionally, it may be important in some circumstances to know how to manage relationships with people who deenergize us for learning with unnecessary critique and discouragement and withheld support and affirmation. Finally, there are times in the process where our progress is most likely to be assisted by periods of solitude. This is the social choreography of emergent learning.

We live in a dynamic age, continuously moving through experiences, organizations, and communities. Not only are we exponentially challenged to reconsider current assumptions and beliefs, but also we are equally challenged to expand and navigate in wider, more varied circles of relationships as a corollary to our amplified learning curve. We also have vastly expanded possibilities of maintaining face-to-face relationships (initially) over distance, and in creating virtual networks of association.

Finally, a crucial dimension of social choreography in emergent learning is our relationship with those we see as credible authorities in relation to the learning challenge. One of the unique contributions of the original study recounted in Chapter 3 was our critical moment of rapprochement with a person we regard, at least ambivalently, as a credible authority and who we may regard as having created so much distress for us. Affirmation of us by a relevant credible authority figured into the transition out of distress and disorientation—the Red Zone—into the Exploration Phase and this is typically not only pivotal, but challenging. There is the subtle act of trust we must evince in being willing to expose ourselves to their response. It involves overcoming our expectation of a negative evaluation (like our own self-evaluation) in order to become receptive to their response. Depending on our characteristic relationship to authorities whom we are not able to trust—fight-or-flight, counterdependent, or dependent—we typically create a familiar "dance" that can include avoiding them entirely or being around them without risking a significant exchange about themes that matter (hiding in plain sight). The first task is to become conscious of who, in a particular emergent learning context, are our credible authorities, that is, people whose affirmation would release our energy to fully engage the challenge. The second task is to position ourselves in relation to the person(s) creating the opportunity for that affirmation to occur. This act requires a critical minimum level of self-esteem, and is a significant example of what

Hampden-Turner (1971) called "trying to bridge the distance to the other(s)" (p. 37). The affirmation from the credible authority does not have to be verbalized; it can occur in a subtle gesture (e.g., a smile of acknowledgement, an invitation). This is a genuine risk because, of course, the quality of the response is not within our control. We examine this important point in Chapter 6, as we examine the quality of leadership that is required to foster emergent learning.

REFRAMING (TRANSITION) AND THE EXPLORATION PHASE

. . . at one and the same time half-sure and whole-hearted . . .
Gordon Allport (1962, p. 378)

The transition out of the Red Zone and into the Green Zone is marked, along with the affirmation by a credible other, by the act of reframing of a challenge as learning rather than as a personal short-coming. We stop blaming ourselves, or others, for our confusion, and we are able to relax without resolution to the challenge. Since we are letting go of our expectations that we, or someone else, should have the answers or a formula to find, we enter the unknown; we *suspend* assumptions and beliefs. Central in this moment is trust.

> Trust is a feeling of confidence or conviction that things can unfold within a dependable framework that embodies order and integrity. We may not always understand what is happening to us, or to another, or what is occurring in a particular situation; but if we trust ourselves, or another, or we place our trust in a process or an ideal, we can find a powerful stabilizing element embracing security, balance, and open-ness within the trusting which, in some way, if not based in naïveté, intuitively guides us and protects us from harm or self-destruction. (Kabat-Zinn, 1994, p. 58)

We proceed in an intuitively guided, present-oriented process of exploring the unknown territory.

The Practice of Right-Brain[5] Thinking

Over the past 60 years, we have learned that the each of the two hemispheres of our brain performed distinctive functions. Neurosur-geon Wilder Penfield discovered in the 1950s that each hemisphere controls the body's functioning on the opposite side. Subsequently,

Nobel laureate Roger Sperry found that the functions of each hemi-sphere are hard-wired and specific—the left brain governs language, abstractions, analysis, and sequential thought, and the right brain governs nonverbal communication, big picture or context, metaphor, and simultaneous information processing. Daniel Pink (2006) noted, "the scientific establishment considered the two regions separate but unequal. The left side, the theory went, was the crucial half, the left side made us human" (p. 13). Certainly, this is clearly reflected in our systems of education that primarily develop left-brain thinking, with the consequence that right-brain thinking is undervalued and underdeveloped. Pink's message to us, though, is that it is right-brain thinking that is becoming more critical in a world in which logical, sequential processes can be automated and, in a society with basic needs already likely satisfied, so the "growth areas" are in the domain of aesthetics and creativity. In particular, he highlights the following six areas of rebalanced "high-concept, high-touch abilities," all of which relate to our twenty-first-century learning agenda:

- "Design" as well as function: "Today it's economically crucial and personally rewarding to create something that is . . . beautiful, whimsical, or emotionally engaging" (p. 65).
- "Story" as well as argument: "The essence of persuasion, commu-nication, self-understanding has become the ability to . . . fashion a compelling narrative" (p. 66).
- "Symphony" as well as focus: "The greatest demand today isn't analysis but synthesis—seeing the big picture, crossing the bound-aries, and being able to combine disparate pieces in to an interest-ing whole" (p. 66).
- "Empathy" as well as logic: "What will distinguish those who thrive will be their ability to understand what makes their fellow woman and man tick, to forge relationships, and to care for others" (p. 66).
- "Play" not just seriousness: "Ample evidence points to enormous health and professional benefits of laughter, lightheartedness, games and humour" (p. 66).
- "Meaning" not just accumulation: ". . . a world of breathtaking material plenty . . . has freed hundreds of millions of people . . . to pursue more significant desires: purpose, transcendence, and spiri-tual fulfillment" (pp. 66, 67).

Pink offers a series of specific and practical suggestions about how we can develop these areas of ability, some of which are mentioned below.

As observed earlier in this chapter, while we use our whole brain constantly, the work of the Equilibrium Phase draws especially on the functions of the left brain, and the underlying challenge of the Exploration Phase is to optimize the powers of the right brain. The key word is *connections*—between experience and ideas, or concepts, and among people, fellow travelers both those along with us and those ahead of us. It is about moving from experience to insight, and tacit to explicit knowing. In this section, we touch on the physiological and mental processes of the Exploration Phase and in the next section, on Green Zone social processes.

Metaphorical Thinking
Gareth Morgan (1986) observed that while attention to metaphor in human thought and expression can be traced in philosophy from Aristotle through philosophers Vico in the eighteenth century, to Nietzsche and others in the nineteenth century, the most intense interest in metaphor in the twentieth century lies in a range of disciplines including philosophy, linguistics, and psychoanalysis. As we learn more about "mind," the role of metaphors and analogies is becoming more significant as a central function of human thought. They are critical in emergent learning.

The advances in our understanding of brain structure and function serve to amplify the significance of right-brain thinking. In their groundbreaking work, *Metaphors We Live By,* Lakoff and Johnson (1980) made the case that metaphors are central and pervasive in our thought and expression. They observed that by the age of four we have hundreds of metaphors through which we understand the world. More recently, Lakoff and his colleagues have been conducting a program of research about brain functioning that overturns traditional assumptions about how knowledge is generated. It speaks directly to what we experience in the Exploration Phase and how *learning is literally embodied.* Traditional cognitive science represented the mind as "a functional system whose processes can be described in terms of manipulations of abstract symbols according to a set of formal syntactic rules" (Gallese and Lakoff, 2005, p. 456), accounting for cognition on a purely symbolic plane. Lakoff and his colleagues have found a very different structure of mind based on a combination of neuroscientific and cognitive linguistic evidence indicating that ". . . conceptual knowledge is embodied, that is, it is mapped within our sensory-motor system" (p. 456). They observed that the same circuitry in our brain is activated when we imagine an action and when we are actually carrying out the action. This means that experiencing or doing and knowing or conceptualizing are *physiologically* linked processes.

> Meaning is grounded in our sensory-motor experience and . . . this embodied meaning [is] extended, via imaginative mechanisms such as conceptual metaphor, metonymy, radial categories, and various forms of conceptual blending, to shape abstract conceptualization and reasoning. What the empirical evidence suggests to us is that an embodied account of syntax, semantics, pragmatics, and value is absolutely necessary for an adequate understanding of human cognition and language. You cannot simply peel off a theory of conceptual metaphor from its grounding in embodied meaning and thought. You cannot give an adequate account of conceptual metaphor and other imaginative structures of understanding without recognizing some form of embodied realism. (Johnson and Lakoff, 2002, p. 245)

How does this happen?

> You are a little kid and you watch your mother pouring formula into the bottle or water into a glass over and over every day. What's going on in your brain? Two parts of your brain are activated—one for quantity, one for verticality and they are activated over and over every day—the level always goes up. Or you're held as a child and you feel affection and warmth together over and over and that means your brain is activated in two places—one for affection and one for warmth—temperature. What happens is when they are activated over, and over? The activation starts to spread. The more they are activated the stronger they get, the more they spread, the stronger they get until they find the shortest path between them and form a circuit. That circuit *is* the metaphor—more is up or affection is warmth. These metaphors, called primary metaphors are physical. They are part of your physical brain. And by the time you are six or seven you have learned hundreds. (Lakoff, 2008)

The basic metaphor becomes elaborated so as to guide behavior in relation to different contexts.

We continue to create metaphors as we engage new experiences. "If a new metaphor enters the conceptual system that we base our actions on, it will alter our conceptual system and the perceptions and actions that the system gives rise to" (Lakoff and Johnson, 1980, p. 145). This being the case, the role of experience in evolving new ways of seeing the world—double- and triple-loop learning—is essential. Formation of metaphors is a critical step in bringing to consciousness what we know tacitly—a point of transition from the unconscious to the conscious. This transition is necessary in order to articulate a new understanding, which is, in turn, essential, enabling us to make choices and plans consciously and in being able to communicate our understanding to others, to accomplish common purposes. How do we push tacit knowledge into consciousness? George Prince (1970) pointed out that the substance of the unconscious is presented to the conscious by metaphors though an intuitive process.

Intuitive Process
Theorists and practitioners of creative problem-solving have contributed enormously to the development of approaches and techniques for bringing tacit knowledge to consciousness. Prince (1970) described a widely held model of mind in which the "preconscious" mediates the conscious mind and the unconscious mind.

> The preconscious is like a problem-oriented, opinionated file clerk. It looks over the shoulder of the conscious mind. When a problem that interests the conscious mind is being considered, it conducts a search for clues that it considers relevant. (p. 81)

Malcolm Gladwell (2005) spoke of "the adaptive consciousness," which he describes similarly as "a giant computer that quickly and quietly processes a lot of data we need in order to keep functioning as human beings" (p. 11). Prince characterized the unconscious or subconscious, the source for the preconscious mind, as "a storehouse of immense capacity . . ." (p. 11), "a reservoir of information so vast and rich it seems quite incredible to the conscious mind" (p. 82).

> When provoked by interest or emotional commitment, [the preconscious] goes searching for relevant suggestive data. Its criteria for relevance do not seem logical because often the data that are presented do not appear to the conscious mind to be connected even distantly with the problem at hand. (pp. 81, 82)

The wisdom of those who have practiced and reflected on facilitating creative processes points to a number of essential conditions for intuitive thinking.

1. *A psychologically safe space free of immediate task demands and need for analysis or strategy.*
   Intuitive process is "incredibly fragile. Insight is not a lightbulb that goes off inside our heads. It is a flickering candle that can easily be snuffed out" (Gladwell, 2005, p. 122).

2. *An assembly of "raw materials" in the form of unorganized observations, ideas, experiences.*
   "The first intimations are likely to be embodied in apparently trivial things, objects or experiences out of everyday life that would seem to have little importance or none whatsoever" (Ghiselin, 1964).
3. *An intense but diffuse concentration* (Prince, 1970) *that Koestler (1964) calls paradoxically, "absent-mindedness of the creative obsession,"*
   "absent-mindedness [that] is, of course, in fact, single-mindedness . . ." (p. 119).
4. Patience to wait for insight. While many insights emerge readily, others take time. In both cases, insights cannot be summoned. "Will belongs to the conscious life only. . . . Will tends to arrest the undetermined development, by laying the emphasis on heightened tension upon what is already in mind" (Ghiselin, 1964, pp. 26, 27).
5. "Responsiveness to . . . own impulses or intuitions" "We believe intuition is an early recognition, below the conscious level, that one is on the right track" (Prince, 1970, p. 84).

To illustrate the intuitive process and its relationship to learning, a carefully self-observed and documented example was provided by Marge Denis (1979), who, using her expertise as a weaver, intuitively *wove* her thesis on intuitive learning, as a precursor to writing it. As each of the above conditions is illustrated, it is referred to by number.

Denis had completed interviews with 16 people in diverse occupations either who saw themselves as intuitive or whom she saw as being intuitive as expressed in their writing or her personal knowledge of them. She believed that if the topic was intuition, then intuition should be integral to the conduct of the processing of the data gathered. Being a weaver, she decided to weave a tapestry intuitively, rather than from a predetermined plan: one that would make sense out of the wide array of observations, ideas, and practices she had accumulated through the interviews (#2). In organizing herself to generate the tapestry, she set aside one week for the project in her weaving tutor's studio located in the country (#1). When shown the loom, she observed that it was 45 inches wide. "The first decision was made. . . . I decided if the warp represented the rational mode with its fixed logical order and structure I would rationally choose the warp that would express and support the intuitive: once the loom was warped I would proceed with the weft intuitively" (p. 140). When she first entered the studio, her "eye was caught by a cone of white wool spun in an uneven nubby texture. That cone said 'intuition'" (p. 140) (#5). Beyond that she was unable to select other materials. "The process cannot be forced. Somehow that decision would be made but the timing was not then" (#4). She had a restless night of dreaming about "many coloured warps hanging all around"—and so decided that she would have a multicolored warp (#5). She selected "deliberately in sequence from the dark colours at the edges to the lighter colours and the white somewhere near the centre." With the width of the tapestry determined spatially by the width of the loom, the warp would be determined temporally; with an extra long warp, she would let the end of the week—time—determine the length of the tapestry (or the end of the warp). As it happened "they came together: on Friday afternoon the warp was used up" (pp. 140, 141). At the end of the day of setting up "treading and tying up the loom," she "threw a bunch of colours together in a three-inch border" (p. 141).

> Early the next morning I viewed the border anew, liked it and realized that some of the colours wanted to come out. (#5) My attention was fully focused on the wools and what they wanted me to do. The topic of intuitive learning was the farthest thing from my mind (#3). It was as though each colour had its own energy, which I felt in a physical magnetic way. I found myself clearly defining tightly woven shapes of colours that demanded to be released from the border. At the same time I introduced the white nubby wool to which I had been attracted. It had an energy of its own and seemed to increase in prominence throughout the week. The white was the only colour that didn't break continuity from the bottom to the top. (pp. 141, 142)

> On Friday afternoon I saw the end of the warp emerging over the back of the loom. I felt very drawn to weave a final very open statement of white among the solid shapes. (#5) This white shape was pointing to the border not yet there. (p. 144)

She recounted, "Upon hanging it up and viewing it for the first time, I was awed by the balance, harmony and symmetry of texture, colour and form" (p. 144) created without a rationally determined plan.

> Throughout the process I maintained an attitude of receptivity which is the very opposite of passivity. I was intensely active but it was an activity that was more a response than an initiating energy. What I responded to all week were the revelations or insights inherent in this and in all learning situations (#5). What I learned from the interviewees came out of my fingertips without first engaging the rational mind.

> When one is attentive to the basic processes of intuition described by interviewees, the gift of intuition occurs and learning takes place. Such was the process of weaving this tapestry." (personal communication, June 9, 2010)

So far we have examined intuitive processes that are about bridging the gap between experience and ideas by beginning with particulars evolving into meaningful constructs through the riches of right brain processes; the gap can also be bridged "from the other side" by an interpretive process that begins with a concept that becomes meaningful in relationship to experience.

The Generative Use of Concepts

In our culture it is likely that most of us think of concepts as having an existence of their own, that is, "outside" our minds; they have meaning based on carefully formulated definitions. We go to dictionaries and technical literature to find what they mean, that is, what they represent in the world of objects and events. We might think of concepts entirely as stable points of reference "out there" to which we adapt; we make them into "things." Building on intellectuals like Nietzsche and Marx in the nineteenth century, the past century was an intensifying record of challenge to this value-perspective, in every discipline, as part of the shift beyond this modernist (rational-empirical) viewpoint. The generative use of concepts in a learning process contrasts with this definitional approach—meaning is generated from associating a concept with a particular experience; it is not simply given by the concept itself.

From philosophy, theology, and literary theory, hermeneutics which is the practice of interpretation, is one of these intellectual challenges to the claims of rational-empiricism. "Aristotle was right to situate the moment of interpretation earlier than the processes of logical analysis" (Palmer, 1969, p. 22). The word "hermeneutics" derives from *hermeios,* referring to the priest at the Oracle of Delphi. Hermes was the Greek god, messenger "bringing a thing or situation from unintelligibility to understanding" (p. 13). What began as a way to treat literary text (in theology, the Bible) evolved into an approach in interpreting lived experience. The notion of *context* is central in hermeneutic thought, and practice is the notion of the hermeneutic circle. In text, the word takes its meaning from the whole sentence, and conversely, understanding the sentence depends on the meaning of the word. Wilhelm Dilthey, a late-nineteenth-century literary historian, transferred this notion into the human sciences. "An event or experience can so alter our lives that what was formerly meaningful becomes meaningless . . . The sense of the whole determines its function and meaning of the parts" (p. 118). Meaning is contextual and historical, and thus is seen from a temporal standpoint. Explaining twentieth-century philosopher Martin Heidegger's development of hermeneutic thought, Palmer explained:

> the being of something is disclosed not the contemplative analytic gaze but in the moment in which it suddenly emerges from hiddenness in the full functional context of the world. Likewise, the character of understanding will be best grasped not through analytical catalogue of its attributes, nor in the full flush of its proper functioning, but when it breaks down, when it comes up against a wall, perhaps when something it must have is missing. (p. 133)

It is in the moments when concepts and experiences converge in our attention that we find illumination—insight. Concepts take on new meanings and become useful in advancing our understanding.

Another way to bridge the gap from concept to experience comes to us in the form of a new wave of thinking in cognitive linguistics and cognitive psychology. A leading spokesperson for this new trend is psychologist Eleanor Rosch who co-authored, with Evan Thompson and the late Francisco Varela (1991), *The Embodied Mind: Cognitive Science and Human Experience,* an extensive and comprehensive treatment of this theme and its significance. The authors invite us to see ourselves as part of, rather than separate from, our environment, a positioning that reflects the experience of present-oriented engagement in the Exploration Phase. Rosch (1999) observed:

> Concepts are the natural bridge between mind and world to such an extent that they require us to change what we think of as mind and what we think of as world; concepts occur only in actual situations in which they function as *participating parts* of the situation rather than as either representations or as mechanisms for identifying objects; concepts are open systems by which creatures can learn new things and can invent; and concepts exist in a larger context—they are not the only form in which living creatures know and act. (p. 61) [emphasis added]

Focusing the convergence of concept and experience, she emphasizes the context, both conceptual and nonconceptual: "Concepts only occur as part of a web of meaning provided both by other concepts and by interrelated life activities" (p. 70). Importantly for our purposes, Rosch frames the potential for concepts to generate novelty: "In the new view, concepts are not representations but functioning, participating parts of total situations. Thus concepts allow for all the novelty of the situations themselves, and there can be genuine surprises, learning, and invention" (p. 72).

Applying the wisdom of the hermeneutics and the interpretative approach, and open system concepts to Green Zone exploration, we can see that spoken or written conceptual formulations can become passages to meaning for us. The richer the reservoir of our conceptual resources, the more possibilities there are for range, depth, and elegance in our understanding of our experience. We know this as we are intuitively drawn to certain titles in a bookstore, library, or now on the Internet. They will be useful to us only at this point in the emergent learning process, however, if we read and listen for meaning rather than for assimilation or replication. In so doing, we are implicitly juxtaposing our experience with the questions and puzzlement it represents to the expressed idea. Marge Denis calls it "dialoguing with the materials" (personal communication, June 15, 2010).

Reconnecting back to our discussion of metaphor, this time not our own but to the symbolic expressions of others, we can add to our store of "illuminate material" stories from authors of fiction and cinema, musicians, visual artists, and choreographers. If Daniel Pink (2006) is right, namely that we are entering an age of the "right brain," this domain of cultural wealth may become our primary connection to the world of ideas.

The Practice of Collaborative Inquiry[6]

To this point, we have focused on the intrapersonal processes that occur in the course of Green Zone exploration. However, intersecting with our own mental processes are the social dynamics of exploration—the nexus between our own search for understanding and that of others. How we locate and engage with partners in inquiry is a pivotal element in progressing through an emergent learning process. There has been an explosion in the uses of groups in education, the workplace, and the community in the past 40 years. The specific group form that enhances our abilities, especially for Green Zone exploration, are those in which the agenda is evolved by participants within the broad purpose of meaning-making (i.e., connecting ideas and our experience), in which the discourse engages all participants in a spirit of inquiry focused primarily in present thought and experience.

Group Dynamics

In our own culture, beginning over the past 60 years with Kurt Lewin's work with group dynamics and attitude change, the phenomenon of learning to work in leaderless or process-facilitated groups has become an increasingly prevalent practice. Self-managed learning in groups and teams in organizations and in communities is matched with the increasing level of education and increasing interest in autonomy in the population (e.g., Michael Adams, 2003). Increasing autonomy is also driven by the need for adaptability in the face of an increasing pace of change. In other cultures, notably aboriginal cultures, and some faith traditions such as the Religious Society of Friends (Quakers), "open process" inquiry and decision-making date back centuries and millennia. Since the 1940s in the Western world, both the prevalence and forms of collaborative learning have evolved. Collaborative inquiry is meant as *a quest for understanding in collaboration with others who have similar or complementary learning interests in self-directed or facilitated groups in which everyone begins without or reaches a point that they realize they do not have "the answer" or "the conclusion."* Several forms of collaborative inquiry that began 60 years ago are the Training Group, or T-group, that developed out of Lewin's applied social psychology in the American National Training Laboratories for Group Dynamics (NTL), and the Tavistock Institute's Work Conferences in the UK, both aimed at developing awareness and high quality in how we relate to each other in groups. These collective inquiry innovations were designed as residential sessions, affording uninterrupted time and providing a safe "container" for reflective exploration. The motivation of scholar practitioners who fostered the development of these social technologies might be represented by the following question of Dorwin Cartwright (2008), professor and director of the Research Center for Group Dynamics at MIT founded by Kurt Lewin:

How can we change people so that they neither restrict the freedom nor limit the potentialities for growth of others; so that they accept and respect people of different religion, nationality, color, or political opinion; so that nations can exist in a world without war, and so that the fruits of our technological advances can bring economic well-being and freedom from disease to all people of the world? (p. 59)

In both traditions, group participants learned through experience to be aware of and to influence group formation, group processes and dynamics, with a view to influencing those processes to foster equitable participation and to optimize productivity. Both traditions organized learning as extended residential sessions away from home, and the workplace. As part of these approaches, there was continuous, collaborative inquiry about our own contributions and their value, through self-observation and feedback from others that generates intense and accelerated real-time learning. Since the focus is on personal responsibility for our own behavior in interdependent relationships with others, the experience of working in collaboratively led groups is novel, and it implies an emergent learning experience. But in all cases, these experiences develop powerful collaborative learning abilities that can be extremely effective in organizational and community settings. It also develops a conversance with preconscious sources of knowledge, and how to work with them in relationships with others.

Based on group observations of training groups, several associates of Lewin, Warren Bennis and Herb Shepard (2009), described a common model of group process, as did Wilfred Bion at Tavistock. While reflective of group development process specifically, the developmental patterns reported by these authors describe emergent process at the level of the group, which is distinct from, but influenced by, individual emergent learning process.

"Maturity for the group means something analogous to maturity of the person" (Bennis and Shepard, 2009, p. 441). Anxiety prevents resolution of conflicts and communication within a group, as it does for a person in the Red Zone. The group has to overcome obstacles and find its way to a state in which it "knows very well what it is doing" (p. 441), as do the individuals involved. This view of group development highlights the pattern of dependence (flight) and counterdependence (fight), which occur typically as groups begin to sort out their relationship to authority, personified in the designated leader. This group development stage is particularly similar to the emergent learning Red Zone, which is resolved with (a) a statement of self-affirmation, taking responsibility for our own learning, rather than blaming self and/or others, and (b) an experience of affirmation by a credible other, typically the designated leader. The second phase in the Bennis and Shepard formulation concerns the challenge of relating productively to peers in valued relationships. "Although the distribution of power was the cardinal issue in phase one, the distribution of affection occupies the group during phase two" (p. 455). While the formulation diverges at this point somewhat from a focus on intuitively guided individual learning and meaning making, it does so in focusing primarily on group relationships that are the conditions or social requirements of collaborative inquiry and dialogue.

Wilfred Bion's (1961) group process model is broadly similar to Bennis and Shepard's patterns of group development. It is perhaps not surprising that, as a psychoanalyst, Bion focused on three different emotional states reflecting the tacit assumptions of the group that shape its different stages. Bion's work on small groups reflected three traditional Western culture assumptions that are successively challenged by a facilitated group, namely, tacit notions about group aims, summarized by Margaret Rioch (2009) they are as follows:

1. "to attain security through and have its members protected by one individual" (p. 469);
2. "to preserve itself and that this can only be done by fighting someone or something or by running away from someone or something"; and
3. "to create a new leader, or a new thought, or something that will bring new life, will resolve old problems" (p. 472).

Bion saw these as fantasies that "interfere with getting work done" (p. 473) by reality-based, responsible, and collaborative members.

Both the NTL and Tavistock group work were early innovations in what is now a wide range of collaborative intensive formats that foster reflective inquiry and dialogue, which leads to a deeper appreciation of a domain of experience and a significantly wider range of approaches to active engagement. The NTL and Tavistock small group innovations have evolved over the past six decades, both being adapted to such central themes as leadership development, diversity and inclusion, and engaging change and are offered internationally. Programs that comprise similar opportunities are offered across the world by the longstanding and well-recognized Center for Creative Leadership. These kinds of "learning spaces" are offered in professional development programs offered by universities, and are integrated into many leadership development degree programs, such as the MA in Leadership, the MBA program, and related certificate programs at Royal Roads University, Victoria, BC, where I am appointed as a professor. All of these enduring and evolving innovations attest to the need for practical, significant, reflective strength that enables us to adapt to our unpredictable context. Large system innovations evolved from both NTL and Tavistock Institute relevant to emergent learning and twenty-first-century flux are what we touch on in the next chapter.

Dialogue

While NTL and Tavistock group work focused attention on social relationships, a later development, that of "dialogue" in groups in the same nondirective process structure, is focused at thought and discourse. Gergen et al. (2004) make the point that Lewin's work, and that of others in this tradition, achieved attitude and behavior change without knowing very much about "the essential process of dialogue itself." It is within the past several decades that there has been an especially careful attention to the process of dialogue. Edgar Schein (1995b) observed that dialogue "is so essential . . . in the context of global changes" (p. 3). Gergen et al. observed that there are diverse meanings of the referent, "dialogue"—such as curiosity driven inquiry (Bohm, 1996), conflict reduction (Hawes, 1999), equalizing voices for minorities (Eisenberg and Goodall, 1993), or collective inquiry into everyday experience (Isaacs, 1993).

Gergen et al. suggested that we think of dialogue as "coordinated action" and "generative dialogue [as] dialogue that brings into being a mutually satisfying and effective organization." They compare generative dialogue "to the fluid and synchronized movements of dancers." The etymology of the word, dialogue, as "flow of meaning" (Bohm, 1996; Isaacs, 1993) conveys a similar theme.

David Bohm (1996) summarizes the process:

> The object of a dialogue is not to analyze things, or to win an argument, or to exchange opinions. Rather, it is to suspend your opinions and to look at the opinions—to listen to everybody's opinions, to suspend them, and to see what all that means. If we can see what all of our opinions mean, then we are sharing a common content, even if we don't agree entirely. It may turn out that the opinions are not really very important—they are all assumptions. And if we can see them all, we may then move more creatively in a different direction. We can just simply share the appreciation of the meanings; and out of this whole thing, truth emerges unannounced—not that we have chosen it. (p. 26)

William Isaacs (1993) traces the evolution of dialogue through different genres of discourse. It begins with conversation (begin to speak) to deliberation (weighing different views) to a choice point between discussion (analysis of different views) and suspension (examining assumptions and feelings and what sustains them). Bohm (1996) stated about the suspension of assumptions:

> You neither carry them out nor suppress them. You don't believe them, nor do you disbelieve them; you don't judge them as good or

bad. Normally when you are angry you start to react outwardly, and you may just say something nasty. Now suppose I try to suspend that reaction. Not only will I now not insult that person outwardly, but I will suspend the insult that I make inside of me. (p. 20)

In the evolution of the dialogue process, Isaacs describes this as a crisis point that, at a group level, parallels the individual Red Zone experience:

People feel that they can't tell where the group is heading; they feel disoriented, and perhaps marginalized and constrained by others. Polarization comes up. Extreme views become stated and defended. All of this "heat" and instability is exactly what *should* be happening. (Isaacs, 1993, p. 36)

The shift occurs if, as participants, we are able to express and together examine the views and feelings we have developed about each other. The constructions that, hidden, have held us apart become the object of our collective attention. Recurrence of these polarizing moments, then, is met with questions, rather than immediate conclusions, questions such as: "What is this? What is the meaning of this? . . . Where am I listening from? What is the disturbance going on in me (not others)? What can I learn if I slow things down and inquire (to seek within)?" (p. 37). If participants, at least most of them, can maintain this inquiring stance, dialogue—"the flow of meaning" (p. 34)—can begin. "The energy that had been trapped in rigid and habitual patterns of thought and interaction begins to be freed up" (p. 37). Isaacs observed that, at this point, it is characteristic for us, as participants, to experience a level of pain when we realize the cost of fragmented thinking to ourselves and our world. There is also a sense of loss of our familiar, "comforting beliefs" (p. 37). This further crisis can lead to another shift in the experience—"people begin to know that they are participating in a pool of common meaning . . ." (p. 38). Isaacs calls this "metalogue," in which the process and content become fused: "This kind of exchange entails learning to think and speak together for the creation of breakthrough levels of thought, and to know the . . . beauty of shared speech" (p. 38).

The rise of interest in dialogue of this nature and the prevalence of its practice is timely in our context of mounting global intensity and the meeting of difference. Bohm (1996) observed:

We could say that practically all the problems of the human race are due to the fact that thought is not proprioceptive [self-reflective].

Thought is constantly creating problems that way and then trying to solve them. But as it tries to solve them it makes it worse because it doesn't notice that it's creating them, and the more it thinks, the more problems it creates—because it's not proprioceptive of what it's doing. If your body were that way you would very quickly come to grief and you wouldn't last very long. And it may be said that if our culture were that way, our civilization would not last all that long, either. (p. 25)

Experience with collaborative inquiry in ways that develop our process awareness and skills—social, emotional, and thought—in contexts that amplify uncertainty conditions, provide us with the ability to meet complex systemic challenges in our organizations and communities. We are unable to influence processes unless we are aware of them, and have developed confidence and skill in dealing with them. There are many sources for learning to engage in and conduct dialogue. Again, it seems we are developing the resources for learning that we need as we are faced with unpredictability. We will consider some of the large system applications of dialogue in Chapter 6.

REFLECTING (TRANSITION) AND TRANSFORMATION PHASE

The eye altering, alters all.

William Blake

Under the best conditions what is, is valued. . . . This fusion . . . is the ability to simultaneously perceive in the fact—the *is*—its particularity *and* its universality.

Abraham Maslow (1971, p. 111)

The Transformation Phase of the emergent learning process spontaneously arises from a period of intense reflection—a review of insights and salient ideas gathered over the period of the open-ended, intuitively guided Exploration Phase. The Transformation Phase is an intense period of hyperawareness in which we are fully engaged simultaneous with being fully aware of ourselves, our thoughts, and our context. We glimpse a whole new perspective that makes sense of many of the elements of our experience and insights generated through the sequence to this point. The assembled collage becomes a coherent big picture. The new perspective includes us in it; that is, we understand ourselves differently.

The Practice of Reflection

To reflect is "to bend or turn (something) back, to give a backward bend or curve to . . . to fold back (a flap of tissue) to expose underlying structures" (*Oxford English Dictionary*). Reflection has been an inherent feature of the entire emergent learning sequence, triggered at the outset by a surprise. "Surprise leads to reflection within an action-present. Reflection is at least in some measure conscious, although it need not occur in the medium of words" (Schön, 1987, p. 28). This draws on the analogy of good jazz musicians who, in listening to self and others, "'feel' where the music is going and adjust their playing accordingly" (p. 30). Donald Schön saw "reflection-in-action [as] a process we can deliver without being able to say what we are doing" (p. 32). It is largely intuitive. In white water kayaking, we cannot stop and think or we are more likely to capsize. Schön suggested that this form of reflection is the first of four possible levels of reflection (p. 115–116). The next, reflection *on* action, enables us to describe what we have done. When we have completed the kayak run of the rapids, we recollect and describe the route we followed, what the experience was, and how we might improve the next run. This level of reflection sounds straightforward but is not easily done when faced with a Red Zone experience, that is, when the context is in question and we are in confusion. It is the accomplishment of the Red Zone to be able to describe experience without a preoccupation with negative judgment. The next level is to reflect on the reflection on the action, that is, to inquire about what it means, and how it relates to other aspects of what we know. What does it mean that I took a more challenging route than I had to, for example? How do people who are really experienced kayakers understand what kayaking is about? This is the work of the Exploration Phase. The fourth level of reflection is to think about how we are thinking and talking about our experience with respect to a challenging sport and risk. This is the work of the reflecting transition. Participants in the original study were making sense out of the notes, readings, and their key ideas as the work of the reflecting transition. Pink (2006) noted the value in "the ability to grasp *relationships between relationships* . . . systems thinking, gestalt thinking, holistic thinking . . . seeing the big picture," which is critical to our times. It is what he calls "Conceptual Age" (p. 141) and is characterized by "high concept and high touch" (p. 51).

We will recall that these levels of reflection are also present in the collective inquiry practices we reviewed earlier in this chapter. Collective inquiry into the dynamics of groups and the quality of our participation necessarily engages us in the first three levels of reflection—thoughtful participation, reflection on the events and our actions, reflection on our description to identify recurring process patterns in the group's and my own behavior, and reflection on the deeper significance of those patterns. This sequence of reflection may, over time, trigger us into thinking about the big picture, or "framing" (Torbert, 2004) our position in the world differently. Certainly, collaborative inquiry as dialogue is specifically designed for us to work through these levels of reflection as we have seen in Isaacs's description of the process earlier in the chapter.

The Practice of Courage

In two ways, courage is required in the Purple Zone with the experience of transformation. One has to do with the fact that *inner* experiences are culturally suspect, and intense inner experiences are intensely suspect. As Richard Tarnas (1991) observed, "The very nature of the *objective* universe turns any spiritual[1] faith and ideals into courageous acts of *subjectivity* constantly vulnerable to intellectual negation" (p. 31). Abraham Maslow (1970) made a similar comment: ". . . the pure positive rejects any inner kind of experiences of *any* kind as being 'unscientific,' as not in the realm of human knowledge, as not susceptible of study by the scientific method, because such data are not objective, that is to say, public and shared" (p. 6). More broadly, in Western culture we tend to be skeptical of states of mind that go beyond day-to-day consciousness. Adding to the concerns is a frequent association of extraordinary states of consciousness with unreflective religious and sectarian practices that have led to divisiveness and, in some cases, destructive outcomes. Therefore, it takes courage to venture into the domains of extraordinary cognition. Nevertheless, Maslow, who toward the end of his career became interested in understanding "self-actualizing people . . . [with] a high level of maturation, health and self-fulfillment" (1968, p. 71), found that they had "a higher frequency of peak-experiences" (p. 26). Csíkszentmihályi and Rathunde (1990) observed that "ecstatic" means literally "to place outside," in this case, outside "ordinary awareness" (p. 39). "One does not need to think of this process as involving a transcendence to a metaphysical realm, but a more limited self-transcendence that arrives at a new *betweenness* with the world, through perceptions (or thoughts) being experienced for the first time" (p. 39).

In addition to the absence of cultural sanction for the extraordinary, there is also the requirement that we take our own insight and experience seriously, that we treat them as important events, especially if they are extraordinary. Maslow (1968) understood that European existentialism had much to offer American psychology with respect to dimensions of the human experience having to do with our uniqueness as a species and as individuals. He also believed that the existentialist perspective highlighted the gap between "human aspirations and human limitations" (p. 10), that is, who we want to become as well as who we are. Moving beyond the normative implies choice and responsibility. This *is* the heart of transformation. One person in the original study clearly expressed her decision to draw back from this choice:

> If I do a lot of learning and get very excited with that, I think, "Oh, where am I going? Am I going to be left all alone doing that?" . . . The scare is something like standing on my own two feet—being responsible for all that stuff. I have such a glorious wish to lean and hang on to everybody—"Please tell me what to do. Am I doing it the right way? Tell me I'm okay." . . . Taking on a question is not my style. . . . I have the feeling that if I take that on I'll really be on my own. (Taylor, 1979, p. 268)

A further and related aspect of the requirement for courage here is that transformational change is irreversible. William Bergquist (1993) pointed out that second-order change, and we could add third-order change, cannot be "undone." Drawing on Nobel Laureate Ilya Prigogine's work in chemistry, "sciences of being" focused on states, and "sciences of becoming," focused on processes that are best symbolized by fire. Bergquist noted that the same distinctions apply in the social world. "Equilibrium has been disturbed, chaos often follows, and we ourselves are not the same as we were before. Time moves in one direction and cannot be reversed" (p. 5). Transformational moments are defining moments of our lives; we will not be the same as we were before. Very often, we sense that we are in the face of a choice that demands the courage to make an irreversible change.

Otto Scharmer (2007) alluded to all of these features in what he calls the "Voice of Fear" as an "enemy at the gate to open will" (p. 43). "It prevents us from letting go of what we have and who we are. It can show up as fear of losing economic security. Or fear of being ostracized. Or fear of being ridiculed. Of death" (p. 43).

Fostering our capacity for courage begins with our recognition of our challenge, reflection about what our particular fears characteristically are, and what context-specific and personally relevant options we have available to us in augmenting our courage and confidence in emergent learning. In the end, the word courage derives from *coraticum*, Latin for "heart." Several of the meanings of courage situate its meaning and the challenge we face: "The heart as the seat of feeling, thought, etc.; spirit, mind, disposition, nature" and "that quality of mind which shows itself in facing danger without fear or shrinking" (*Oxford English Dictionary*). The Exploration Phase not only generates new ideas and insights, but also is constituted by collaboration and active engagement in learning *with* others, so as to amplify confidence that supports courage. Otto Scharmer (2007) and his colleagues also noted that "open heart" precedes "open will" (p. 41) in realizing our possibilities.

The Practice of Mindfulness (Part II)

> Sitting still or lying still, in any moment we can reconnect with the body, transcend the body, merge with the breath, with the universe, experience as whole and unfolded into larger and larger wholes. A taste of interconnectedness brings deep knowledge of belonging, a sense of being an intimate part of things, a sense of being at home wherever we are. (Kabat-Zinn, 1994, p. 226)

The mindfulness practice we considered at the beginning of this chapter as support in sustaining ourselves through the distress of the Red Zone now becomes a pathway to apprehending the big picture. Brown et al. (2007) noted the relationship between mindfulness and integrative awareness, "an assimilatory, non-discriminatory interest in what serves the function of promoting synthesis, organization and integration of functioning" (p. 217).

There is an important distinction between reflexive self-awareness and mindfulness. "The two functions are somewhat independent although . . . they are often intertwined" (Brown et al., 2007, p. 216). To the extent that reflection on our own experience and behavior is self-attention with *intention*, that is, we are observing with a prior purpose to accomplish something from observing it, this is a distinct practice from mindfulness. However, the fourth level of reflection described above can readily become an accepting, receptive observation of a flow of thought. What is clear is that intensive reflection on one's insights and meaningful ideas leads to an extraordinary state of presence in which one achieves the kind of clarity associated with the practice of mindfulness.

The Practice of Presence

Intense attention—*mindfulness with intention*—can generate a similarly transformative experience.

Abraham Maslow (1968) invited people to tell him about their "happiest moments, ecstatic moments, moments of rapture" (p. 71) and identified a series of patterns in "peak-experiences" or "Being cognition"—"B-cognition," including

"the experience or object tends to be seen as a whole, as a complete unit, detached from its relations, from possible usefulness, from expediency, and from purpose" (p. 74).

"*the precept is exclusively attended to.* This may be called 'total attention'. . . . In such attention the figure becomes *all* figure and the ground, in effect, disappears" (p. 74).

"*The peak experience is felt as a self-validating, self-justifying moment which carries its own intrinsic value with it.* That is to say it is an end in itself, what we may call an end-experience rather than a means-experience" (p. 79).

"*There is a very characteristic disorientation in time and space.* It would be accurate to say that in these moments the person is outside time and space subjectively" (p. 80).

"*the peak experience is only good and desirable, and is never experienced as evil or undesirable.* The experience is intrinsically valid; the experience is perfect, complete and needs nothing else. It is sufficient to itself" (p. 81).

"B-cognition is much more passive and receptive than active [suggesting the relationship to mindfulness]" (p. 86).

"many dichotomies, polarities, and conflicts are fused, transcended or resolved" (p. 91).

"One aspect of the peak-experience is a complete, though momentary, loss of fear, anxiety, inhibition, defense and control, a giving up of renunciation, delay and restraint. . . . This too implies a greater openness of perception since fear distorts" (p. 97).

One of the participants in the original study described the experiences of the Transformation Phase over a period of a week—intense reflection on her experiences and insights of the Exploration Phase. Her account was provided in great detail, some of the experience occurring during the interview. Since the transformation "moment" is not a commonly discussed experience, her description is presented here as an example that illustrates some of the features Maslow identified.

She began talking in one of the interviews about information she was organizing for her studies—it began with a metaphor. She recounted that earlier in the week she had been making connections among new ideas she was encountering. "It's not totally active; it's partially passive—partial in the sense that I'm letting things in" (p. 166).

> It's this huge funnel. . . . I'm just sifting. . . . I should find an analogy because I *feel* the pieces and I don't know quite what to say about it. It's my jigsaw puzzle again [she used the analogy of the jigsaw puzzle to describe the gathering of apparently unrelated insights in the Exploration Phase], but it's one step removed . . . I'm starting to pick out particular key pieces . . . I know it *will* come together eventually, and some of them are starting to click already. (p. 165)

She went on to discuss some other aspect of her experience with others in the educational setting and the physical sensations that arose; suddenly she interrupted herself to describe physical sensations that were occurring at that very moment in the interview, creating a simultaneity of experience and self-observation.

> I get a physical reaction to it. . . . It's an expansion in the chest area. What I'm talking about right now is how I feel in the moment and that is very—"hyped" is the word, but it's a different kind of hype . . . than I've been experiencing [in the educational setting but similar to others] in my personal life. For some reason the image of a mushroom crossed my mind and I don't know why. (p. 165)

She then linked the physical sensation to poet John Keats' notion of the convergence of the apparent dichotomies of pleasure and pain forming a circle with an opening, forming something like a container that having received "a lot of stuff," closes.

> Suddenly, instead of being polar opposites it's like a magnetic or an electrical charge and it just goes "kapoom" and . . . it's all going around at the same time—opposite directions but at the same time. . . . What it creates for me is physical terms from my waist to my neck—like the whole inside part of me which is heart and lungs and soul . . . starts literally expanding and it almost makes it hard for me to talk at times. I'm very aware of that pressure. (p. 166)

The imagery she described is compatible with an atomic particle accelerator that creates high energy; she later identified that the mushroom signified an atomic explosion. The imagery and physical sensations point to the power of the experience. She stated that I, as an interviewer, was "watching . . . a flip-flop," which was what she called insights. She was physically shaken, prompting me to inquire after the interview whether she felt fully able to return to her home.

She reported a second wave of insight the next week when thinking about perceptual frames. Sleepless, she began that evening producing a diagram of the pleasure-pain continuum as an "almost closed circle," which took her into a cascade of further insights until 3 A. M. Through the process she had evolved a new embodied perspective on learning and knowledge, and herself as a participant in creating, and that she understood from the inside-out.

Later she described the transformation experience using the following imagery:

> If you've looked at the sun from the bottom of some kind of depth, there's a different quality. It's a diffuse, all pervading quality that you don't get when you're on the surface of the earth. Then it's more a pin point—darkness and shadows. It's a fully expanded sort of awareness. I don't think I've ever felt that before . . . It's gut level. It's *total*. It runs from the top of my toes to the top of my head and beyond. It almost creates an aura around me.

This example of the transformation experience is also well described by Otto Scharmer's (2007) "Theory U," which was reviewed in Chapter 4. Specifically, the Transformation Phase in an *individual's* experience of emergent learning is that described by Scharmer in a facilitated social process of "presensing" (present + sensing). It is the "social field" of the "*I-in-now*: what I understand from the source or bottom of my being, that is, from attending with my open will" (p. 11). "It deals with the fundamental happening of letting go and letting come" (p. 41). Scharmer outlines four principles of presensing, the first of which we have mentioned:

1. "Letting go and surrendering": "Letting go concerns the opening process, the removal of barriers and junk in one's way, and surrendering is moving into the resulting opening." (p. 185)
2. "Inversion: Going through the eye of a needle": "When you pass through the eye of a needle—the threshold at which everything that isn't essential must go—you shift the place from which you operate to 'those who are surrounding us'; you begin to see from a different direction, you begin to move forward your self *from* future." (p. 185)
3. "The Coming into being of a Higher (Authentic) Presence and Self": ". . . a forward pull from a different kind of opening or possibility that somehow connected with the embodiment of an emerging or different kind of self—the authentic or essential: Self." (p. 187)

The fourth condition applies especially to facilitated social contexts intended to foster transformation or presensing, while as individuals it is helpful to be aware of the places we choose and their qualities, which may be similar. The conditions for dialogue, as observed in Chapter 3, are also instructive.

4. Creating a Holding Space for Deep Listening": Scharmer outlined three conditions: "unconditional witnessing or no judgment, impersonal love, and seeing the essential self." (p. 187)

The Transformation Phase is a crucible within which our value-perspective changes; it can "provide a complete and coherent explanation of [our] . . . place . . . within the world . . . [that facilitates the [our] experience of [ourselves] as a goal directed agent[s]" (Owen, 1994, p. 97). The intensity of the experience appears to match the pervasiveness of the change that results.

The Practice of Wisdom

There is growing recognition that we are entering a paradigmatically different era, and are facing sustainability challenges such as are represented on our twenty-first-century learning agenda (e.g., O'Sullivan, 1999; Friedman, 2005, 2008; Appadurai, 2006; Gore, 2006; Laszlo, 2006; Senge et al., 2008). There is also increasing attention to more dimensional, holistic ways of thinking associated generally with the practice of wisdom that more adequately match our twenty-first century challenges than the solely empirical rational emphasis of the modern era. Csíkszentmihályi and Rathunde (1990) observed:

> With the important challenges that face modern society, one-dimensional technological thinking will not suffice for finding our location with respect to many critical survival problems. There is no question that now more than ever we need a holistic, long-range understanding of actions and events—let us call it wisdom—so as to avoid unforeseen consequences of narrowly specialized interests and ways of knowing. (p. 36)

They proposed that "perpetual historical association of wisdom with perfect joy, self-transcendence, ecstasy . . . may have an evolutionary significance that needs to find new expression . . ." (p. 38) without necessary orientation to the metaphysical realm. Orwoll and Perlmutter (1990) draw on the work of Erik Erikson, Carl Jung, and Heinz

Kohut to situate wisdom as a quality evolved through self-development and self-transcendence: focus on "ultimate concerns" and "social radius eventually accompanies humankind in general" (Erickson); "unabsorbed by individualistic passions" and "self-transcendent themes as precipitated by an inner shift toward collective consciousness" (Jung) (p. 163); "self suspends its own importance, experiences others empathically, and responds to its own impermanence with humor and an expanded sense of self" (Kohut) (p. 163).

The renewed attention to wisdom highlights integration of many features we have examined in the emergent learning process, suggesting that the development of wisdom both contributes to and arises from full cycle emergent learning. A number of conceptualizations of wisdom underline the integration of aspects of human personality and functions.

- Csíkszentmihályi and Rathunde (1990):
  The great "width" (empathy), "height" (intelligence), and "depth" (reflexivity) of the wise person allows him or her to form a more complex or *concrete and abstract* perspective on some problem and thus attain the possibility of the wisest course of action. (p. 35)
- Labouvie-Vief (1990):
  I have proposed to define wisdom as the grounding of intellectual operations—those usually associated with *logos*—in *mythos*, an organismic core of interpersonal and intrapersonal processes (p. 76). *Mythos* means *speech, narrative, plot,* or *dialogue* (p. 55). *Logos* derives from *gather, read,* and came to connote *counting, reckoning, explanation, rule,* or *principle* and, finally, *reason.* (p. 56)
- Birren and Fischer (1990):
  Wisdom is an *integration of the affective, conative, and cognitive aspects* of human abilities in the response to life's tasks and problems. Wisdom is a balance between the opposing valences of intense emotion and detachment, action and inaction, and knowledge and doubts. (p. 326)

Another set highlights multiple forms of intellect in combination with practical experience, emphasizing recognition of our knowledge and understanding.

- Baltes and Smith (2008)
  We define *wisdom* as expert knowledge in the fundamental pragmatics of life that permits exceptional insight, judgment, and advice about complex and uncertain matters. (p. 351)

- Kramer (1990)

  Wisdom was seen as . . . involving the application of relativistic and dialectical modes of thinking . . . through the recognition of individuality, context, possibilities for change and growth, and both cognition and affect and by allowing for effective interpersonal skills. (p. 305)

- Sternberg (1990)

  The wise person is characterized by a metacognitive stance. Wise people know what they know and what they do not know as well as the limits of what can be known and what cannot be. . . . Wise people welcome ambiguity, knowing that it is an ongoing part of life, and try to understand the obstacles that confront themselves and others in life. They are motivated toward in-depth understanding of phenomena, and at the same time they recognize the limitations of their own understanding. They seek understanding of what will "work" not only for them but for society as well. (p.157)

Robert Sternberg and his colleagues actively promote learning wisdom for youth in schools (pp. 113–126). Here are the six guidelines they offered, which have been adapted and expanded on here:

1. Reading and inquiry into the wisdom traditions—philosophy and theology—and outstanding literary fiction and cinema—classic and contemporary, consciously articulating the lessons we learn from what we undertake and apply them to our lives;
2. Reflect on public issues and personal dilemmas in light of the values at stake and the ethical principles involved;
3. Create opportunities to discuss your observations, thoughts and questions with others;
4. Exercise our "critical, creative, and practical thinking in service of the common good" (p. 117);
5. Reflect on how we are using our skills and knowledge "for better or worse ends" with the potential of adding a new way to contribute to the common good;
6. Identify examples of wisdom being exercised (not overlooking our own) and contemplate the examples of "role models" (p. 125) in the practice of wisdom.

NAMING (TRANSITION) AND EQUILIBRIUM PHASE

First enlightenment, then the laundry.

Buddhist saying

The final phase of the emergent learning sequence is the return to equilibrium, a relatively stable state, where changes are elaborations or applications of the new perspective generated through intense open-ended inquiry and major insight. As individuals, we become independent of others with respect to exploration and sense-making but our challenge is now to establish relationships with others in the application of what we have learned. Our mode of thinking becomes more analytical and strategic, and our relationships with people more instrumental as we pursue the practical goals and aspirations. The transition to the Blue Zone, or Equilibrium Phase, is naming our new perspective and confirming its intelligibility to others—communicating the extraordinary experience and major insight to others whom we expect would understand. As we emerge from the intensity of the Transformation Phase, our opportunity is to carry the new perspective into our lives and our work, along with pursuing new possibilities that the new perspective opened up for us.

The Practice of Vision with Flow

The challenge of moving into a period of equilibrium is to translate the essence of a new perspective into practical terms, without losing the passion associated with the initial breakthrough insight. Joseph Jaworski's (1998) book, *Synchronicity,* is a detailed description of his journey from the moment in which his "whole life had been shattered" (p. 40), through his discovery of a deep sense of purpose and all the phases of realizing his dream—the American Leadership Forum dedicated to enabling men and women as leaders "to see their larger purpose in life, to see their special destinies in life, and to reach for that which is truly worthy of them" (p. 60). What is exemplary about his story is that, at no point as he recounted it, did he lose his connection with his "inside-out" process. He modeled maintaining a sense of presence while pursuing practical project development; he modeled the message of his book, namely, "the inner path of leadership."

Otto Scharmer (2007) called this "crystallizing," that is, "sustaining the connection and beginning to operate from it" (p. 195). The risk is that we disconnect from the source of energy and inspiration we discovered in the Transformation Phase and leave behind the new perspective and the possibilities that it provides us. "Getting into [or we could say, from the Transformation Phase, *staying* in] the flow of deep intention and going with it" (Scharmer, 2007, p. 199) is not something exotic and accessible only to the few, though it may be that only a small proportion of us live with deep intention. Csíkszentmihályi and Rathunde (1990) called this "optimal experience" (p. 3), that is, "times when, instead of being buffeted by anonymous forces, we do feel in control of our own actions, masters of our own fate. . . . We feel a sense of exhilaration, a deep sense of enjoyment that is long cherished and becomes a landmark in memory for what life should look like" (p. 3)

> It is when a sailor holding tight to her course feels when the wind whips through her hair, when the boat lunges through the waves like a colt—sails, hull, wind, and sea humming a harmony that vibrates in the sailor's veins. It is what a painter feels when the colors on the canvas begin to set up a magnetic tension with each other, and a new *thing*, a living form, takes shape in front of the astonished creator. (p. 3)

> Contrary to what we usually believe, moments like these [and writing this book!], the best moments of our lives, are not the passive, receptive, relaxing times . . . The best moments usually occur when a person's body and mind are stretched to its limits in a *voluntary* effort to accomplish something difficult and worthwhile. Optimal experience is something we *make* happen. . . . For each person there are thousands of opportunities, challenges to expand ourselves. . . . In the long run optimal experiences add up to a sense of mastery—that comes as close to what is usually meant by happiness as anything we can conceivably imagine. (p. 3) [italics added]

Csíkszentmihályi depicts flow as a channel between anxiety (measured on the "*y*" or vertical axis), on the one hand, and boredom (measured on the "*x*" or horizontal axis), on the other. Flow is a diagonal channel from lower left to upper right, indicating that flow can occur no matter what is either the potential intensity of anxiety or the potential vacuousness or the boredom (p. 74).

There is here a paradoxical relationship between "control" and "letting go/letting come" (Scharmer, 2007), or between "active" and "receptive." The paradox resolves itself when we focus on "control over consciousness, which in turn leads to control over the quality of experience" (Csíkszentmihályi, 1990) and when we combine it with a systemic awareness, that is, recognition that we are inextricably connected to all that is around us. As such, we are not in control of the changing environment, but we do choose our relationship to it and, following from that, how we will influence it (as discussed in Chapter 6).

The role of vision *with* flow is to hold intention and, as Scharmer termed it, "learning from the *future* as it emerges" (p. 7). Drawing on the work of Robert Fritz (1984), Peter Senge elevated our awareness of the power of personal vision 20 years ago with his best-selling classic, *The Fifth Discipline*. An authentic personal vision is a critical element in "personal mastery," and is the *"ability to focus on ultimate intrinsic desires, not only on secondary goals"* (Senge, 2006, p. 137). It is distinguished from our purpose, which is "a general heading" and "abstract," versus the vision which is "a destination," in the form of "a concrete picture." In speaking about an artistic creation, Fritz (1984) recommended that we "learn to form pictures of what [we] want" (p. 123) and consider it from multiple angles. "The conception period has the feel of play to it" (p. 127). He saw us moving from "concept to vision" (p. 127). The difference between concept and vision *"is in focus, and focus is made possible by limitation.* When you focus a concept into a vision, *you are limiting many ways into a single way"* (p. 127). Fritz advised us to consider what we want *"independently of consideration of process"* (p. 134) of attaining it, and *"from questions of possibility"* (p. 135). The gap between our vision and our current reality is a "structural conflict" that generates a tension between our desire to achieve the vision, and limiting beliefs we may have (not all of them conscious) that we cannot have or do not deserve what we want, and so on. Fritz (1989) observed that the closer we get to achieving our vision, the greater that tension will become. We have to resist the temptation to let go of the vision in order to reduce discomfort from the tension. In order to do that, we have to become aware of our typical forms of resistance.

Lessem (1994) identified criteria for quality visions that we can add to authentic, "ultimate intrinsic desires" as noted above. The first is "consciousness," or being "obsessed with your vision." The second is "internal consistency." If we have narrowed our focus to our highest priority elements in a coherent vision, there should be no competing features. The third is "clarity." It should communicate clearly to others. Our vision is one of several critical means of locating and aligning with potential partners who have complementary commitments. The fourth criterion is "intensity, the strength of its attraction as compelling and powerful statement—"impactful, colorful, captivating, and energizing" (p. 108). The fifth is "confidence"—focus on the positive. The sixth is "recognition" its capability to draw recognition from others. Finally, our "faith" in the vision is expressed by "act[ing] as if it were a reality" (p. 109).

The Practice of Values Fluency

The focus on values has been amplified in our current global context; it is at the heart of each of our twenty-first-century challenges outlined in Chapter 1. In order to successfully navigate the complexities at the ever accelerating pace of our daily lives, our purposes, choices and actions need to be anchored deeply and explicitly in what matters most to us if we are to remain flexible and yet stay "on course." In a culturally diverse context, we need "values fluency," the capability to articulate our own values, live to them, recognize others' values that may or may not be the same as ours, and find common ground. The most threatening challenges of our time—the deterioration of the environment, corruption in private enterprise and government, lagging productivity and quality of workplaces—all confront us with our views and values that contribute to the intractability of these problems.

Milton Rokeach (1973) was one of the most widely known social science thought leaders in the domain of values. In his definition of values he highlights a distinction between values pertaining to goals ("terminal values"), and those related to means ("instrumental values"):

> A *value* is an enduring belief that a specific mode of conduct or end-state of existence is personally or socially preferable to an opposite or converse mode of conduct or end-state of existence. A *value system* is an enduring organization of beliefs concerning preferable modes of conduct or end-states of existence along a continuum of relative importance. (p. 5)

Their importance as anchors derives from the observation that values have been regarded as being mostly stable over time. However, they are also seen to be susceptible to change under some conditions, including experiences of dissatisfaction (Rokeach, 1973; Meglino and Ravlin, 1998); thus Red Zones are the likely origins of values shifts.

As salient as values are becoming in our lives and discourse, we are still refining our understanding of what they are (Meglino and Ravlin, 1998) and how to work with them on a practical level. An important distinction was articulated by Chris Argyris and Donald Schön (1974), between the values we say we have ("espoused"), and those that are evident through our actions ("values-in-use"). Alignment between what we say and what we do is a matter of personal integrity; it requires us to become more conscious of our behavior in relation to our values. Recognizing misalignment becomes a helpful, though discomforting source of Red Zone learning toward values fluency. Argyris and Schön fostered practices and developed tools for applying this insight, especially in a range of professional practices.

William Gellermann and his colleagues (1990) highlighted the centrality of values in ethical decision-making, situating values as a foundation for ethics. They offered an important distinction between "ethics as morality" in which "the notion of a code of moral conduct plays a critical role" (p. 42), and "ethics as the quest for a good life" which "focuses on the idea of flourishing, or fulfillment" (p. 53). The former emphasizes concern about instrumental values or how we act, and the latter looks at terminal, end-state values, or why we act. They suggested that ethical practice goes beyond moral compliance and it is more than an act. We are not refined in our thinking and behavior because it is a taboo topic, especially when we make ethical errors; we dare not discuss our inevitable shortcomings and therefore we are less likely to learn from them. Gellermann and his colleagues described a process that holds some similarities to emergent learning, one that enhances consciousness of ethical practice through a series of steps in a self-facilitated inquiry connecting ethical sensitivity, thought and action. "Increasing ethical sensitivity to situations that require ethical thought and action" (p. 64) launches a process of structured reflection through problem analysis in relation to our values. This is an ethical analysis that includes attention to the desired results, facts, and assumptions and then to decision and action followed by reflection. Gellermann and his colleagues used the term fluency to describe the "the smoothness with which that dialogue [conversation with one's self] flows" in this process. The more specific use of the term is "values fluency." What is clear is that ethical practice depends on an increasing level of awareness and ease of conversance about our values as they relate to our behavior.

Emergent learning is central to the question of personal values in several ways. First, the process provokes us to examine the beliefs, assumptions, and expectations that are important to us. Values are beliefs that have both cognitive and emotional aspects. They are fundamental, not only to how we behave, but even to how we see the world; they comprise our value-perspective. Charles Taylor (1989) called this our "operational framework," about which we have a "strong evaluation" (p. 20). Second, emergent learning means re-examining that "operational framework" or "value-perspective," and perhaps examining it consciously for the first time as an object of reflection, provoked by something of significance that calls it into question. An outcome of emergent learning is some change in our values and value-perspective, a significant shift of mind with greater self-awareness and, with it, more of an explicit sense of personal responsibility. Greene and Burke (2007) in revisiting Maslow's notion of self-actualization, noted that in his later work, specifically *The Farther Reaches of Human Nature* (1971), he associated people who reported peak experiences with evidence of the movement "from self to other" (Green and Burke, 2007, p. 120), and they were "without a single exception, involved in a cause outside their skin: something outside of themselves, some calling or vocation" (Maslow, 1971, p. 42, cited in Greene and Burke, p. 120). This has enormous implications for our twenty-first century challenges and learning agenda. How we act to influence our world is how we exercise leadership, and this is the focus of the next chapter, in which we consider, among other contributions, Richard Barrett's (1998, 2006) evolution of Maslow's work related to what Greene and Burke have called "selfless-actualization" (p. 120) differentiated into four distinctive levels of values adapted to leadership, organizational, and national cultures.

The Practice of Entering the Field of Action

Entering the field of action is to realize our vision and purpose; it is to "bring to fruition" (*Oxford English Dictionary*). Here, emergent learning, as a process, blends with the act of leadership. From the standpoint of practice, this is an enormous domain to consider. Here we touch on first steps only, and several elements of the practice intended to optimize the realization of our vision, all with the common theme of *connecting* with people and social structures—finding and developing common purpose.

Prototyping and Performing

Otto Scharmer (2007) noted that getting into action requires an integration of "head, heart, and hand" and navigation between "two major dangers and pitfalls: mindless action and actionless minds" (p. 205). He suggested that "prototyping" is the first step into action that obviates these potential traps—we "present a concept before [we] are done" (p. 203). Maintaining our connection to our "inspiration" and our "intention" we "sense and seize opportunities that arise" (Scharmer, quoting Jaworski, p. 207). He observed that we need "to be sheltered, supported, nurtured and helped" (p. 210) in fledgling innovations; he suggested we need "strategic microcosms," describing them with the metaphor of "landing strips" (pp. 210, 211). "Performing means to operate from a larger field" (p. 216)—institutional settings. Scharmer pointed to the movement of innovation into the wider context of a society and engaging an inter-institutional ecology. This structural perspective is one of the themes in Chapter 6.

Maintaining a Process Perspective

In pursuing a vision and purpose we have an agenda; there are cherished goals we dream of achieving. We will be called upon to remember our learning from the Red Zone, namely, that things never unfold as we expect. While holding our cherished goals, it is helpful to balance our content perspective with a process perspective. We live the paradox of having a clear personal agenda and, to the extent that agenda concerns broader social purposes, that is, making a difference for the better, the results have to be *ours, not mine.* I have missed this powerful subtlety numerous times in my career, so I have a special appreciation for it!

Though consultation is not our specific focus here, entering into relationships with people in pursuing our practice purposes is. Edgar Schein's (1999) principles of process consultation are so fundamental to building a firm relationship foundation for action, that they are adapted here to include an introduction to collaborative change. Some of the principles need to be interpreted using the perspective that we may be bringing a project idea to the relationship, whereas Schein's perspective was that of a consultant to a client who is the origin of a stated purpose. Our task in any action-based partnership is to reach a point where all stakeholders own the purpose. He contrasts three different relationships: "telling the client what to do"; "selling solutions . . . or tools," or "engaging the client in a process that will in the end be seen as helpful to the client" (p. 4). Schein's principles of process consultation:

1. "always try to be helpful" (p. 6); without adhering to this principle, success is unlikely.
2. "always stay in touch with current reality" (p. 6); "By *reality* I mean some sense of what is going on inside me, what is going on inside the other person or persons in the situation and what the nature of that situation is" (p. 6).
3. "access your ignorance (p. 11);" "The only way to discover my inner reality is to learn to distinguish what I know from what I assume I know" (p. 11).
4. "everything is an intervention" (p. 17); how we communicate is paramount and we are always communicating verbally and nonverbally.
   (In a different scenario than the consultation process, the first principle is changed from "the client owns the problem and the solution" (p. 20), to we all own the problem and solution.)
5. "the client owns the problem and solution" (p. 20); in partnerships in which we are one of the sponsors of the initiative, ownership belongs to us as well.
6. "go with the flow" (p. 39); build adequate trust with the partner, though an unpredictable process, the capability to do so is essential.

7, 8, and 9. "confrontive inquiry" (p.49); putting our own ideas on the table, which may challenge our partner, understanding that "timing is crucial," and to "be constructively opportunistic with confrontive interventions" (p. 49), and expect that "errors will occur and will be the prime source of learning" (p. 50).

10. "when in doubt, share the problem" (p. 55); establish the level of mutual trust and credibility, when necessary—the quality of our relationships with partners and stakeholders, consciously constructed, is the platform required for realizing our vision.

Building a Support/Challenge Team

In a complex environment, we can expect that many perspectives will be required to keep us on track with our vision and purpose, as well as to ensure that our intentions are fully realized. In a wide field of engagement, while working with change, it is important to consciously create a social environment for ourselves that fosters innovation. Currently, few environments come ready-made to assist us in optimizing effective action and continuing the learning that will maintain our resilience in an environment of flux. Robert Kegan (1994) commented on the quality of such an environment:

> If I were asked to stand on one leg, like Hillel, and summarize my reading of centuries of wise reflection on what is required of an environment for it to facilitate the growth of its members, I would say this: people grow best where they continuously experience an ingenious blend of support and challenge; the rest is commentary. Environments that are weighted too heavily in the direction of challenge without adequate support are toxic; they promote defensiveness and constriction. Those weighted too heavily toward support without adequate challenge are ultimately boring; they promote devitalization. In contrast, the balance of support and challenge leads to vital engagement. (p. 42)

A significant element of our success in action comes from not only our fellow travelers, but also from our advisors, coaches, and mentors. We need to socially choreograph our Equilibrium Phase world, as we did our emergent learning process.

SUMMARY

We have reviewed 14 practices that enhance our expertise at emergent learning. They are offered in response to the question: How might we catalyze the development of our abilities to learn and act for the greatest benefit in meeting our increasingly urgent twenty-first-century challenges? The description of each practice is meant to be an introduction, pointing to possibilities for further exploration. The practices have been juxtaposed to aspects of the emergent learning process to which they seem to relate most, but clearly many of them touch on all aspects of our journey. The practices are interrelated, so that developing the quality of our practice of one will contribute to the quality of many of the others as well. As we strengthen our self-esteem and self-compassion, we will find ourselves more capable in collaborative inquiry. Both contribute to the quality of our practice of presence, and so on. Wherever we begin (or continue, as the case may be) will have a positive effect and represents commitment to improving our lives and the planet.

CHAPTER 6

GLOBAL IMPERATIVES, EMERGENT LEARNING, AND LEADERSHIP

In the human world, unlike in nature, [the future] can be decisively influenced by conscious will and considered purpose. Human will and purpose decide whether the world heads toward breakdown or toward breakthrough. This sensitivity to human intervention is a remarkable feature of today's civilization. It places a unique opportunity in our hands: the opportunity to tip the scales of human destiny.

Ervin Laszlo (2008, p. 3)

NO PROMISES BUT A PROMISING DIRECTION

Our focus to this point has been on navigating ourselves adaptively through an environment of accelerating and unpredictable change in the face of critical demands. Anticipating continual turbulence and uncertainty, we have considered what it is to take an *emergent learning process* perspective. We examined this pattern in detail and considered its relevance across different contexts as reflected in multiple second- and third-order learning process configurations that have been articulated over the past 40 years. This emergent learning perspective holds promise as a means of navigating through unfamiliar territory, as a way to interpret the significance of particular events in the experience, and as a means of evolving an unwelcome surprise into a more expansive perspective. Finally, as an aspect of leading ourselves, we considered some of the practices we could undertake to improve our abilities to engage and benefit from emergent learning.

Through strengthening our capacities as emergent learners through *successive iterations* of this process, we as individuals are better positioned to make progress on the following dimensions of our twenty-first-century learning agenda:

1. *The capacity to surmount fear, and to engage change and challenges with confidence in the midst of uncertainty and ambiguity*
   Each experience of engaging the unknown strengthens our confidence in a process that we come to recognize, itself, as familiar. Our anxiety is reduced and we are able to avoid the pitfalls of the Red Zone. Our tendencies to engage in self-blame, blaming others, and collusion with others in negatively focused alliances is also minimized as we recognize these patterns and their significance in the overall process. Our confidence is more likely to be anchored in our ability to manage our own experience and ourselves than in externally observable performance and others' assessments. It becomes easier to acknowledge that we do not know and/or that we are "not there yet." We are likely to use the resources of others more wisely, and because our energy and attention are not completely consumed by self-concern, we are more likely to be a resource to others. We recognize the value of being in the present, so we are likely to be more aware and more able to generate more insight for ourselves.

2. *Values-based leadership with "global intelligence," that is, values that endure in a time of flux and that serve the interests of the whole*
   We have taken a step toward recognizing our values because there is a contrast between what we now believe is important and what we recognize we tacitly believed earlier. In Maslow's terms, we shift from being dedicated exclusively to satisfying deficit needs of survival, belonging, and self-esteem to being open to learning and change in the direction of fulfilling our best possibilities. These values are now expressed in our behavior, not only in our talk. Richard Barrett (2010) has highlighted this even more clearly in his further development of Maslow's thinking as the movement from "'I' to 'we'" (elaborated below). But most of us have only just begun; we will have to engage more Red Zones as we directly connect with what it means to develop "global intelligence," but we are now more able to do so. We may have become more open to seeing connections between our own experience and self-interest, on the one hand, and the well-being of the planet and the rest of

its inhabitants, on the other. We are more able to acknowledge the hard realities "that we don't know we don't know."

3. *Widely practiced informed and responsible participation in communities and organizations—active engagement based on a sense of personal agency, creative thinking informed by diverse perspectives*

We will differ as to the extent to which we have been engaged in our communities and organizations beyond doing our particular job or looking after our particular family. However, we will have a greater sense of personal responsibility for our views of the world and enhanced confidence and abilities to act on what we believe to be important. We may also have developed our right-brain abilities to think beyond "what we know that we know" in order to generate creative alternatives. We will have recognized that our own perspective is not immutable, so we may be less likely to take our identity primarily from what we know. Having generated insights with others that led us to a new perspective, we may be more able to treat our ideas as our own constructions, or those of others that we choose to adopt, rather than given truth.

4. *Respect for cultural, gender, generational difference, and equitable world citizenship with differences appreciated as a potential source of innovation*

This same recognition of different perspectives may enable us to recognize that the viewpoints we hold come with a particular history; they are the ways that we all make sense out of our experiences and they help us navigate through our lives. For those reasons, they are valued. We might be more likely to treat cultural, gender, and generation differences with respect and curiosity, rather than with judgment. If we have connected with our own vulnerability through the experience of "not knowing," we may also be more likely to recognize other kinds of vulnerabilities. If we are more secure in ourselves, and more in touch with the rich possibilities we have yet to experience, we may be better able to engage differences and to appreciate them as a source of creativity, and be more open to the positive opportunities they may offer.

5. *The natural world cared for and recognized as our home, that is to say, repositioning of ourselves* within *the natural world*

If we reflect deeply on our experience of emergent learning, we may recognize how learning goes far beyond conscious thought. We may notice how thought, feeling, and sensation are intricately connected, and that we have a means through our intuition of accessing what we know that is not yet conscious. Over time, we may see a deeper significance in our patterns of emergent learning as representing the rhythm in living systems as they evolve. It may be more difficult to primarily objectify that natural world in an instrumental way. As we develop more strength to engage surprise and the unknown, we may also be more open to recognizing the harsh evidence of environmental devastation as a by-product of our civilization, and our way of life.

Emergent Learning and Leadership

While learning is inherently satisfying, the real significance of learning lies in how we act as a consequence, and particularly in the context of where our choices have the possibility of making a difference between destructive and enhancing prospects. John Macmurray (1957) stated it best: "All meaningful knowledge is for the sake of action, and all meaningful action is for the sake of friendship" (p. 15).

Emergent learning yields much more than content learning; it opens us to a different approach to engaging the world. For that reason, leadership flows very directly from emergent learning because we have not "left" the practical realities in order to learn—we have connected with them more fully. The value-perspective shift we have begun frames a different way of leading, as well as a different way of learning. The first part of the rest of this chapter examines *emergent learning for leadership*, that is, the nature of leadership made possible by the spirit and practice of emergent learning. In the second part of the chapter, we will consider the reverse—*leadership for emergent learning*, that is, what opportunity there is for us to take leadership in catalyzing emergent learning.

LEADERSHIP REIMAGINED

Expertise at emergent learning actually develops the same domain of competencies that scholar-practitioners have been calling for in leadership in our postconventional, postindustrial, postmodern era. Joseph Rost (1992) conducted a comprehensive review of leadership definitions from the beginning of the twentieth century to the 1990s. He noted that the typical themes over that time tended to be "the great man theory that was popular in the early part of this century, group theory in the 1930s and 1940s, trait theory in the 1940s and 1950s, behavior theory in the 1950s and 1960s, contingency/situational theory in the 1960s and 1970s, and excellence theory in the 1980s" (http://library.books24x7.com.ezproxy.royalroads.ca/

book/id_7399/viewer.asp?bookid=7399&chunkid=244334001).
He concluded that the vast array of definitions had one underlying
theme:

> Leadership as good management is a perfect summary of what leader-
> ship has meant in the industrial era. Good management is the apex
> of industrial organizations, the epitome of an industrial society, the
> consummate embodiment of an industrial culture. Industrialism is
> unthinkable without good management, and understanding leadership
> as good management makes perfect sense in an industrial economy.
> Thus, the twentieth-century school of leadership takes on a title, a
> name that fits naturally and easily. *Leadership as good management is
> the industrial paradigm of leadership.* (http://library.books24x7.com.
> ezproxy.royalroads.ca/book/id_7399/viewer.asp?bookid=7399&chu
> nkid=0223649039)

He observed that the Industrial Age leadership meanings "reveal a
fundamental understanding of leadership that is rational, management oriented, male, technocratic, quantitative, goal dominated, cost-
benefit driven, personalistic, hierarchical, short term, pragmatic, and
materialistic" (http://library.books24x7.com.ezproxy.royalroads.ca/
book/id_7399/viewer.asp?bookid=7399&chunkid=0223649039).

As we move beyond the Industrial Age, he proposed a postindustrial definition: "*Leadership is an influence relationship among leaders
and followers who intend real changes that reflect their mutual purposes.*" It communicates "four essential elements" of leadership.[1] First,
"influence" is "multidirectional" (anyone can be a leader) and it is
"noncoercive." Second, there are not only multiple followers but also
multiple leaders with unequal influence all actively involved. Third, all
intend to achieve substantive change. Fourth, leaders and followers
develop noncoercively "mutual purposes" that the "changes reflect"
(http://library.books24x7.com.ezproxy.royalroads.ca/book/id_
7399/viewer.asp?bookid=7399&chunkid=559712967).

Good management[2] is important and it is not enough for a
dynamic age that we are now encountering.

Converging Views: Leadership We Need Now

Since Rost published this work nearly 20 years ago, the rich literature on leadership has continued to point in a similar direction. It
emphasizes different aspects of the same orientation in noncoercive
relationships, mutual purpose, and the strong commitment to making a difference—*stepping beyond egocentrism, fostering leadership in*

others and genuinely caring for them, taking personal responsibility and accountability, and maintaining their integrity and authenticity through proactive reflection on their practice. The following exemplify the "conversation" that has been occurring about leadership in the past decade relevant to our twenty-first-century environment.

Jim Collins (2001), in *Good to Great: Why Some Companies Make the Leap and Others Don't,* was not looking for leadership to be a significant factor in outstanding performance by companies measured by sustained exemplary financial performance, but he found it anyway. He and his team called it "Level Five Leadership" distinguished by a "paradoxical mix of professional will and personal humility"—people who exhibit "compelling modesty" (p. 39). "They are ambitious . . . but ambitious first and foremost for the company, not themselves" (p. 39). They took "full responsibility" for poor performance but credited others with successes. They "set up their successors for even greater success in the next generation" (p. 39).

Joseph Raelin (2003), as an S. Knowles Chair at Northwestern University, suggested that there were four key qualities of leadership practice needed for a "chaotic" environment. He called it "leaderful practice" emphasizing a wide engagement of people. The first and "most revolutionary" is "that leadership is *concurrent,*" that is, "more than one leader can operate at a time, so leaders are willing and naturally share power with others" (p. 13). It is "*collective*"—leadership may emerge from multiple members of the community" (p. 15); it is "*collaborative*" (p. 15)—"everyone counts, every opinion and contribution sincerely matter" (p. 16); and it is "*compassionate*"—"each member of the community is valued" (p. 16).

Robert Quinn (2004), Margaret Elliott Tracy Collegiate Professor in Business Administration, Ross School of Business at University of Michigan, and his colleagues identified "fundamental state of leadership" they saw as needed for our stormy environment. Four qualities comprising this orientation are as follows:

- Other Focused: . . . transcending my ego, putting the common good and welfare of others first, increasing in authenticity, nurturing trust, and enriching the levels of connectivity in my networks;
- Internally Directed: . . . continually examining my hypocrisy and closing the gaps between my values and my behavior. . . . reaching higher levels of personal security and confidence;
- Externally Open: . . . moving outside my comfort zone, experimenting, seeking real feedback, adapting, and reaching

exponentially higher levels of discovery, awareness, competence, and vision;

- Purpose-Centered: . . . clarifying what I want to create. . . . committed and engaged, full of energy and holding an unwavering standard as I pursue a meaningful task. (p. 22)

Harrison Owen (2008) talked about "Wave Riders" as people in a variety of settings who "flow" with unfolding events.

> They do not command, they invite. They do not envision themselves at the apex of a hierarchy but rather in a circle with peers and colleagues. The source of their power comes from their own unique passion linked to responsibility, which attracts others to join a common venture. A venture which is at once productive and fulfilling for those who care to join. Wave Riders are leaders who enable individuals and organizations to fulfill their potential—with distinction. (p. 4)

Henry Mintzberg (2004), Cleghorn Professor of Management Studies at the Desautel Faculty of Management at McGill University, defined leadership as part of management.

> Leadership is not about making clever decisions and doing bigger deals, least of all for personal gain. It is about energizing other people to make good decisions and do better things. In other words, it is about helping to release positive energy that exists naturally within people. Effective leadership inspires more than empowers; it connects more than controls; it demonstrates more than decides. It does this by *engaging*—itself above all and consequently others.

> To do so, leadership has to be legitimate, meaning that it has to be not only accepted but also respected by those subjected to it. Above the will to manage must be the right to manage. . . . If democracy is to have real meaning, it must extend to the organizations where most of us function every day. (p. 143)

Bill George (2003), professor of management practice at Harvard Business School, described similar and complementary features of leadership needed in a business context that has been plagued with corruption and greed.

> Authentic leaders genuinely desire to serve others through their leadership. They are more interested in empowering the people they lead to make a difference than they are in power, money, or prestige for

themselves. They are as guided by qualities of the heart, by passion and compassion, as they are by qualities of the mind.

Authentic leaders use their natural abilities, but they also recognize their shortcomings and work hard to overcome them. They lead with purpose, meaning, and values. They build enduring relationships with people. Others follow them because they know where they stand. They are consistent and self-disciplined. When their principles are tested, they refuse to compromise. Authentic leaders are dedicated to developing themselves because they know that becoming a leader takes a lifetime of personal growth. (http://library.books24x7.com.ezproxy. royalroads.ca/book/id_9528/viewer.asp?bookid=9528&chunkid=42 6655370)

Developmental Frameworks of Leadership

Two of the commentaries described the evolution of leadership in a direction that appears critical in reversing the dangerous trajectory we are on at this historical moment and in building a positive future. We can recognize similarities between the two developmental schemas presented here, as well as differences. William Torbert's (2004) formulation of "transformational leadership" was formulated from a vantage point that highlighted single-, double-, and triple-loop learning as features. It speaks directly to the nexus of learning and leadership. Richard Barrett's (in press) "full spectrum leadership" is constructed from the standpoint of human values and fosters connections to the cultural context.

Transformational Leadership
William Torbert (2004) articulated a seven-stage developmental framework organized according to the "action-logics" or "strategy that so thoroughly informs our experience that we cannot see it" (p. 66). This first set we will readily recognize—"conventional action-logics appreciate for *similarity and stability*" (p. 93).

- "The *Opportunist* treats the physical or outside world territory of experience as the primary reality and concentrates on gaining control of things there. This action-logic views unilateral power as the only effectual type of power and works within a very short time horizon . . . grasping opportunities and firefighting emergencies . . ." (pp. 66, 67).
- "The *Diplomat* treats his or her own sensed performance territory as what really matters and concentrates on gaining self-control in

order to act effectively. . . . experiences referent power and current norms that such power generates most strongly. . . . focuses on routine tasks . . ." (p. 67).

- "The *Expert* treats the strategic territory of experience as the primary reality and concentrates on mastering his or her cognitive grasp of one or more disciplines" (p. 67).
- "The *Achiever* concentrates on making incremental single-loop changes in behavior to eventually reach planned results. Timely action occurs when 'I' successfully juggle the need for occasional immediate wins, observance of agreed-on deadlines, efficient work, and effective outcomes as judged by the market or other constituency" (p. 67).

The second set we find less familiar—"postconventional action-logics appreciate *differences* and participating in ongoing, creative *transformation* . . ." (p. 93). With the first "action-logic" in this set, "Individualist" is a "transition stage" that leads to the "Strategist" and the "Alchemist," "action-logics" matched to the dynamism of our context.

- "The *Individualist* is a bridge between two worlds. One is the pre-constituted, relatively stable and hierarchical understandings we grow into as children, as we learn how to function as members of a pre-constituted culture. The other is the emergent, relatively fluid and mutual understandings that highlight the power of responsible adults to lead their children, their subordinates, and their peers in transforming change" (p. 102).
- "The *Strategist* . . . is self-awareness in action. . . . intuitively recognizes all action as either facilitating or inhibiting ongoing transformational change . . . (p. 104). . . . will develop ways to detect disparities between mission and strategy, strategy and operations, operations and outcomes so that ineffective and unethical processes can be connected. . . . keen awareness of inequities in race, ethnicity, class, gender, and development among colleagues and subordinates. . . . expressions are spontaneous, combining genuineness and intensity" (p. 106).
- "The *Alchemist's* interest in the fresh quality of awareness is not as a means to something else, but as an end in itself" (p. 180). ". . . active attention to analogies across . . . scales of development . . . and . . . use of personal 'charism' . . . to challenge [others] in collaborative action inquiry. . . . stands in the tension of opposites, seeks to blend them. . . . treats time and events as symbolic, analogical, metaphorical (not merely linear, digital, literal)" (p. 182).

Torbert's schema locates emergent learning (double- and triple-loop learning) clearly in the postconventional stages of development. It also reveals something of a fusion of emergent learning qualities and leadership practice—emergent understanding, responsibility, self-awareness, intuitive recognition, active attention, holding a "tension of opposites," and fluency with metaphorical thought.

Full Spectrum Leadership
As reviewed in Chapter 2, in his work on "full spectrum consciousness," Richard Barrett (1998, in press) adapted and elaborated Abraham Maslow's hierarchy of needs into seven levels—survival, relationship, self-esteem, transformation, internal coherence, making a difference, and service. These levels are depicted in table 6.1 as they pertain to identity, leadership, and corporate sustainability. The first three levels (survival, relationship, and self-esteem) are deficit needs that, in being met, establish us as *viable* beings, or entities. We can accomplish viability largely by relying on single-loop learning, acquiring the necessary conventional and technical knowledge.

Barrett (in press) saw the fourth level, transformation, as comprising three stages: "personal mastery" ("managing, mastering or releasing our conscious or unconscious fears"); "individuation" ("uncovering [the] authentic self" beyond our conventional legacy); and "self-actualization" (finding our purpose) (p. 70). The emergent learning process represents an intense engagement in this fourth level of consciousness. It fosters a breakthrough from the world of form to the world of process—continuous change and learning. Barrett expanded Maslow's self-actualization into the four remaining levels of consciousness he described. The fifth level of consciousness is "internal coherence," which is associated with the development of a clear sense of personal purpose and vision. He characterized this level of consciousness as the adaptive requirement of any individual or entity being able "to bond with others to form group structures based on shared values" (p. 93). He emphasized that the associated ". . . ability to display and engender trust corresponds to the fifth level of personal consciousness. It requires that you develop a deep level of authenticity . . ." (p. 98). Together the fourth and fifth levels of consciousness accomplish overall internal coherence of the person or entity.

External coherence is accomplished through "making a difference" and "service"—levels six and seven, respectively. "Making a difference" is about fulfilling our purpose in action, which, inevitably, involves partnerships with others with complementary or similar purposes (p. 171). A feature value is "empathy," that is, "the ability

Table 6.1 Richard Barrett's Leading Others and Organizations

Stages of Evolution		Levels of Consciousness and Leadership Role	Description of Leading Others	Description of Leading Organizations
Stage 1: Team/Organizational Mastery	1	**Survival** *Crisis Director*	Focusing on the health, safety, and welfare of employees and the financial stability of the organization.	Focus on financial stability, shareholder value, and the health, safety, and of employees. Reduce control, caution, micromanagement, corruption, greed, and exploitation.
	2	**Relationships** *Relationship Manager*	Building employee and customer loyalty through direct open and caring communication.	Focus on employee and customer loyalty, employee recognition, and open communication. Reduce manipulation, blame, internal competition, internal politics and gender, or any form of discrimination.
	3	**Self-esteem** *Manager/Organizer*	Building employee pride through best practices and efficient systems and processes.	Focus on systems, processes, quality, productivity, branding, and professional growth. Reduce bureaucracy, hierarchy, elitism, silo-mentality, power and status seeking, and confusion.

(continued)

Table 6.1 Continued

Stages of Evolution	Levels of Consciousness and Leadership Role	Description of Leading Others	Description of Leading Organizations
Stage 2: Internal Cohesion	4 **Transformation** *Facilitator/Influencer*	Empowering employees to grow and develop personally and professionally by giving them responsible freedom.	Focus on adaptability, accountability, responsibility, empowerment, continuous learning, personal growth and development, and diversity.
	5 **Internal Cohesion** *Integrator/Inspirer*	Creating a cohesive team culture based on a shared mission/purpose and a shared set of values.	Develop shared vision and shared values, and focus on trust, integrity, honesty, fairness, openness and transparency, creativity, enthusiasm, and commitment.
Stage 3: External Cohesion	6 **Making a difference** *Mentor/Partner*	Cooperating with other teams across institutional boundaries for the overall benefit of the organization.	Cooperate with internal and external partners in strategic alliances and focus on employee fulfilment, coaching and mentoring, and becoming a servant-leader.
	7 **Service** *Wisdom/Visionary*	Building an ethical framework of standards to guide the team in its day-to-day operations.	Focus on social responsibility, sustainability and ethics, long-term perspective, human rights, social justice, compassion, humility, and forgiveness.

Source: From Barrett, R. (2010). *The New Leadership Paradigm: Leading Self, Leading Others, Leading an Organization, and Leading in Society.*

to imagine oneself in another's place, experience and understand their feelings and desires, and communicate this understanding to the other person" (p. 252). "Service" is "when making a difference becomes a way of life" (p. 172). A feature value is "compassion," that is, "The ability to imagine oneself in another's place, experience and understand their feelings and have an overwhelming desire to alleviate their suffering" (p. 252).

Barrett proposed that optimal living and leading need to be "full spectrum"; that is, *all levels of consciousness interplay to generate outcomes that simultaneously serve individual and social interests.* Our civilization has emphasized pursuit of individual "viability." Service to others is an act, not a way of life. Barrett's perspective represents more than that; he regards our capacity to function on any level as contributing to strength on all levels. In particular, he demonstrated that, counterintuitively in conventional culture, contributing to external cohesion—making a difference in and serving the wider community and world—creates practical benefits to our own viability.

Themes on the Role of Emergent Learning in Leadership

These commentaries about the nature of leadership in the postconventional era reflect a common direction, but with different emphases. One theme is that leadership goes beyond being self-serving to serving the common good. This theme that was articulated over three decades ago by Robert Greenleaf (1977) as the "servant-leader" described as "the natural feeling that one wants to serve, to serve *first*" (p. 27). The priority is the interests of the whole, not our own needs for material benefit or recognition. The second theme is that many of the aspects of the emergent learning process reflect the same qualities that scholar-practitioners highlighted as inherent in postconventional leadership (e.g., driven by personal purpose and responsibility, values-focused, shared leadership and collaboration, authenticity, and transparency). The third theme related to how the boundary between learning and leading becomes less distinct as we shift to *leadership focused on influencing processes* rather than primarily content. Emergent learning is both an entry point and a source of practices for postconventional leadership.

Our Leadership Context As a Complex Adaptive System

We began in Chapter 2 distinguishing conceptions and practices of learning framed in an Industrial Age modernist perspective and the conceptions and practices of learning based in a mechanistic meta-phor, from a postindustrial postmodern era—emergent, embodied, embedded—typified by the unfolding story of a contextual metaphor (Pepper, 1961). Emergence is a key feature of what has been called a complex adaptive system. A complex adaptive system consists of mul-tiple interacting agents. While machines are closed systems, complex adaptive or living systems are open systems in that they interact and evolve with their environments. Observers of the system as part of its environment can affect or change the observed system. Interactions in complex adaptive systems are nonlinear; that is, there is not a simple cause–effect relationship. Small causes can have big effects. The pat-terns that emerge are generated by the interactions, not a single source. Diversity of composite elements increases the systems' adaptability, as does a balance of order and chaos, or flux. A living system is self-organizing in that it can generate new and more complex configura-tions from simpler ones in order to adapt to a changing environment. Systems are nested within larger systems, each level of organization having the potential to effect change in the other, as illustrated in the Panarchy Model of Holling and Gunderson (2002) in Chapter 4.

In a complex adaptive environment, leadership becomes a very different proposition than it does in an environment imagined as a well-oiled machine. We see the recognition of a dynamic adaptive context in the above-mentioned conceptualizations of twenty-first-century leadership.

LEADING FROM WHERE WE ARE

William Bergquist (1993) observed, "during the postmodern era, great leadership takes place in a specific place and context, at a specific time in history" (p. 99). Location and timing are paramount since, as leaders, we are interacting agents within a dynamic system. We consider ourselves as leaders in four "locations" as we briefly glimpse at leadership in light of the challenges of our time in a complex and dynamic global context.

Leadership in Relationships

As parents, friends, teachers, colleagues, mentors, and "bosses," we find ourselves having unique opportunities to exercise influence that fosters others' constructive engagement in the world, as well as their emergent learning process. Erik Erikson (1950) spoke to the devel-opment of the foundational quality for engagement in the world, namely, "basic trust," which he believed depended "on the quality of the maternal relationship" (p. 249).

> This forms the basis in the child for a sense of identity which will later combine a sense of "being all right," of being oneself, and of becoming what other people trust one will become. There are, therefore, . . . few frustrations in either this or the following stages which the growing child cannot endure if the frustration leads to the ever-renewed experience of greater sameness and stronger continuity of development, toward the final integration of the individual life cycle with some meaningful wider belongingness. (p. 249)

We saw the critical role of self-esteem in meeting the unexpected and challenging differences and their impact in Red Zones. Parenting may be the most powerful leadership opportunity to foster strength in the face of daunting twenty-first-century challenges. Later, others will have opportunities to augment or diminish that ability to trust others and the processes of change. Especially important are those times when we carry institutional authority and have credibility with our employees, or our students, so that our affirmation releases them from an episode of self-doubt allowing them to then relax in the face of uncertainty, exist in a state of not knowing, and be open to the opportunity to explore and to learn. As such, we have the power in some moments to be gatekeepers—to open the door to learning, or to close it.

Providing timely affirmation is one of the many events in an emergent learning process that becomes more recognizable with an awareness of emergent learning patterns. Knowing the likely contours of the process would enable us to know what the learning significance of specific moments is for people; it would clarify our place in "their stories." We would recognize other opportunities we have to catalyze learning—when to offer encouragement, how to respond to challenges to our authority, when to provide resources, when to give "space," how to foster their awareness of their own process, and when and how to pose smart and useful questions. As leaders, we are what Barrett has identified as Facilitators/Influencers and possibly Integrator/Inspirers. This is the function of coaches, but it is also the work of any of us perceived by others as being "credible" authorities.

Another form of leadership in relationships is "modeling the way" (Kouzes and Posner, 2007) and "use of self" (Patwell and Seashore, 2006; Curran et al., 1995; Larrison, 2009). While these two forms of leadership are somewhat different, they both emphasize the authentic presentation of ourselves, the congruence between espoused values and our behavior, and the embodiment of stated beliefs. We know that most of our important learning moments begin in our experience and only tacit awareness through sensing and feeling. Morley Segal (1997) observed that leaders have opportunities to influence others, especially at certain key moments: as they join the organization; when they are confronted with some form of stress or conflict; and when they have some other form of growth experience in professional life. Kouzes and Posner (2007) identified the importance of modeling our values in action as we respond to critical incidents. It is at these particular times, in Red Zones, when, as leaders, our *behavior* communicates more powerfully than usual. Patwell and Seashore (2006) developed a coach training approach in order to foster "use of self"—attention to self and one's impact in action—for people working with others as coaches. Virginia Satir believed that "the person of the practitioner was the single most impactful aspect of the therapeutic relationship" (Satir, Banmen et al., 1991, cited in Larrison, 2009), an observation that has been expressed by others about other kinds of leadership roles.

Leadership as a Citizen: Local and Global

Postconventional leadership is exemplified in the exercise of influence generated from personal responsibility working with others who share common purposes. As such, leadership is not restricted to formal positions of authority. In working on twenty-first-century challenges, leadership can begin from wherever we are. Our location affects both our possibilities and our limitations, but both can evolve as we engage the challenge.

Social innovators and social entrepreneurs, both defined as making a *social* difference for the better, often initiate highly successful ventures designed to make a difference from outside existing organizations. We often build organizations around an action purpose. In examining the outstanding case of Bob Geldof and Live Aid in 1985 for Ethiopian famine relief, Frances Wesley (1991), the J. W. McConnell Chair in Social Innovation, observed that his success in raising money was aided by his "role as a rebel/outsider" and his insistence that it be based in a *temporary* organization.

> Temporary or self-designing systems represent an interesting option for the management of global issues. The dependence of such systems on loose networks, as opposed to traditional organizations for manpower and resources, allows such organizations to avoid some issues of territoriality and even regulation. It also allows advocates to tap in

to constituencies which are not drawn on by traditional organizations. (p. 1027)

Geldof and a network of leading popular musicians of the day raised over £60 million through a worldwide series of concerts broadcast by satellite television. But we do not have to be rock stars to accomplish audacious dreams. Craig Kielberger, at the age of 12, was gripped by a newspaper article that described the murder of a Pakistani boy his own age who was killed after speaking out against the child slavery he had endured. Beginning with his fellow students, Kielberger launched a network to free children around the world from child labor. His efforts led to the founding of Free the Children, "the largest network of children helping children through education," and it has "changed the lives of over one million children" (p. 11). Wesley and her colleagues (2006) described the miraculous accomplishments of many of these special individuals as they explored the nature of successful social innovation. And many of us can name our own exemplars in this field.

We all begin with no idea how things will transpire. Wesley et al. (2006) called the beginning, "getting to maybe."

> Their first tentative steps were not part of some grand strategy, but rather experiments they were compelled to try. Often to their own surprise, the response to their initiatives was not only positive, but also as if they catalyzed a chemical reaction: the system seemed to shift in ways they had never imagined. (p. 37)

As we bring the qualities of postconventional leadership—purpose, passion, partnership, possibility, and a project for the common good—into a wider pattern of relationship in a particular social context, energy is created and momentum becomes self-generating. Goldstein et al. (2008) examined the "mixed success" of massive aid programs and suggested that assumption of "the heroic leader" compromises the results. They point, as Wesley and her colleagues do, to an underpinning complexity perspective that holds more promise for framing a social entrepreneurship approach that will achieve the desired benefits for the investment of time and resources. In this perspective, social entrepreneurship is characterized as a network configuration, a flow of "*rich* information," "learning emerging from macro system interactivity," and "heterarchical cooperation" (pp. 13, 14). "The requisite complexity" in the social entrepreneurial context leads to "emergence," that is, "the arising of novel patterns, novel structures, and novel properties in complex systems" (p. 20) that cannot be accounted for by a single "cause." Thus our initial contribution becomes the opening line to a larger story with no pre-planned plot line and an ending that cannot be precisely predicted.

In Organizations as Positional Leaders

The principles of working mindfully with people in relationships and groups to enable others and to foster constructive change processes apply to us as organizational leaders, but we have a further opportunity to exercise positive influence toward change related to our twenty-first-century challenges. To this point, we have considered our own values, beliefs, and observable behavior as avenues through which we can exercise influence. As organizational leaders, we have greater opportunities to influence organizational culture, structure, and processes that in turn affect the possibilities for emergent learning.

One of Ken Wilber's valuable contributions was his four-quadrant model constructed in the intersection of the horizontal dimension from "interior" on the left and "exterior" on the right and the vertical dimension with "individual" on the top and "collective" on the bottom. The upper left quadrant concerns our individual consciousness and character, the upper right our individual behavior, the lower left our collective culture (e.g., organizational culture), and the lower right the collective structure (e.g., organizational structure). Wilber shows the intersection of person and system simultaneously with the visible (external) and invisible (internal) components. Richard Barrett, in his practice as an organizational consultant, observed that organizational leaders will have credibility *if*, in addition to being technically competent, they model their espoused values in action. If they achieve credibility, they will have opportunities to shape the culture (shared values) of the organization so that daily work life reflects the shared values. The culture and shared values then inform decisions concerning organizational structure and policies that express the culture. Optimal cohesion and productivity in a system is achieved when there is a values alignment between the individual and the organization (upper and lower left quadrants), when there is personal alignment between an individual's personal values and his or her behavior (upper two quadrants), when there is mission alignment between the person's work behavior and the social structures of the organization (upper and lower right quadrants), and when there is structural alignment between the organization's culture and structure (lower two quadrants). The quality of each quadrant affects, and is affected by, all others. An organizational culture can inspire members to recognize and practice personal values, and the influential people in an organization can engage members in processes that strengthen organizational culture and align structures.

Edgar Schein (1995b) was one of the first scholars to highlight the significance of organizational culture as part of a positional leader's responsibility, suggesting that a role of the leader is as *"culture manager."* He suggested a definition: *"a pattern of basic assumptions— invented, discovered, or developed by a given group as it learns to cope with its problems of external adaptation and internal integration—that has worked well enough to be considered valid and, therefore, to be taught to new members as the correct way to perceive, think, and feel in relation to those problems"* (p. 9). Schein fostered an appreciation of the importance and challenge of understanding and changing organizational culture; he pointed out the constraints organizational culture can have on the implementation of strategy, the success of mergers and acquisitions, and organizational innovations.

Since Schein's initial work 25 years ago, the pace of change in the world has continued to accelerate. Organizational cultures and structures that worked in the twentieth century cannot adapt quickly enough to our twenty-first-century pace. Fashioned for a more predictable industrial culture, most of our organizations lack the agility needed to meet external demands and, at the same time, provide optimal workplace conditions that develop and benefit from the creative potential of their employees. If we consider the typical organizational workplace as a context for emergent learning, we find adequate challenge of the unexpected, but we do not have the conditions that would enable us to evolve Red Zones into learning, exploration, and innovation. The more the world speeds up, the less time we have to reflect on our experience ourselves or with others and create structures and processes effective in responses to the demands of a dynamic environment. Contrary to the models of leadership considered in this chapter, many current organizational cultures call for a few individual decision makers at the apex of a hierarchy far beyond where the product of the organization are delivered, and where the practical demands of the environment are palpable. The challenge then is to invite double-loop learning by individuals, by organizational leaders in particular, and for the organization as a whole to confront fundamental assumptions that are no longer relevant in the current environment. In Chapter 1 we noted that Emery and Trist (1965) foresaw the changing environment long ago, and in response, proposed a fundamental change in the way we are organized; they called it participative design, informed by the specifications of complex adaptive systems. Drawing on the work of Fred Emery, Eric Trist, and Merrelyn Emery, Ronald Purser and Steven Cabana (1998) described the self-managing organization as having six "critical human requirements" (p. 32): "autonomy and discretion" (p. 32), "opportunity to learn and continue learning on the job," "optimal level of variety," "need for social support and an opportunity to exchange help and respect," "sense of meaningful contribution," and "prospects for a desirable future" (p. 33). They noted that in addition to the capacity for partnerships in a global economy, organizations face a "creativity imperative" (p. 34).

> In a world where the future is becoming increasingly uncertain and more complex, organizations that can foster creativity will have an easier time reinventing themselves as shifting discontinuities demand new responses, new thinking, new strategies, and new products. . . . Organizational creativity cannot be forced or engineered into systems—we can't order people to be creative or simply pull a tool off the shelf for people to use, expecting creativity to flow on demand. Instead, self-managing organizations are designed in ways that allow *social creativity* to flourish. Organizing for social creativity means developing work environments that promote creative collaboration and interactive learning. (pp. 34, 35)

Whether or not we embrace fully self-managing organizations, the direction for change is toward authority and responsibility that is more widely distributed. Joseph Raelin (2003) suggested some similar workplace qualities for leaderful organizations: "task—high discretion," "decisions—autonomous," "sphere of activity—beyond the job," "commitment—intrinsic," and "culture—trust oriented" (p. 58). These are all features of the workplace that foster emergent learning.

On our twenty-first-century learning agenda is the challenge to generate responsible participation. The capacity for organizations to function effectively and adaptively is also a critical condition for tackling the rest of our agenda. For example, C. S. Holling and his Resilience Network colleagues observed that the organizations established to foster action on the environment became inflexible and ineffective over time, therefore constraining the work on the environmental agenda.

Finally, as noted in Chapter 2, Robert Kegan (1994) reminded us that our environments have a hidden curriculum. We take lessons from our workplace about our capacity to accomplish goals together, whether it is a sense of efficacy or defeat, hope or despair, trust or mistrust in others, and so on. What we learn there has far-reaching implications for our approach to twenty-first-century challenges.

Marvin Weisbord (2004) reviewed the evolution of organizational forms and organizational change in the twentieth century and concluded with this observation, among others:

> Democracy is a rough way to live. With all its flaws, I think it beats the alternatives. I do not wish to have someone else, no matter how well educated, well-intentioned, wealthy, or wise, decide unilaterally what's best for me. Unless we are deeply involved in our work, we cannot feel good about ourselves. Unless we work with others toward valued goals, we cannot infuse hope and aspiration into our lives. Unless we treat one another as equals, we cannot find dignity, meaning, and community in work. Unless we make our own mistakes, and learn to forgive ourselves, we cannot learn at all. Unless we cooperate, we cannot survive. (p. 482)

Leadership in Educational Settings

The work of this book began with a study of graduate students learning in what we can now call education for leadership in complex adaptive systems; it generated the detailed "inside-out" description of the emergent learning process that we have been examining. The context for the study was a graduate course that Dr. Virginia Griffin had the courage and insight to structure in a way that required learners to approach the course with autonomy and self-direction, cooperation and collaboration, awareness of one's own experience as it unfolded, and genuine engagement with relevant knowledge. It provided the experience of an adaptive democracy in the classroom, recognizing that we do not learn new ways of being and acting paradigmatically without living them, no matter how compelling the ideas. We do not know their real meaning unless we have an experience that provides us with a context of meaning for them. We cannot *think* our way into a radically new perspective; we need to have an embodied experience of, at minimum, a replica of that new way of being and acting. As educators, we have an opportunity to provide settings that are structured to foster emergent learning expertise. Over the past 30 years, a facilitative process-oriented approach to education has become more widely practiced and a more frequent focus in the literature. This new form of educational practice is especially relevant for education and professional development related to practical engagement in social realities.[3] There has been an explosion of professional and personal development programs and many formal educational innovations that address the development of emergent learning expertise and/or some of the practices discussed in Chapter 5. It is not possible in this limited space to address adequately the range of innovations exemplified in a recent publication by Edward Taylor, Jack Mezirow, and their colleagues (2009). However, there are some educational design and leadership principles that characterized many of these approaches.

The orientation to leadership in educational settings that fosters emergent learning is similar to the approach of positional leaders articulated earlier in this chapter. It means being conscious of, and enacting, one's role as a positional and perceived authority in a way that transfers authority, responsibility, and accountability for learning to learners as a model for organizational leadership that distributes authority, responsibility, and accountability in an organization. As such, the teacher is a critical feature of learners' stories of developmental change that runs "under" the educational business of the day. I approach teaching continuously with questions about the meaning of the educational moment for learners, and who I am in the story they are constructing. Major gains in the practice of effective leadership frequently require quantum changes in understanding the challenge, and reframing one's position as a leader. The opportunity to model distributed authority and collaboration is also important. The role of educators in this form of education is beautifully summarized by Berger (2004):

> Although finding the edge sometimes requires a guide and staying there requires support, ultimately the way through the confusion is to grow, and only the person at the edge can do that growing. This means (as I see it) that a transformative teacher has the following three major responsibilities to his or her students:
> 1. helping students find and recognize the edge,
> 2. being good company at the edge, and
> 3. helping to build firm ground in a new place. (pp. 345–346)

Other principles that govern how education is designed and delivered that are critical to fostering emergent learning include "primacy of practice" (practical experience as the ground for learning); "systemic perspective"; "process orientation"; "learning-as-process"; and "reflexivity" (M. Taylor et al., 2002). Edward Taylor (2009) observed common elements—"individual experience, critical reflection, and dialogue"—in his review of "transformative learning" and more recently added themes of "a holistic orientation, awareness of context, and an authentic practice" as "core elements" (p. 4). He also noted the increasing recognition of the importance of affect as part of reflection and learning. Assessment for emergent learning is characterized by a significant responsibility by the learner, and an integration of theory and practice in demonstrating competency.

Such programs require intensive format teaching and learning, that is, extended periods of contact time of the cohort and instructors in order to integrate action, reflection, and conceptualizing into the practice. Educational and professional development programs that incorporate any of the practices outlined in Chapter 5 will be contributing to expertise in emergent learning, but it also requires structuring of the learning setting to replicate a complex adaptive system. This includes a venue for practice, the space for reflection, relationships to support reflective dialogue, a rich source of relevant conceptual material, a process of self-assessment incorporating genuine feedback from others, and the "container" for the experience provided by a courageous, knowledgeable, facilitative leader who models the practice with integrity. Finally, teaching teams afford a critical opportunity to model effective leadership as collaborative, the origin of knowledge from multiple sources, and, even on occasion, differing perspectives among people in authority as valuable in a complex world.

This form of education is becoming more common, but it is as much a shift of values-perspective for educational institutions as it is for individuals. Most schools, colleges, and universities are organized for a twentieth-century industrial culture. Knowledge is a commodity to be transferred from one who possesses it to another who does not. We (M. Taylor et al., 2002) examined some of the assumptions about learning that affect how the educational context is designed and managed, including qualifications for faculty appointments that require practical experience integrated with theoretical accomplishments, scheduling of class time for intensive format teaching and learning, flexible facilities to accommodate multiple configurations for learning, and admissions requirements that address experience as well as academic performance. Each of these specific issues can be resolved practically, but what is more challenging is the underlying institutional value-perspective that generates its current practices and is taken for granted by institutional leaders.

> The paradigmatic differences in this new educational practice are often opaque to those who approach the educational task from a conventional university standpoint. . . . The risk is always that the prevailing assumptions of the academy will obscure, obliterate and, inadvertently, overwhelm or disaggregate core elements of the new approach. . . . In its favour is that the global changes now occurring demand approaches

to leadership that are profoundly different from those that have served well in the past. While the university is often regarded as out of touch with the "real world," it is now being challenged, along with other institutions in our culture. (p. 366)

Part of educational leadership for a dynamic and complex world is to work at the paradigmatic interface with an institutional setting that was designed for a more predictable and stable context.

EPILOGUE

We are living in a time between "stories"—in the transition space between radically different epochs. In order to survive and thrive in the future, we will need to learn and lead in a fundamentally new way. A value-perspective that provided the foundation for success in the modern era has not proven adequate to the current turbulent global context. In fact, force fitting it to our current environment appears to make things worse. A technical imagination applied to nontechnical challenges as problem-solving does not foster the resilience in people and living systems, nor does it generate constructive, enduring solutions needed in our historical moment. Here, by "solution" is meant "the action of releasing or setting free; deliverance, release" (*Oxford English Dictionary*), rather than an ending from a quick answer. The central theme of this book is to explore the significance and practical value of moving forward in *an approach of not knowing* that is, by necessity, our experience between stories.

Thomas Homer-Dixon (2006) suggested that we "cultivate a prospective mind":

> We can't hope to preserve at least some of what we hold dear—unless we're comfortable with change, surprise, and the essential transience of things, and unless we are open to radically new ways of thinking about our world and about the way we should lead our lives. We need to exercise our imaginations so that we can challenge the unchallengeable and conceive the unconceivable. Hunkering down, denying what's happening around us, and refusing to countenance anything more than incremental adjustments to our course are just about the worst things we can do. These behaviours increase our rigidity. . . . (p. 282)

Homer-Dixon defined "prospective mind" as one that "aggressively engages this new world of uncertainty and risk. A prospective mind recognizes how little we understand, and how we control even less" (p. 28). He concluded, "it's time we turned passengers into drivers" (p. 30).

I invite us to take Homer-Dixon's challenge a step further, and to reconsider our vantage point. Instead of being a conscious mind focusing primarily on an external problem with the intent of acquiring knowledge to fix it, we should engage our environment as an *embodied* consciousness having turned "inward" first to access not only our thoughts but also our senses, emotions, and intuition that arise as we are *embedded* in our context with a major challenge so that we have the possibility of developing not only knowledge but also *wisdom* with which to address it. In doing so we accept *not knowing* and engaging in a learning process that we are confident will illuminate best prospects in relationship to others for exercising our influence that is leading optimally. Possibly it would be helpful to think of ourselves as *proactive passengers*, rather than "drivers" (a term that may seduce us back into thinking we stand out from others in that we have the answers).

We return again to Labouvie-Vief's (1990) observation in Chapter 5 about "the adaptive significance and the heuristic importance of the inward turn" (p. 72):

> The mature individual . . . realizes that *subjective* and communal are a necessary part of one's endeavours to be objective. Still, they do not remain a goal in themselves. Rather, they become a vantage point from which the individual searches for a new concept of objectivity—however, no longer one that is rooted in a "God's-eye-view" of certainty but one that is more open, tentative, and human-sized. (p. 72) [italics added]

For those of us who have been socialized in Western cultures, the "inward turn" may be one of our greatest hurdles to overcome. Among the ways that we diminish the value of going "inside" is the assumption it is a form of self-preoccupation, egocentrism, and self-indulgence, that it distracts us from responsible service to others, our community, and our workplace. It is seen as antithetical to social participation—a form of selfishness. Certainly, self-attention can be narcissistic, but we need a more refined consideration of "inside," distinguishing "inside-in" that is a destination from "inside-out" that is a process in order to engage beyond ourselves. Paradoxically,[4] "inside-out" process is a means of *connecting*, not disconnecting. It is a way of bringing our whole selves to a task. The "inside-out" perspective that reveals not only our thought patterns in learning but also the messages from our senses and our emotional landscape illuminates the critical role of right-brain thinking—intuition and insight. It also reveals the patterns of relationship integral to learning and enables us to identify significant others critical to our endeavor. Also, paradoxically, what may seem chaotic from the "outside" assembles into an ordered *process* when perceived from "inside-out." It is a structure of experience that appears to be as much a feature of a "self-organizing" universe as any other emergent evolutionary process from the cellular level on through more complex forms of living systems (Maturana & Varela, 1987).

Typically, we think of wisdom as something that comes with age for at least some of us. In the face of our twenty-first-century challenges, catalyzing the development of wisdom seems crucial. For 40 years at least, we have been assembling the "tools" and constructs we need to navigate a turbulent world more wisely. We have the possibility of shifting our perspective, changing our approach to acting in the world, as well as reshaping the cultures, structures, and processes of the social systems we inhabit so as to create the world we desire. This will involve living, learning, and leading in ways that now seem strange. Our first task may be to make the extraordinary ordinary.

Notes

Introduction

1. dian marino, who insisted that her name be spelled without capital letters, was a dear friend and colleague through the inception of this work, which began when we were students at the Ontario Institute for Studies in Education of the University of Toronto, and continued as a fellow traveler while she was a Professor in Environmental Studies at York University in Toronto, until her untimely death in 1993. dian was also a talented artist with a strong social consciousness; this quote is the title of one of her serigraphs.
2. Norman White (1981) in *The Health Conundrum: Explorations in Health Studies* states, "The biomedical strategy has been implemented, earnestly and energetically, in many jurisdictions. Its results do not correspond to our expectations. Virtually, without exception, morbidity measures and costs do not fall—they rise" (p. 6).

Chapter 1

1. Bureau of Labor Statistics, Economic News, July 2, 2009. http://www.bls.gov
2. CNNMoney.com, June 5, 2008, 2:09 p.m. One million housing foreclosures. http://money.cnn.com/2008/06/05/news/economy/foreclosure/?postversion=2008060514
3. *New York Times*, July 11, 2008. U.S. weighs takeover of two mortgage giants. http://www.nytimes.com/2008/07/11/business/11fannie.html
4. *Wall Street Journal*, September 16, 2008. Deal and deal makers, AIG bailout. http://online.wsj.com/article/SB122156561931242905.html
5. *New York Times*, September 15, 2008. Lehman files for bankruptcy. http://www.nytimes.com/2008/09/15/business/15lehman.html
6. CNNMoney.com, September 29, 2008, 9:10 p.m. DOW: Biggest single-day point loss ever. http://money.cnn.com/2008/09/29/markets/markets_newyork/index.htm?cnn=yes
7. CNNMoney.com, March 6, 2009, 6:32 p.m. DOW hits 6469.95. http://money.cnn.com/2009/03/06/markets/markets_newyork/index.htm

8. National Values Assessment is a values survey format that originated with Richard Barrett and administered through the Barrett Values Centre. Further information can be found at www.valuescentre.com.

9. In surveys conducted by Environics Research and Communication (Adams, 2003) in response to the question "The father must be master in his own house," the percentage of respondents agreeing were as follows: Sweden 10%, Germany and Canada 18%, France 26%, United Kingdom and Spain 29%, Italy 34%, Mexico 43%, and the United States 52%. (In Canada, the percentage of respondents agreeing has climbed to 24%, a change that is associated with immigration, especially Asian.

10. The Global Commission on International Migration, consisting of 19 members from diverse regions of the world, was established in 2003 with the encouragement of then UN Secretary-General Kofi Annan, with the support of the governments of Switzerland, Sweden, the Netherlands, United Kingdom, Norway, Australia, and Germany in addition to the MacArthur Foundation, Ford Foundation, and World Bank.

11. Countries receiving the most migrants in 2000 were the United States (20% or 35 million of the total), the Russian Federation (7.6% or 13.3 million), Germany (4.2% or 7.3 million), Ukraine (4.0% or 6.9 million), and India (3.6% or 6.3 million). The leading sources of migration were what the GCIM called the Chinese diaspora (35 million), the Indian diaspora (20 million), and the Filipino diaspora (7 million).

12. These were findings in an IPSOS Public Affairs poll conducted between May 1 and May 22, 2006, for Associated Press International.

13. Homer-Dixon (2006) identified "high-quality" energy as highly concentrated energy, such as in gasoline, and "low-quality" energy as diffuse energy, such as is contained in the ground. The former can power vehicles while the latter may be used for heating homes.

14. Spariosu M. (2004) refers to "global intelligence" as "work[ing] toward what is in the best interest of and will benefit human beings and all life on the planet" (p. 6).

CHAPTER 2

1. Jack Mezirow (1990) spoke of "meaning perspective . . . [or] the structure of cultural assumptions within which new experience is assimilated to—and transformed by—one's past experience" (p. 101). Beck and Cowan (1996), whose schema developed out of Clare Graves's (1970) "levels of existence," coined the term "ᵛMEME" (a psychocultural equivalent to the biochemical gene in DNA), which "reflects a worldview, a valuing system, a level of psychological existence, a belief structure, and organizing principle, a way of thinking or a mode of adjustment . . . [that among other things] *impacts upon all life choices* as

a decision-making framework" (p. 4). Formulations of value-perspective transformation fostered by forms of education have been described by William Perry (1999) as "stages of intellectual and ethical development" and by Paulo Freire (2000) as "levels of consciousness." Those schemas explicitly connected to life stages through adulthood began with Erik Erikson (1950) and include Daniel Levinson and Roger Gould. Carol Gilligan (1982) highlighted differences in value-perspectives of women from those described by theorists whose developmental stages described primarily the journey of men through the life span. Belenky et al. (1986) documented among women different perspectives on knowing from "received knowledge" to "connected knowledge." Other development stage schemas not specifically linked to age cohorts include Jane Loevinger's (Loevinger and Blasi, 1976) stages of ego development, James Fowler's (1981) faith orientations, William Torbert's (2004) "developmental stages" among organizational leaders, and Richard Barrett's (1998) levels of human consciousness based on Abraham Maslow's (1954) hierarchy of needs.

CHAPTER 3

1. The participants in the initial study, six women and two men, ranged in age from 25 to 50 years and volunteered to be interviewed. Among them were a training officer and consultant in government, a professor of social work, a counselor and group worker, a dietetic nutritionist, a high school teacher in Theatre Arts and English, an adult educator in a university extension department, a consultant in the provincial education ministry, and a reference librarian. Learners' progress through the sequence varied in pace, and not all learners moved through the entire sequence. One participant did not progress past the first phase of the process and a further four were in the second phase of the process during the period in which the interviews were conducted. The learners were participants in a graduate course entitled "Basic Processes of Facilitating Adult Learning" instructed by Dr. Virginia Griffin. The course was designed in every respect to place the participants in the "driver's seat" in designing, implementing, and assessing their own learning and, additionally, invited them to participate collaboratively in designing the third to thirteenth of the course sessions.

2. In their study of organizations and leadership across 62 countries, House et al. (2004) found that power distance ("The degree to which members of a collective expect power to be distributed equally" [p. 30]) in organizations prevailed in every culture in the study though they also found that "[s]ocietal Power Distance practice is negatively and significantly correlated to all measures of economic health (e.g., economic prosperity, government support for prosperity, societal support for competitiveness, world competitiveness index)" (p. 38).

3. Unconscious incompetence is the first of four levels of competency that has become well known in the domain of training and education for the practical world. They are:

    1. unconscious incompetence, where a person is unaware that he does not know;
    2. conscious incompetence, where she knows that she does not know;
    3. conscious competence, where he knows that he knows and is aware how he is applying the knowledge; and
    4. unconscious competence, where she is unaware that she knows and unaware how she is applying the knowledge.

CHAPTER 4

1. "ᵛMEMEs" stands for "value memes" by which Beck and Cowan (1996) mean "organizing principles" or "the amino acids of our psycho-social DNA [that] act as the magnetic force which binds memes and other kinds of ideas in cohesive packages of thought" (p. 31). They are "initially shaped in each human mind, ᵛMEMEs are so vital they reach across whole groups of people and begin to structure mindsets on their own" (pp. 31, 32).

CHAPTER 5

1. Eleanor Roosevelt quote http://www.quotationspage.com/quote/35592.html
2. By 2006, 16.5 million Americans practiced yoga, as reported in Winston, K. (2006), *In Search of Wholeness*, www.publishersweekly.com, retrieved May 28, 2009.
3. GoPubMed reported the number of publications about Yoga increased from 30 in 1999 to 136 in 2009 http://www.gopubmed.com/web/gopubmed/WEB1lOWEB10O00h00100090000100h001000j100200010, and those on meditation increased from 56 in 1999 to 197 in 2009 http://www.gopubmed.com/web/gopubmed/WEB1lOWEB10O00h00100090000100h001000j100200010, retrieved May 28, 2009.
4. Progoff cited this passage from Jung, C. (1928) *Two essays on analytical psychology*, H. Baynes and C. Baynes (trans.). NY: Dodd, Mead.
5. "Right brain" is shorthand for the hemisphere that governs the non-dominant hand; for left-handed people it would be left-brain thinking.
6. The term "collaborative inquiry" is often associated with formal research process, but here it is meant to emphasize an open-ended process of exploration by individual and group learning.

CHAPTER 6

1. Joseph Rost (1992) elaborated "four essential elements" of his definition as follows:

    1. "The relationship is based on influence.
    a. The influence relationship is multidirectional.
    b. The influence behaviors are noncoercive.
    2. Leaders and followers are the people in this relationship.
    a. The followers are active.
    b. There must be more than one follower, and there is typically more than one leader in the relationship.
    c. The relationship is inherently unequal because the influence patterns are unequal.
    3. Leaders and followers intend real changes.
    a. *Intend* means that the leaders and followers purposefully desire certain changes.
    b. *Real* means that the changes the leaders and followers intend must be substantive and transforming.
    c. Leaders and followers do not have to produce changes in order for leadership to occur. They intend changes in the present; the changes take place in the future if they take place at all.
    d. Leaders and followers intend several changes at once.
    4. Leaders and followers develop mutual purposes.
    a. The mutuality of these purposes is forged in the noncoercive influence relationship.
    b. Leaders and followers develop purposes, not goals.
    c. The intended changes reflect, not realize, their purposes.
    d. The mutual purposes become common purposes."
    (http://library.books24x7.com.ezproxy.royalroads.ca/book/id_7399/viewer.asp?bookid=7399&chunkid=559712967)

2. Henry Mintzberg (2004) defined leadership within "managing" but made the same argument: "Management without leadership is sterile; leadership without management is disconnected and encourages 'hubris.'" (p. 4).
3. I have not addressed elementary and high school education here. I recognize, however, the extreme importance of supporting educational initiatives to reexamine basic design practices with a view to enhancing and developing approaches to fostering emergent learning at an early age.
4. To the extent that something is paradoxical to us is the extent to which we are using a mindset that did not arise from the world we are experiencing. This is the nature of living "between stories."

References

Ackoff, R. (1979). The future of operational research in the past. *Journal of Operational Research Society, 30*(2), 93–104.

Adams, M. (2003). *Fire and ice: The United States, Canada, and the myth of converging values.* Toronto: Penguin Canada.

———. (2006). Fire and Ice: The United States, Canada, and the Myth of Converging Values: Focus on Work and Leadership. Presentation to the 11th Annual Values and Leadership Conference, 5 October, Victoria, BC.

———. (2007a). *Unlikely utopia: The surprising triumph of Canadian pluralism.* Toronto: Penguin Canada.

———. (2007b). The Future of Leadership. Presentation to the Human Resource Professional Association of Ontario, 10 January, Toronto.

Allport, G. (1962). Psychological models for guidance. *Harvard Educational Review, 32,* 373–381.

Appadurai, A. (2006). *Fear of small numbers: An essay on the geography of anger.* Durham, NC: Duke University Press.

Argyris, C., and D. Schön. (1974). *Theory in practice: Increasing professional effectiveness.* San Francisco: Jossey-Bass.

Baltes, P., and J. Smith. (2008). Fascination with wisdom: Its nature, ontogeny, and function. *Perspectives on Psychological Science, 3,* 56–64.

Bar-On, R. (1997). *Bar-On emotional quotient inventory: Technical manual.* Toronto: Multi-Health Systems.

Barrett, M. (1994). Communication, excerpt from convocation address on the occasion of having been conferred LL.D., *honoris causa.* November, Concordia University, Montréal, QC.

Barrett, R. (1998). *Liberating the corporate soul: Building a visionary organization.* Boston: Butterworth-Heinemann.

———. (2006). *Building a values-driven organization: A whole system approach to cultural transformation.* Boston: Butterworth-Heinemann.

———. (in press). *The new leadership paradigm: Leading self, leading others, leading an organization, and leading in society.*

Barrett, W., and D. Suzuki. (1996). *Zen Buddhism: Selected writings for D. T. Suzuki.* New York: Doubleday.

Bateson, G. (1972). *Steps to an ecology of the mind,* Chicago: Chicago University Press.

Bateson, G., and M. Bateson. (1987). *Angels fear: Towards an epistemology of the sacred.* New York: Macmillan.

Beck, D., and C. Cowan. (1996). *Spiral dynamics: Mastering values, leadership and change*. Malden, MA: Blackwell Publishing.

Beckhard, R., and W. Pritchard. (1992). *Changing the essence: The art of creating and leading fundamental change in organizations*. San Francisco: Jossey-Bass.

Belenky, M., B. Clinchy, N. Goldberger, and J. Tarule. (1986). *Women's ways of knowing: The development of self, voice and mind*. New York: Basic Books.

Bennis, W., and H. Shepard. (2009). A theory of group development. In W. Burke, D. Lake, and J. Paine (eds.), *Organization change: A comprehensive reader*. San Francisco: Jossey-Bass, pp. 441–465.

Berger, J. (2004). Dancing on the threshold of meaning: Recognizing and understanding the growing edge. *Journal of Transformative Education*, 2(4), 336–351.

Berger, P., and T. Luckmann. (1966). *The social construction of reality*. New York: Doubleday.

Bergquist, W. (1993). *The postmodern organization: Mastering the art of irreversible change*. San Francisco: Jossey-Bass.

Bion, W. (1961). *Experiences in groups, and other papers*. London: Tavistock Institute.

Birren, J., and L. Fisher. (1990). Elements of wisdom: Overview and integration. In R. Sternberg (ed.), *Wisdom: Its nature, origins and development*. New York: Cambridge University Press, pp. 317–324.

Blake, W. http://thinkexist.com/quotation/the_eye_altering-alters/175345.html.

Bohm, D. (1996). *On dialogue*. New York: Routledge.

Bowes, B. (2007/2008). The business case for workplace diversity. *CMA Management, 81*(8), 14–16.

Boyatzis, R. (2009). Competencies as a behavioural approach to emotional intelligence. *Journal of Management Development, 28*(9), 749–770.

Boyatzis, R. E., and D. Goleman. (1996). *Emotional competency inventory*. Boston: The Hay Group.

Branden, N. (1994). *Six pillars of self-esteem*. New York: Bantam.

Bridges, W. (2004). *Transitions: Making sense of life's changes*. (2nd edition) Cambridge, MA: Da Capo Press.

Brill, A. (trans. and ed.) (1995). *The basic writings of Sigmund Freud*. New York: The Modern Library.

Brown, K., R. Ryan, and J. Creswell. (2007). Mindfulness: Theoretical foundations and evidence for salutary effects. *Psychological Inquiry, 18*(4), 211–237.

Buber, M. (1970). *I and thou*. Walter Kaufmann (trans.), New York: Touchstone.

Burke, W. (2008). *Organizational change: Theory and practice*. Thousand Oaks, CA: Sage Publications.

Buunk, A., and F. Gibbons. (2007). Social comparison: The end of a theory and emergence of a field. *Organization Behavior and Human Decision Processes, 102*, 3–21.

Buunk, B., A. Nauta, and E. Molleman. (2005). In search of the true group animal: The effects of affiliation orientation and social comparison orientation upon group satisfaction. *European Journal of Personality, 19,* 69–81.

Capra, F. (2002). *The hidden connections: Integrating the biological, cognitive and social dimensions of life into a science of sustainability.* New York: Doubleday.

Carson, S., and E. Langer. (2006). Mindfulness and self-acceptance. *Journal of Rational-Emotive & Cognitive Behavior Therapy, 24*(1), 29–43.

Cartwright, D. (2008). Achieving change in people: Some applications of group dynamics theory. *Group Facilitation: A Research and Applications Journal, 9,* 59–65.

Coffman, P. (1989). Inclusive language as a means of resisting hegemony in theological education: A phenomenology of transformation and empowerment of persons in adult higher education. Unpublished doctoral dissertation, Northern Illinois University, Dekalb, IL.

Collins, J. (2001). *Good to great: Why some companies make the leap and others don't.* New York: Harper Collins.

Courtney, B., S. Merriam, and P. Reeves. (1996). The centrality of meaning-making in transformative learning: How HIV-positive adults make sense of their lives. 37th Annual Adult Education Research Conference. (pp. 73–78). May, Tampa, FL: University of South Florida.

Csíkszentmihályi, M. (1990). *Flow: The psychology of optimal experience.* New York: Harper & Row.

———. (1992). Introduction. In M. Csíkszentmihályi and I. Csíkszentmihályi (eds.), *Optimal experience: Psychological studies of flow in experience.* New York: Cambridge University Press.

Csíkszentmihályi, M., and R. Rathunde. (1990). The psychology of wisdom: An evolutionary approach. In R. Sternberg (ed.), *Wisdom: Its nature, origins and development.* New York: Cambridge University Press, p. 25–51.

Cuervo-Cazurra, A., and L. Dau. (2009). Promarket reforms and firm profitability in developing countries. *Academy of Management Journal, 52*(6), 1348–1368.

Curran, K., C. Seashore, and M. Welp. (1995). Self as an Instrument of Change. Paper presented to the Organization Development Network National Conference, 17 November, Seattle, WA.

d'Aquino, T. (1996). Globalization, Social Progress, Democratic Development and Human Rights: The Responsibility of a Multinational Corporation. Vital Speeches of the Day; 12/01/96, 63(4), p. 107, 4pA. Presentation to the Academy of International Business Annual Meeting, 27 September, Banff, AB. Retrieved May 18, 2008 from http://web.ebscohost.com.ezproxy.royalroads.ca/ehost/pdf?vid=5&hid=115&sid=60fccba9-62a6-417a-a2b7-1eea29621b6a%40sessionmgr107.

de Guerre, D. (2001). Industrial and Organizational Management Are Gone. Presentation on the Human Systems Intervention MA degree program. Concordia University: Montréal, QC.

de Guerre, D., and M. Taylor. (2004). Sustainable learning organization development: Participative design and organizational coaching.

International Journal of Knowledge, Culture and Change Management.
4, 513–520.

Denis, M. (1979). Toward the development of a theory of intuitive learning in adults based on a descriptive analysis. Thesis, Ontario Institute for Studies in Education of the University of Toronto: Toronto.

Dewar, A. (2003). Boosting strategies for self-esteem: Enhancing self-esteem of individuals with catastrophic illnesses and injuries. *Journal of Psychosocial Nursing, 41*(3), 26–32.

Dewey, J. (1916). *Democracy and education.* New York: The Macmillan Company.

———. (1967). *Experience and education.* Chicago: Random House.

Donkin, R. (2008). Work drives us to distraction. *Human Resources,* January, 16.

Edwards, R. (2010). Global conference agrees deal to cut pollution. *The Herald-Scotland,* 12 December. http://www.heraldscotland.com/news/transport-environment/global-conference-agrees-deal-to-cut-pollution-1.1073907.

Einstein, Albert. (n.d.). Online. Retrieved April 26, 2010, from http://www.brainyquote.com/quotes/authors/a/albert_einstein.html.

Einstein, A. (n.d.). thinkexist.com. Retrieved July 14, 2010, from http://thinkexist.com/quotation/no_problem_can_be_solved_from_the_same_level_of/222376.html.

Eisenberg, E., and H. Goodall, Jr. (1993). *Organizational communication: Balancing creativity and constraint.* New York: St Martin's Press.

Eliade, M. (1967). *Myths, dreams and mysteries.* Philip Mairet (trans.), New York: Harper & Row.

Elias, D. (1993). Educating leaders for social transformation. Thesis, Teachers College, Columbia University: New York.

Eliot, T. S. (1959). *Four quartets.* London: Faber.

Emery, F., and E. Trist. (1965). The causal texture of organizational environments. *Human Relations, 18,* 21–32.

Erikson, E. (1950). *Childhood and society.* New York: W. W. Norton.

Fowler, J. (1981). *Stages of faith: The psychology of human development and the quest for meaning.* San Francisco: Harper Collins.

Friedman, T. (2005). *The world is flat: A brief history of the twenty-first century.* New York: Farrar, Strauss and Giroux.

———. (2008). *Hot, flat, and crowded: Why we need a green revolution and how it can renew America.* New York: Farrar, Straus and Giroux.

Freire, P. (1973). *Education for critical consciousness.* New York: Seabury Press.

———. (2000). *Pedagogy of the oppressed.* New York: Continuum.

Fritz, R. (1984). *The path of least resistance: Learning to become the creative force in your own life.* New York: Fawcett Books.

———. (1991). *Creating: A practical guide to the creative process and how to use it to create anything—a work of art, a relationship, a career or a better life.* New York: Fawcett Columbine.

Gallese, V., and G. Lakoff. (2005). The brain's concepts: The role of the sensori-motor system in conceptual knowledge. *Cognitive Neuropsychology,* 22(3/4), 455–479.

Gellermann, W., M. Frankel and R. Ladenson. (1990). *Values and ethics in organizations and human systems development: Responding to dilemmas in professional life.* San Francisco: Jossey-Bass.

Gendlin, E. (1996). *Focusing-oriented psychotherapy: A manual for the experiential method.* New York: Guilford Press.

George, B. (2003). *Authentic leadership: Rediscovering the secrets to creating lasting value.* San Francisco: Jossey-Bass.

George, B., and A. McLean. (2007). The transformation from 'I' to 'we.' *Leader to Leader, 45* (Summer), 26–32.

Gergen, K., M. Gergen, and F. Barrett. (2004). Dialogue life and death of the organization. *The SAGE handbook of organizational discourse.* Thousand Oaks, CA: Sage Publications. http://www.sage-ereference.com. ezproxy.royalroads.ca/hdbk_orgdiscourse/Article_n2.html.

Ghiselin, B. (ed.) (1964). *The creative process.* New York: Mentor Books.

Gilligan, C. (1982). *In a different voice: Psychological theory and women's development.* Cambridge, MA: Harvard University Press.

Gladwell, M. (2005). *Blink: The power of thinking without thinking.* New York: Back Bay Books, Little, Brown & Company.

Gleick, J. (1987). *Chaos: Making a new science.* Markham, ON: Penguin Canada.

Global Commission on International Migration (GCIM). (2005). *Migration in an Interconnected World: Report of the Global Commission on International Migration.* Retrieved April 27, 2008, from http://www.gcim. org/attachements/gcim-complete-report-2005.pdf.

Goldstein, J., J. Hazy, and J. Silberstang. (2008). Complexity and social entrepreneurship: A fortuitous meeting. *E-CO, 10*(3), 9–24.

Goleman, D. (1995). *Emotional intelligence.* New York: Bantam Books.

———. (1998). *Working with emotional intelligence.* New York: Bantam Books.

Goleman, D., R. Boyatzis, and A. McKee. (2009). Primal leadership. *Leadership Excellence, 26*(10), 9–10.

Gore, A. (2006). *An inconvenient truth.* New York: Rodale.

Gould, R. (1978). *Transformations: Growth and change in adult life.* New York: Simon & Schuster.

Graves, C. (1966). Deterioration of work standards. *Harvard Business Review,* 44 (5), 117–125.

———. (1970). Levels of existence: An open system theory of values. *Journal of Humanistic Psychology, 10*(2), 131–155.

———. (1974). Human nature prepares for a momentous leap. *The Futurist,* 72–87. Retrieved May 9, 2008, from http://www.clarewgraves.com/ articles_content/1974_Futurist/1974_Futurist.html.

Greene, L., and G. Burke. (2007). Beyond self-actualization. *Journal of Health and Human Services Administration, 30*(2), 116–128. http://proquest.

umi.com.ezproxy.royalroads.ca/pqdweb?index=1&did=1440913571&Src hMode=2&sid=1&Fmt=6&VInst=PROD&VType=PQD&RQT=309&V Name=PQD&TS=1279298813&clientId=4565.

Greenleaf, R. (1977). *Servant leadership: A journey into the nature of legitimate power and greatness.* Edited by Larry C. Spears. 25th anniversary edition. Mahwah, NJ: Paulist Press.

Gunderson, L., and C. S. Holling. (2002). *Panarchy: Understanding transformations and natural systems.* Washington, DC: Island Press.

Hampden-Turner, C. (1971). *Radical man: The process of psycho-social development.* New York: Anchor Books.

Harris, J. (1998). *The learning paradox: Gaining success and security in a world of change.* Toronto: Macmillan.

Hawes, L. (1999). The dialogics of conversation: Power, control, and vulnerability. *Communication Theory, 9,* 229–264.

Haxton, B. (trans.) (2001). *Fragments: The collected wisdom of Heraclitus.* Toronto: Penguin Canada.

Heifetz, R., and D. Laurie. (2001). The work of leadership. *Harvard Business Review, 79*(11), 131–141. http://wp6eu6tz5x.search.serialssolutions. com/directLink?&atitle=The%20work%20of%20leadership&author=Ron ald%20Heifetz%3B%20Donald%20Laurie&issn=00178012&title=Harvar d%20Business%20Review&volume=79&issue=11&date=20011201&spa ge=131&id=doi:&sid=ProQ_ss&genre=article&lang=en.

Hilgard, E. (1975). *Theories of learning.* (4th edition) Englewood Cliffs, NJ: Prentice-Hall.

Holling, C. S., and L. Gunderson. (2002). Resilience and adaptive cycles. In L. Gunderson. and C. S. Holling (eds.), *Panarchy: Understanding transformations in human and natural systems.* Washington, DC: Island Press, pp. 25–62.

Hollinger, P. (2008). Experts stress the need to reverse workplace trend. *Financial Times,* February 2, 10.

Holman, P., and T. Devane. (eds.) (1999). *The change handbook: Group methods for shaping the future.* San Francisco: Berrett-Koehler.

Holt, M. (1994). Retesting a learning theory to explain intercultural competency. In K. Obloj (ed.), *High speed competition in new Europe.* Published in the proceedings of the 20th Annual Conference of the European International Business Academy. (pp. 53078). 11–13 December, Warsaw, Poland: University of Warsaw International Management Centre.

Homer-Dixon, T. (2006) *The upside of down: Catastrophe, creativity and the renewal of civilization.* Toronto: Alfred A. Knopf Canada.

House, J., P. Hanges, M. Javidan, P. Dorfman, and V. Gupta. (2004). *Culture, leadership, and organizations: The GLOBE study of 62 societies.* Thousand Oaks, CA: Sage.

Hunter, M. (1980). Perspective transformation in health practices: A study in adult learning and fundamental life change. Thesis, University of California: Los Angeles.

Imparato, N., and O. Harari. (1994). *Jumping the curve: Innovation and strategic choice in an age of transition.* San Francisco: Jossey-Bass.

Intergovernmental Panel on Climate Change (IPCC). (2007). *Climate Change 2007: Fourth Assessment Report.* Retrieved July 14, 2010, from http://www.ipcc.ch/publications_and_data/publications_and_data.htm.

International Labor Organization (ILO). (2007). *Equality at Work: Tackling the Challenges. Report on the ILO on Fundamental Principles and Rights at Work.* Retrieved May 19, 2008, from http://www.ilo.org/dyn/declaris/DECLARATIONWEB.DOWNLOAD_BLOB?Var_DocumentID=6779.

Internet World Stats. (2009). Internet usage statistics: World internet users and population stats. Retrieved July 1, 2010, from http://www.internetworldstats.com/stats.htm.

Isaacs, W. (1993). Taking flight: Dialogue, collective thinking, and organizational learning. *Organizational Dynamics, 93*(22), 24–39.

———. (1999). *Dialogue and the art of thinking together: A pioneering approach to communicating in business and in life.* New York: Currency/Doubleday.

Jaworski, J. (1998). *Synchronicity: The inner path of leadership.* San Francisco: Barrett-Koehler.

Jung, C. (1958). *The undiscovered self.* Boston: Little, Brown & Company.

———. (1969). *Collected works, Volume 8: The structure and dynamics of the psyche.* Princeton, NJ: Princeton University Press.

Kabat-Zinn, J. (1994). *Wherever you go, there you are: Mindfulness meditation in everyday life.* New York: Hyperion.

Kauffman, S. (1991). Antichaos and adaptation. *Scientific American, 265*(2), 78–84.

Kegan, R. (1982). *The evolving self: Problem and process in human development.* Cambridge, MA: Harvard University Press.

———. (1994). *In over our heads: The mental demands of modern life.* Cambridge, MA: Harvard University Press.

Kegan, R., and L. Lahey. (2009). *Immunity to change: How to overcome it and unlock the potential in yourself and your organization.* Cambridge, MA: Harvard Business School Publishing.

Keim, B. (2007). Memories of the earth seen from space. *Wired Science,* April 20. Retrieved July 14, 2010, from http://www.wired.com/wiredscience/2007/04/memories_of_the.

Kelly, G. (1963). *A theory of personality: The psychology of personal constructs.* New York: Norton.

Kelly, K. (2008). Web & Where 2.0+. Presentation to Northern California Grantmakers and the William and Flora Hewlett Foundation. 14 February. Retrieved June 22, 2010, from http://www.youtube.com/watch?v=J132shgIiuY&feature=related.

Kiersey, D. (1998). *Please understand me II: Temperament, character, intelligence.* Del Mar: CA: Prometheus Nemesis Books.

Knowles, M. (1975). *Self-directed learning: A guide for learners and teachers.* Englewood Cliffs, NJ: Prentice Hall.

Knowles, M., G. Lucas, D. Molden, W. Gardner, and K. Dean. (2010). There's no substitute for belonging: Self-affirmation following social and non-social threats. *Personality and Social Psychology Bulletin, 36*(2), 173–186.

Koestler, A. (1964). *The act of creation.* London: Pan Books Ltd.

Kolb, D. (1984). *Experiential learning: Experience as a source of learning and development.* Upper Saddle River, NJ: Prentice Hall.

Kouzes, J., and B. Posner. (2007). *The leadership challenge.* (4th edition) San Francisco: Jossey-Bass/Wiley.

Kramer, D. (1990). Conceptualizing wisdom: The primacy of affect-cognition relations. In R. Sternberg (ed.), *Wisdom: Its nature, origins and development.* New York: Cambridge University Press, pp. 270–313.

Krueger, R., and D. Gibbs. (eds.) (2007). *The sustainable development paradox: Urban political economy in the United States and Europe.* New York: Guilford Press.

James, W. (1949). *Essays in pragmatism.* New York: Hafner Press.

Johnson, M., and G. Lakoff. (2002). Why cognitive linguistics requires embodied realism. *Cognitive Linguistics, 13*(3), 245–263.

Labouvie-Vief, G. (1990). Wisdom as integrated thought: Historical and developmental perspectives. In R. Sternberg (ed.), *Wisdom: Its nature, origins and development.* New York: Cambridge University Press.

Lakoff, G. (2008). How Framing and Metaphor Contribute to the Way We Think. Address to the Commonwealth Club of California, 20 June, San Francisco.

Lakoff, G., and M. Johnson. (1980). *The metaphors we live by.* Chicago: University of Chicago Press.

Langer, E. (1997). *The power of mindful learning.* Cambridge, MA: Perseus Books.

Larrison, T. (2009). Capturing the space in-between: Understanding the relevance of professional "use of self" for social work education through hermeneutic phenomenology. Thesis, University of Illinois at Urbana-Champaign: Urbana/Champaign, IL.

Laswell, T. (1994). *Adult learning in the aftermath of job loss: Exploring the transformative potential.* 35th Annual Adult Education Research Conference Proceedings. (pp. 229–234). 20–22 May, Knoxville, TN: University of Tennessee.

Laszlo, E. (2006). *The chaos point: A world at the crossroads.* Charlottesville, VA: Hampton Roads Publishing.

———. (2008). *Quantum shift in the global brain: How the new scientific reality can change us and our world.* Rochester, VT: Inner Traditions.

Lessem, R. (1994). From vision to action. In W. Bennis, J. Parikh, and R. Lessem (eds.), *Beyond leadership: Balancing economics, ethics, and ecology.* Cambridge, MA: Blackwell, pp. 87–112.

Lewin, K. (1952). Group decision and social change. In G. Swanson, T. Newcomb, and E. Hartley (eds.) *Readings in social psychology.* (Rev. Ed.) New York: Holt, Rinehart and Winston.

Levinson, D. (1978). *Seasons of a man's life.* New York: Ballantine Books.

Lindeman, E. (1926). *The meaning of adult education.* New York: New Republic.

Lindley, D. (2007). *Uncertainty: Einstein, Heisenberg, Bohr, and the struggle for the soul of science.* New York: Anchor Books.

Loevinger, J., and A. Blasi. (1976). *Ego development: Conceptions and theories.* San Francisco: Jossey-Bass.

Macmurray, J. (1957). *Self as agent.* London: Faber & Faber.

———. (1961). *Persons in relation.* London: Faber & Faber.

Mahoney, M. (1991). *Human change processes: The scientific foundations of psychotherapy.* New York: Basic Books.

Mansfield, V., and J. Spiegelman. (1991). The opposites in quantum physics and Jungian psychology: Part I theoretical foundations. *Journal of Analytical Psychology, 36,* 267–287.

Marris, P. (1974). *Loss and change.* London: Routledge & Kegan Paul.

Marshak, R. (2009). *Organizational change: Views from the edge.* Bethel, ME: The Lewin Center.

Martin, A. (2009). *The anti-anxiety workbook; Proven strategies to overcome worry, phobias, panic and obsessions.* New York: Guildford Press.

Maslow, A. (1943). A theory of human motivation. *Psychological Review, 50,* 370–396.

———. (1954). *Motivation and personality.* New York: Harper.

———. (1968). *Toward a psychology of being.* (2nd edition) New York: D. Van Nostrand Company.

———. (1970). *Religions, values, and peak experiences.* New York: Penguin Books.

———. (1971). *The farther reaches of human nature.* New York: Penguin.

Matthew 6:34, *Holy Bible* Revised Standard Version.

Maturana, H., and F. Varela. (1987). *The tree of knowledge: The biological roots of human understanding.* Boston: Shambhala.

Mayer, J. (2004). Be realistic. In leading by feel. *Harvard Business Review, 82*(1), 27. http://wp6eu6tz5x.search.serialssolutions.com/directLink?&atitle=Leading%20by%20feel&author=John%20D%20Mayer%3B%20Daniel%20Goleman%3B%20Colleen%20Barrett%3B%20Steven%20Gutstein%3B%20et%20al&issn=00178012&title=Harvard%20Business%20Review&volume=82&issue=1&date=20040101&spage=27&id=doi:&sid=ProQ_ss&genre=article&lang=en.

Mayer, J. D., P. Salovey, D. R. Caruso, and G. Sitarenios. (2003). Measuring emotional intelligence with the MSCEIT V2.0. *Emotion, 3,* 97–105.

McLuhan, M. (1962). *The Gutenberg galaxy: The making of typographic man.* Toronto: University of Toronto Press.

Meglino, B., and E. Ravlin. (1998). Individual values in organizations: Concepts, controversies, and research. *Journal of Management, 24,* 351–389.

Mezirow, J. (1978). Perspective transformation. *Adult Education Quarterly, 28,* 100–110.

———. (1990). *Fostering critical reflection in adulthood: A guide to transformative and emancipatory learning.* San Francisco: Jossey-Bass.

————. (2000). Learning to think like an adult: Core concepts of transformation theory. In J. Mezirow and Associates, *Learning as transformation: Critical perspectives on a theory in progress*. San Francisco: Jossey-Bass/Wiley, pp. 3–33.

Mezirow, J., V. Marsick, and Columbia University. (1978). Education for Perspective Transformation. Women's Re-entry Programs in Community Colleges. ERIC Document Reproduction Service No. ED166367, January 1. Retrieved September 13, 2008, from ERIC database.

Mintzberg, H. (2004). *Managers not MBA's: A hard look at the soft practice of managing and management development*. San Francisco: Jossey-Bass.

Morgan, G. (1986). *Images of organization*. Beverly Hills, CA: Sage Publications.

Morgan, J. (1987). Displaced homemaker programs: The transition from homemaker to independent person. Thesis, Teachers College, Columbia University: New York.

Myers, I. (1980). *Gifts differing: Understanding personality type*. Mountain View, CA: Davies-Black Publishing.

Myers, T., and Crowther, J. (2009). Social comparison as a predictor of body dissatisfaction: A meta-analytic view. *Journal of Abnormal Psychology, 118*(4), 683–698.

Neff, K. (2009). The role of self-compassion in development: A healthier way to relate to oneself. *Human Development, 5,* 211–214.

Neff, K., and R. Vonk. (2009). Self-compassion versus global self-esteem: Two different ways of relating to oneself. *Journal of Personality, 77*(1), 23–50.

Organization of Economic Cooperation and Development (OECD). (2008). *International immigration outlook*. Retrieved April 25, 2010, from http://www.oecd.org/document/26/0,3343,en_2649_33931_41292762_1_1_1_1,00.html.

————. (2009). *International immigration outlook*. Retrieved April 25, 2010, from http://www.oecd.org/document/63/0,3343,en_2649_33931_43214335_1_1_1_1,00.html.

Orwoll, L., and M. Perlmutter. (1990). A study of wise persons: Integrating a personality perspective. In R. Sternberg (ed.), *Wisdom: Its nature, origins and development*. New York: Cambridge University Press.

O'Sullivan, E. (1999). *Transformative learning: Educational vision for the 21st century*. Toronto: University of Toronto Press.

Owen, D. (1994). *Maturity and modernity; Nietzsche, Weber, Foucault and the ambivalence of reason*. New York: Routledge.

Owen, H. (2008). *Wave rider: Leadership for high performance in self-organizing world*. San Francisco: Berrett-Koehler.

Oxford English Dictionary Online (blue). Retrieved October 5, 2008, from http://dictionary.oed.com.ezproxy.royalroads.ca/cgi/entry/50024005?query_type=word&queryword=blue&first=1&max_to_show=10&sort_type=alpha&result_place=2&search_id=iob7-qK0Kqz-2751&hilite=50024005.

———— (change). Retrieved December 30, 2010, from http://www.oed. com.ezproxy.royalroads.ca/search?searchType=dictionary&q=change&_ searchBtn=Search.

———— (courage). Retrieved June 18, 2010, from http://dictionary.oed. com.ezproxy.royalroads.ca/cgi/entry/50052293?query_type=word&qu eryword=courage&first=1&max_to_show=10&sort_type=alpha&result_ place=1&search_id=Ivr3-h5Bwzh-6978&hilite=50052293.

———— (disorientation). Retrieved September 29, 2008, from http:// dictionary.oed.com.ezproxy.royalroads.ca/cgi/entry/50066462? single=1&query_type=word&queryword=disorientation&first=1&max_ to_show=10.

———— (emergent). Retrieved August 9, 2009, from http://dictionary.oed. com/cgi/entry/50073966?single=1&query_type=word&queryword=e mergent&first=1&max_to_show=10.

———— (equilibrium). Retrieved October 5, 2008, from http://dictionary. oed.com.ezproxy.royalroads.ca/cgi/entry/50077253?single=1&query_ type=word&queryword=equilibrium&first=1&max_to_show=10.

———— (insight). Retrieved April 19, 2010, from http://dictionary.oed. com.ezproxy.royalroads.ca/cgi/entry/50118013?query_type=word&q ueryword=insight&first=1&max_to_show=10&sort_type=alpha&result_ place=1&search_id=gPmj-sno45s-14180&hilite=50118013.

———— (intuition). Retrieved April 25, 2010, from http://dictionary.oed. com.ezproxy.royalroads.ca/cgi/entry/50120301?single=1&query_type= word&queryword=intuition&first=1&max_to_show=10.

———— (metánoia). Retrieved September 30, 2008, from http://dictionary. oed.com.ezproxy.royalroads.ca/cgi/entry/00307409?single=1&query_ type=word&queryword=metanoia&first=1&max_to_show=10.

———— (purple). Retrieved September 30, 2008, from http://dictionary.oed. com.ezproxy.royalroads.ca/cgi/entry/50192948?query_type=word&q ueryword=purple&first=1&max_to_show=10&sort_type=alpha&result_ place=1&search_id=CRaB-81I6Fv-4080&hilite=50192948.

———— (realize). Retrieved June 30, 2010, from http://dictionary.oed. com.ezproxy.royalroads.ca/cgi/entry/50198441?query_type=word&q ueryword=realize&first=1&max_to_show=10&sort_type=alpha&result_ place=2&search_id=o5B8-50KejF-13221&hilite=50198441.

———— (reflect). Retrieved June 15, 2010, from http://dictionary.oed. com.ezproxy.royalroads.ca/cgi/entry/50200804?query_type=word&q ueryword=reflect&first=1&max_to_show=10&sort_type=alpha&result_ place=3&search_id=Pux5-X2Di9R-12141&hilite=50200804.

———— (resilience). Retrieved July 15, 2010, fromhttp://dictionary.oed. com.ezproxy.royalroads.ca/cgi/entry/50204032?single=1&query_type= word&queryword=resilience&first=1&max_to_show=10.

———— (solution). Retrieved July 17, 2010, from http://dictionary.oed. com.ezproxy.royalroads.ca/cgi/entry/50230506?query_type=word&qu eryword=solution&first=1&max_to_show=10&sort_type=alpha&result_ place=1&search_id=Ga1G-whj7zK-2691&hilite=50230506.

———— (spiritual). Retrieved June 17, 2010, from http://dictionary.oed.com.ezproxy.royalroads.ca/cgi/entry/50233686?single=1&query_type=word&queryword=spiritual&first=1&max_to_show=10.

———— (tipping point). Retrieved July 18, 2010, from http://dictionary.oed.com.ezproxy.royalroads.ca/cgi/entry/50253235/50253235se4?single=1&query_type=word&queryword=tipping+point&first=1&max_to_show=10&hilite=50253235se4.

———— (transformation). Retrieved July 18, 2010, from http://dictionary.oed.com.ezproxy.royalroads.ca/cgi/entry/50256220?single=1&query_type=word&queryword=transformation&first=1&max_to_show=10.

————(transition). Retrieved July 18, 2010, from http://dictionary.oed.com.ezproxy.royalroads.ca/cgi/entry/50256294?query_type=word&queryword=transition&first=1&max_to_show=10&sort_type=alpha&result_place=1&search_id=shqr-35yC0O-2350&hilite=50256294.

Palmer, R. (1969). *Hermeneutics: Interpretation theory in Schleiermacher, Dilthey, Heidegger, and Gadamer.* Evanston, IL: Northwestern University Press.

Parkes, C. M. (1971). Psycho-social transitions: A field for study. *Social Science & Medicine, 5,* 101–115.

Patwell, B., and E. Seashore. (2006). *Triple impact coaching: Use of self in the coaching process.* Columbia, MD: Bingham House Books; and Victoria, BC: Patwell Consulting.

Pepper, S. (1961). *World hypotheses: A study in evidence.* Berkeley, CA: University of California Press.

Perry, W. (1999). *Forms of intellectual and ethical development in college years: A scheme.* San Francisco: Jossey-Bass.

Petrie, H., and R. Oshlag. (1993). Metaphor and learning. In A. Ortony (ed.), *Metaphor and thought.* (2nd edition) Cambridge, MA: Cambridge University Press, pp. 579–609.

Piaget, J. (1951). *The psychology of intelligence.* London: Routledge & Kegan Paul.

Pink, D. (2006). *A whole new mind: Why right-brainers will rule the future.* New York: Riverhead Books.

Polanyi, M. (1967). *The tacit dimension.* Garden City, NY: Anchor Books.

Pope, S. (1996). Wanting to be something more: Transformations in ethnically diverse working class women through the process of education. Thesis, The Fielding Institute: Santa Barbara, CA.

Poscente, V. (2008). *The age of speed: Learning to thrive in a more-faster-now world.* Austin, TX: Bard Press.

Prince, G. (1970). *The practice of creativity.* New York: Collier Books.

Progoff, I. (1973). *Jung's psychology and its social meaning.* Garden City, NY: Anchor Books.

Purser, R., and S. Cabana. (1998). *The self managing organization: How leading companies are transforming the work of teams for real impact.* New York: Free Press.

Quenk, N. (2000). *In the grip: Understanding type, stress and the inferior function*. (2nd edition) Palo Alto, CA: Consulting Psychologists Press.

Quinn, R. (2004). *Building the bridge as you walk on it: A guide for leading change*. San Francisco: Jossey-Bass.

Raelin, J. (2000). *Work-based learning: The new frontier of management development*. Upper Saddle, NJ: Prentice-Hall.

———. (2003). *Creating leaderful organizations: How to bring leadership out in everyone*. San Francisco: Berrett-Koehler.

———. (2007). Toward an epistemology of practice. *Academy of Management Learning and Education, 6*(4), 495–519.

Rioch, M. (2009). The work of Wilfred Bion on groups. In W. Burke, D. Lake, and J. Paine (eds.), *Organization change: A comprehensive reader*. San Francisco: Wiley, pp. 466–479.

Rokeach, M. (1973). *The nature of human values*. New York: Free Press.

Rooke, D., and W. Torbert. (2005). Seven transformations of leaders. *Harvard Business Review, 83*(4), 66–78. http://wp6eu6tz5x.search. serialssolutions.com/directLink?&atitle=7%20Transformations%20of%20 Leadership&author=David%20Rooke%3B%20William%20R%20Torbert& issn=00178012&title=Harvard%20Business%20Review&volume=83&iss ue=4&date=20050401&spage=66&id=doi:&sid=ProQ_ss&genre=articl e&lang=en.

Rosch, E. (1999). Reclaiming concepts. *The Journal of Consciousness Studies, 6*(11–12), 61–77.

———. (2007). More than mindfulness: When you have a tiger by the tail, let it eat you. *Psychological Inquiry, 18*(4), 258–264.

Rosenberg, M. (2005). *The heart of social change: How to make a difference in your world*. Encinitas, CA: Puddledancer Press.

Rost, J. (1992). *Leadership for the 21st century*. New York: Praeger. http:// library.books24x7.com.ezproxy.royalroads.ca/book/id_7399/viewer. asp?bookid=7399&chunkid=559712967.

Royal Pingdom. (2010). *Internet 2008 in numbers*. Retrieved July 14, 2010, from http://royal.pingdom.com/2009/01/22/internet-2008-in-numbers.

Schachter, S. (1959). *The psychology of affiliation*. Palo Alto, CA: Stanford University Press.

Scharmer, O. (2007). *Theory U: Leading from the future as it emerges*. Cambridge, MA: Society for Organizational Learning.

Schein, E. (1995a). *Kurt Lewin's change theory in the field and in the classroom: Notes toward a model of managed learning*. Retrieved November 22, 2008, from http://www.solonline.org/res/wp/10006.html.

———. (1995b). Dialogue and learning. *Executive Excellence. 12*(4), 3–4.

———. (1999). *Process consultation revisited: Building the helping relationship*. New York: Addison-Wesley.

Schön, D. (1983). *The reflective practitioner: How professionals think in action*. New York: Basic Books.

————. (1987). *Educating the reflective practitioner: Toward a new design for teaching and learning in the professions.* San Fransciso: Jossey-Bass.

Schweizerische Eidgenossenschaft. (n.d.). *Worldwide migration.* Retrieved April 27, 2008, from http://www.bfm.admin.ch/bfm/en/home/themen/laenderinformation/weltweite_migration.html.

Segal, M. (1997). *Points of influence: A guide to using personality theory at work.* San Francisco: Jossey-Bass.

Senge, P. (2006). *The fifth discipline: The art and practice of the learning organization.* New York: Doubleday.

Senge, P., O. Scharmer, J. Jaworski, and B. Flowers. (2004). *Presence: An exploration of profound change in people, organizations, and society.* New York: Currency/Doubleday.

Senge, P., B. Smith, N. Kruschwitz, J. Laur, and S. Schley. (2008). *The necessary revolution: How individuals and organizations are working together to create a sustainable world.* New York: Doubleday.

Shlain, L. (1998). *The alphabet versus the goddess: The conflict between word and image.* Toronto: Penguin Canada.

Siegel, R. (2010). *The mindfulness solution: Everyday practices for everyday problems.* New York: Guildford Press.

Sinnott, E. (1959). Creativeness in life. In H. Anderson (ed.), *Creativity and its cultivation.* New York: Harper Row.

Soros, G. (2008). *The new paradigm for public markets: The credit crisis and what it means.* New York: Public Affairs.

Spariosu, M. (2004). *Global intelligence and human development: Toward an ecology of global learning.* Cambridge, MA: MIT Press.

Statistics Canada. (2007a). *Immigration in Canada: A portrait of the foreign-born population, 2006 Census: Immigration: Driver of population growth.* Retrieved April 17, 2008, from http://www12.statcan.ca/english/census06/analysis/immcit/foreign_born.cfm.

Statistics Canada. (2007b). *Immigration in Canada: A portrait of the foreign-born population, 2006 Census: Immigrants came from many countries.* Retrieved April 17, 2008, from http://www12.statcan.ca/english/census06/analysis/immcit/asia.cfm.

Sternberg, R. (1990). Wisdom and its relations to intelligence and creativity. In R. Sternberg (ed.), *Wisdom: Its nature, origins and development.* New York: Cambridge University Press.

Stinson, A., C. Logel, M. Zanna, J. Holmes, J. Cameron, J. Wood, and S. Spencer. (2008). The cost of lower self-esteem: Testing a self- and social-bonds model of health. *Journal of Personality and Social Psychology, 94*(3), 412–428.

Storr, A. (1973). *Jung.* Glasgow, UK: Fontana/Collins.

Tarnas, R. (1991). *The passion of the Western mind: Understanding the ideas that have shaped our world view.* New York: Ballantine Books.

Taylor, C. (1989). *Sources of the self: The making of the modern identity.* Cambridge, MA: Harvard University Press.

Taylor, E. (1994). Intercultural competency: A transformative learning process. *Adult Education Quarterly, 44,* 154–174.

———. (1997). Building upon the theoretical debate: A critical review of the empirical studies of Mezirow's transformative learning theory. *Adult Education Quarterly, 48,* 34–59.

———. (2007). An update of transformative learning theory: A critical review of empirical research (1999–2005). *International Journal of Life-long Education, 26*(2), 173–191.

Taylor, E., J. Mezirow, and Associates. (2009). *Transformative learning in practice: Insights from community, workplace and higher education.* San Francisco: Jossey-Bass/Wiley.

Taylor, M. (1979). Adult learning in an emergent learning group: Toward a theory of learning from the learner's perspective. Thesis, University of Toronto: Toronto.

———. (1986). Learning for self-direction in the classroom: The pattern of a transition process. *Studies in Higher Education, 11*(1), 55–72.

Taylor, M., D. de Guerre, J. Gavin, and R. Kass. (2002). Graduate education for dynamic human systems. *Management Learning, 33*(3), 349–369.

Tolle, E. (1999). *The power of NOW: A guide to enlightenment.* Novato, CA: New World Library.

Torbert, W. (1972). *Learning from experience toward consciousness.* New York: Columbia University Press.

———. (2004). *Action inquiry: The secret of timely and transforming leadership.* San Francisco: Berrett-Koehler.

Torbert, W., and D. Fisher. (1992). Autobiographical awareness as a catalyst for managerial and organizational development. *Management Education and Development, 23*(3), 184–198.

Tough, A. (1971). *The adult's learning projects: A fresh approach to theory and practice in adult learning.* Toronto: Ontario Institute for Studies in Education.

United Nations. (1992). United Nations Framework Convention on Climate Change. Retrieved July 14, 2010, from http://unfccc.int/resource/docs/convkp/conveng.pdf.

———. (2010). *Keeping the promise: A forward-looking review to promote an agreed action agenda to achieve the Millennium Development Goals by 2015: Report of the Secretary General to the General Assembly.* Retrieved April 26, 2010, from http://www.un.org/ga/search/view_doc.asp?symbol=A/64/665.

Vaillant, G. (1977). *Adaptation to life.* Boston: Little, Brown & Company.

Varela, F., E. Thompson, and E. Rosch. (1991). *The embodied mind: Cognitive science and human experience.* Boston: The MIT Press.

Weisbord, M. (2004). *Productive workplaces revisited: Dignity, meaning, and community in the 21st century.* San Francisco: Jossey-Bass/Wiley.

Wesley, F. (1991). Bob Geldof and Live Aid: The affective side of global social innovation. *Human Relations, 44*(10), 1011–1036.

Wesley, F., B. Zimmerman, and M. Patton. (2006). *Getting to maybe: How the world is changed*. Toronto: Random House Canada.

Wesley, F., S. Carpenter, W. Brock, C. S. Holling, and L. Gunderson. (2002). Systems of people and nature are not just social and ecological systems. In L. Gunderson and C. S. Holling (eds.), *Panarchy: Understanding transformations in human and natural systems*. Washington, DC: Island Press, pp. 103–119.

Wheatley, M. (1999). *Leadership and the new science: Discovering order in a chaotic world*. San Francisco: Berrett-Koehler.

White, J., E. Langer, L. Yariv, and J. Welch. (2006). Frequent social comparisons and destructive emotions and behaviors: The dark side of social comparisons. *Journal of Adult Development, 13*(1), 36–44.

White, N. (1981). *The health conundrum: Explorations in health studies*. Toronto: TV Ontario Publications.

Wilber, K. (2000a). *Integral psychology: Consciousness, spirit, psychology and therapy*. Boston: Shambhala Publications.

———. (2000b). *A theory of everything: An integral vision for business, politics, science, and spirituality*. Boston: Shambhala Publications.

Wortley, R., and S. Smallbone. (2006). *Child pornography on the Internet*. Washington, DC: U.S. Department of Justice, Office of Community-Oriented.

INDEX